W9-BBF-401

# The Pronunciation of Standard English in America

BY

GEORGE PHILIP KRAPP

PROFESSOR OF ENGLISH IN COLUMBIA UNIVERSITY

NEW YORK

OXFORD UNIVERSITY PRESS

AMERICAN BRANCH: 35 WEST 32ND STREET

LONDON, TORONTO, MELBOURNE, AND BOMBAY

1919

police, fire, uti...
...and recreation.

...ll too familiar with the horrors ...by our urban slums. Perhaps the sub... can avoid repeating this tragedy by instituting a program of "suburban renewal" before the slum infection takes hold.

Kulturral

## Cultures of the Americas

One of the most searching discussions of Latin America to be held in this country has been in session in Denver. This conference, sponsored by the United States National Commission for UNESCO, has as its central theme "The Cultures of the Americas: Achievements in Education, Science and the Arts."

The aims of the conference, employed through a new dimension of foreign policy called cultural diplomacy, are to get at the root of many of the existing problems that beset the attending nations.

In demonstrating the deep interest of Latin-American culture and ideas found in the United States, the conference has endeavored to examine various techniques and organizations which will help to solidify the cultural ties between the Latin nations and this country. Many important representatives of labor, science, the business and educational fields from all the Latin and United States participants have been in attendance in addition to those representatives of the cultural areas. A total of 1,500 delegates representing significant fields of human endeavor have taken part in this cultural examination of hemisphere ideas.

with...
back in...
dewy morning...
pleasant memories...
and when, as occas...
arithmetic seems du...
they may be parc...
backward. They al...
mitted a glance f...
summer, when life...
replace life in algeb...
one can speak wi...
cows, of course, bu...
these post-summer...
peaceful days of all...
the collie are at t...
and all is quiet, no...
Chewing a contemp...
at last can settle t...
hand. Better she ...
as milk for appren...
ter for the school...

WINTER IS A...

Down-driven from...
Wandering, floun...
Alien to the heat...
A great bird fee...
Through tendons,...

The great umbre...
Drifts white and...
The wind on pin...
Of predatory we...

WILLIAM...

R

k Times

eard on these stations of the QXR Network: Philadelphia WFIL-FM, M, New Haven WNHC-FM, Albany-Troy-Schenectady WFLY-FM, R-FM, Ithaca WRRA-FM, Jamestown WJTN-FM, Olean WHDL-FM, YR-FM, Utica-Rome WRUN-FM.

41 G
42 Per
43 Con
pres
44 Rep
45 Deb
47 Did

| 1 | 2 |
|---|---|
| 14 | |
| 17 | |
| 20 | |
| 23 | |
| | |
| 33 | 34 |
| 39 | |
| 42 | |
| 45 | |
| | |
| 55 | 56 |
| 61 | |
| 64 | |
| 67 | |

# PREFACE

WHETHER one thinks this should or should not be so, it is a fact that most cultivated persons in America nowadays, and an increasing number in England, are more or less self-conscious about their speech. The present very general interest in the practical applications of the science of phonetics is one of the proofs of the truth of this statement. With our strange mingling of races, our widely separated but rapidly inter-communicating local units of population, our constantly shifting social boundaries between class and class, it is inevitable that, in America at least, such should be the case.

When people become conscious of so familiar an activity as speech, it means that changes are taking place in it. The universal possession of all persons in the land, the rich and the poor, the learned and the unlearned, of farmer, artisan, laborer and merchant, speech is not only the great social solvent which makes the nation one, but also the readiest test by which such differences as exist are measured and known. And where these differences and distinctions arise out of a rapidly developing civilization, as in America, it is often extremely hard to determine their value. If we had but a single standard of speech, universally accepted and practiced, the task undertaken in this book would be easy, though obviously it would be unnecessary. But we have no standard beyond opinion, which in a democratic society must always be many-headed. If therefore in the following pages the author has been at times less dogmatic than some of his readers think he should have been, his plea is that where there is a diversity of opinion and practice among reasonable people, there must be also an equally broad charity in judgment. Could anything be more absurd than to stigmatize as incorrect a pronunciation which is actually in general use, to put down in a dictionary only one pronunciation of a word when several are current among cultivated speakers? All cultivated speakers do not speak alike in America. If we think they should, that is a theory hard to enforce by compelling one group to yield to another. To be sure, opinion may be well-informed or ill-informed, and genuine blunders are usually due to lack of information, not to perversity. It is the purpose of this book to provide a rational method of examining pronunciation, the most important of the practical aspects of speech, in order that those who have a conscience in the matter may exercise it with justice both to themselves and to others.

The materials of the book have been ordered under the several sounds of the language. To one experienced in phonetics, no other plan would seem possible, and though perhaps at first embarrassed by an unfamiliar method, the untrained student will in the end find this the most profitable way of approach to the subject. The important thing is to acquire skill in hearing sounds as sounds, to be able to think of them as sounds apart from their representation in conventional spelling. The market is plentifully provided with dictionaries, with alphabetical lists of words said to be frequently mispronounced. The information contained in these books may or may not be trustworthy, but the best of them can offer little help to the student who wishes to observe the facts for himself and to arrive at his own judgments. And even the fullest of these lists cannot possibly be complete or contemporary. Pronunciation changes day by day, and dictionaries soon become antiquated. The intelligent person is one who makes his own dictionary as he goes along. The author's intention has not been, therefore, to provide exhaustive lists of words which may be mispronounced, but to show how the whole subject should be approached. Such words as are treated, however, will be found in alphabetical order in the index at the end of the book.

Wherever a question of choice between two pronunciations arises, there is rarely any difficulty in making a choice after the facts are once known. It is the province of a book like this to show students how they may become sure of their facts, not to make their choices for them. The author has endeavored, however, not to make trouble where there really is none. It would have been easy to swell the number of 'mis-pronunciations' by culling from the lists of books of the twenty-thousand-words-often-mispronounced kind. But most of the words recorded in such books are not mispronunciations. They are merely rare and learned words which few persons ever have any occasion to pronounce. A word can be said to have acquired a pronunciation in the English language only when it is current on the lips of English-speaking people. Otherwise it is an eye-word, without an established phonetic value. The instances discussed in the present volume are such as the author himself has observed. None are taken at second hand from books. Though they may not correspond to every other person's particular observations and special difficulties in pronunciation, what they may lack in inclusiveness will perhaps be compensated for by the fact that they are neither traditional survivals from books nor fanciful dilemmas of a theorist, but genuine records of present speech in America.

The professional student of phonetics seems to find it hard to resist the fascination which the game of inventing symbols exerts. The conventional alphabet is obviously inadequate for any scientific purposes, and scores of phonetic alphabets have been invented to take its place. If a phonetic alphabet is an evil, it is a necessary evil. But moderation should be practiced in the exercise of this evil, for once started, there is obviously no limit to the number of symbols one may devise as records of his observations. It may be said, moreover, that in the end not even the most elaborate phonetic alphabet can record all the shadings and nuances of speech sounds current daily in good use. For one seeking absolute completeness and precision, some device, richer in possibilities than an alphabet must be discovered.

In this book neither absolute precision nor a very high degree of precision in the notation of sounds has been attempted. The author's aim having been not to elaborate, but to simplify as much as possible, it may occasionally be felt that certain sounds have gone unrecorded. Thus the alphabet employed provides symbols for only two pronunciations of the vowel in **got**, **hot**, **not**, etc., that is the short of the vowels which appear in the first syllables of **father** and **author**. Perhaps a third intermediary sound should have been recorded, representing a vowel approximately with the same tongue position as the vowel of **father**, but with slight rounding of the lips. Likewise the two vowels of a word like **city** are not quite the same, though they have been indicated in the present volume by the same phonetic symbol. Yet again, the initial consonants in pairs of words like **haul** and **heel**, **gone** and **geese**, **call** and **keel** are acoustically different and are organically formed in different ways. The quality of the consonant, in these instances, is dependent upon the vowel by which it is followed. In a word like **city**, the second vowel may be said to be an unstressed variant of the first. And whenever it is possible to take account of sound variations in this way by means of a general explanatory statement, the author has chosen to do this in preference to adding to the number of symbols. Where one has several relatively slight variations in pronunciation, as in the pronunciation of **not, hot, got,** etc., the author has again preferred to indicate what might be called the extremes of tendency by means of phonetic symbols, filling in the modifications between these extremes by means of a descriptive statement. No introductory work on phonetics can read like an algebraic formula, or if it did, no one would read it.

Perhaps a word of explanation, if not of apology, is needed for the use of the word American as signifying the United States. In this the author is merely following general usage and does not mean to imply that the English of Canada either is or should be like the English of the United States. Canada is fortunate in having the adjective Canadian, but we have no adjective form for the United States. If we seem to be appropriating a general term for a specific meaning, we would point out that such is not the case, for American has practically ceased to be a general term. By this same warrant of usage, the term English has been applied to the speech of America, just as it must be applied to every country where the English language is spoken. If a more exact limitation of the general term is required, we must speak of American English, of British English, of Canadian English, of any of the half dozen varieties of English that have established for themselves local homes upon the face of the globe.

Geographical limitations in American speech, especially American standard speech, are extremely difficult to determine with precision, and in this book have been indicated only in the most general terms. The reason for this is that American cultivated speech is extraordinarily mixed. Relatively few Americans spend all their lives in one locality, and even if they do, they cannot possibly escape coming into contact with Americans from other localities. The result is that a 'pure dialect,' if any such thing ever does exist, must be sought elsewhere than in our much-traveling and very adaptable cultivated and educated classes. The universal negative is the last form of dogmatism upon which the careful student of American speech will insist. It is safer to indulge in a universal affirmative, to say that any pronunciation which may occur in cultivated speech, may occur in any region of America. For several large divisions, especially in the speech of the more obviously typical local representatives, we have a fairly defined feeling. We can distinguish with some certainty Eastern and Western and Southern speech, but beyond this the author has little confidence in those confident experts who think they can tell infallibly, by the test of speech, a native of Hartford from a native of Providence, or a native of Philadelphia from a native of Atlanta, or even, if one insist on infallibility, a native of Chicago from a native of Boston. This means of course that geographical distinctions are not of prime importance in the discussion of standard

American speech. Cultivated Americans do not all speak alike, but on the other hand, they do not move in mutually exclusive and self-centered circles in their habits of speech. Holmes insists, in the *Autocrat,* that the accent of a word may tell you all you want to know about the origin and possibilities of a person. Perhaps it may, but it is well to remember that such judgments are likely to place the placer quite as inescapably as they do his victim.

The term standard speech, it will thus be seen, has been used by the author without a very exact definition. Everybody knows that there is no type of speech uniform and accepted in practice by all persons in America. What the author has called standard may perhaps be best defined negatively, as the speech which is least likely to attract attention to itself as being peculiar to any class or locality. As a matter of fact, speech does not often attract notice to itself unless it is markedly peculiar. For the most part when one is listening to the speech of others, one is intent upon getting the meaning, not upon observing the form. In consequence there is likely to be, even in what we may justly call standard speech, a considerable area of negligible variation, negligible, that is, from the point of view of the practical use of language. To the conscientious and critical listener, many of these variations may seem reprehensible, but only so by the test of some theoretical or ideal standard. In the following pages, wherever the author has put down a form or several forms of speech without defining them as provincial, or dialectal, or vulgar, or artificial, he would have the usages taken as being, in his opinion, standard, and if two or more differing standard pronunciations are given, the implication intended is that a speaker is as likely to offend as many critical listeners by using one as by using another of the pronunciations.

Perhaps it is not necessary to say that this book has not been prepared for the purpose of showing the difference between American and British pronunciation, or of proving that either one of these is better than the other. Whenever reference has been made to British pronunciation, the comparison has been made in order to indicate more definitely the facts of American pronunciation. The concern of the book is above all with these facts, and as it cannot well be denied that we have an attained result in the pronunciation of English in America, it would seem that our first obligation is to become aware of the facts, to recognize their existence just as we recognize the existence of our other distinctive social institutions. On the basis of such knowledge, one may at least intelligently proceed to the building of theories for the improvement of American speech, if one is so moved. Yet it seems scarcely credible that one who knows the facts should think it possible to impose British standards upon American speech, or to do anything but ally himself to the best tendencies, as each observer sympathetically views them, of our native American pronunciation.

An important section of the book, to which it is suggested that the student give very special attention, is that at the conclusion, consisting of passages in phonetic transcription. These should be carefully studied in detail, and every student should make similar transcriptions, based upon his observations. The first five transcriptions here presented as examples are representations of standard pronunciation, as observed and recorded by the author himself. Passages six to twelve are records of the pronunciation of several individuals taken down for this book. They represent varieties of standard pronunciation, the intention being that they should be indicative but not exhaustive of the great number of current forms of standard speech. Passages thirteen to sixteen are phonetic transcriptions of literary records of American dialect speech, and they have been included to afford material for the comparison of standard with dialect speech. Finally passages seventeen to nineteen may be used for a comparative study of British and American speech. In England as in America differing opinions are held on the question of standard speech, though both scholars and general public seem pretty well agreed that Southern British has greater right to be regarded as standard than any other form of British speech. Northern British, however, stands a good deal closer to American English than does Southern British. In fact it is only rather extreme forms of Southern British which seem markedly different from American speech.

For permission to reproduce the passage from *Jane Eyre,* the author acknowledges his obligations to Mr. Daniel Jones, Reader in Phonetics in the University of London. A similar obligation extends to other writers who have permitted him to make phonetic transcriptions of passages from their published works, and a greater to those persons who have submitted to his inquisitions and who have sacrificed time and convenience to enable him to make phonetic transcriptions of their pronunciation. Thanks are due to Professor H. M. Ayres for aid with the proof, and Mr. William Tilly who helpfully criticized some of the opening sections of the book. The author is indebted also to the members of various classes before which he has lectured in the Summer Session as well as in the regular sessions of Columbia University. If one cannot travel everywhere in America, the next best substitute is to be seated at a great city university like Columbia, whither students come from every nook and cranny of the country, eager to impart as well as to receive information.

COLUMBIA UNIVERSITY
May, 1918.

# CONTENTS

| | PAGE |
|---|---|
| PREFACE | iii |
| SYMBOLS | xiv |
| I. THE MECHANISM OF SPEECH | 1 |
| II. DESCRIPTION OF SOUNDS | 14 |
| III. SOUNDS AND THEIR OCCURRENCE | 57 |
| EXERCISES | 143 |
| BIBLIOGRAPHICAL NOTE | 149 |
| TRANSCRIPTIONS | 151 |
| INDEX OF WORDS | 213 |

# SYMBOLS

## VOWELS

| SYMBOL | KEY | TRANSCRIPTION |
|---|---|---|
| [ɑ] | *not* | [nɑt] |
| [ɑː] | *father* | [ˈfɑːðəɹ] |
| [aː] | *fast* | [faɪst] |
| [æ] | *hat* | [hæt] |
| [e], [e·], [eː] | *vacation* | [veˈke·ʃən] |
| | *late* | [leɪt] |
| [ɛ] | *get* | [gɛt] |
| [ɛː] | *there* | [ðɛːɹ] |
| [ə] | *about* | [əˈbaʊt] |
| [ə] | *bird* | [bəɹd] |
| [i], [i·], [iː] | *expediency* | [ɛksˈpidɪənsɪ] |
| | *freedom* | [ˈfri·dəm] |
| | *free* | [friː] |
| [ɪ] | *sit* | [sɪt] |
| [o], [o·], [oː] | *locomotive* | [ˌlokəˈmo·tɪv] |
| | *note* | [noːt] |
| [ɔ] | *auditory* | [ˈɔdɪˌtɔrɪ] |
| [ɔː] | *law* | [lɔː] |
| [u], [uː] | *altruistic* | [æltruˈɪstɪk] |
| | *true* | [truː] |
| [ʊ] | *bush* | [bʊʃ] |
| [ʌ] | *but* | [bʌt] |
| [ʌː] | *hurt* | [hʌɪt] |

## DIPHTHONGS

| Symbol | Key | Transcription | Symbol | Key | Transcription |
|---|---|---|---|---|---|
| [eɪ] | *play* | [pleɪ] | [ɑʊ] | *house* | [hɑʊs] |
| [aɪ] | *ride* | [raɪd] | [ɔɪ] | *boil* | [bɔɪl] |
| [oʊ] | *go* | [goʊ] | [ju] | *mute* | [mjut] |

## CONSONANTS

| Symbol | Key | Transcription | Symbol | Key | Transcription |
|---|---|---|---|---|---|
| [b] | *bib* | [bɪb] | [ɹ] | *first* | [fəɹst] |
| [d] | *did* | [dɪd] | [s] | *best* | [bɛst] |
| [g] | *gig* | [gɪg] | [z] | *rise* | [raɪz] |
| [h] | *house* | [hɑʊs] | [ʃ] | *wish* | [wɪʃ] |
| [j] | *yawl* | [jɔːl] | [ʒ] | *pleasure* | [ˈplɛʒəɹ] |
| [k] | *king* | [kɪŋ] | [t] | *talk* | [tɔːk] |
| [l] | *land* | [lænd] | [θ] | *thing* | [θɪŋ] |
| [m] | *man* | [mæn] | [ð] | *that* | [ðæt] |
| [n] | *not, knot* | [nɑt] | [f] | *stiff* | [stɪf] |
| [ŋ] | *sing* | [sɪŋ] | [v] | *drive* | [draɪv] |
| [p] | *tap* | [tæp] | [w] | *wet* | [wɛt] |
| [r] | *very* | [vɛrɪ] | [ʍ] | *whet* | [ʍɛt] |

ː after a sound indicates a long sound, as in **father** [ˈfɑːðəɹ], [jɔːl].

· after a sound indicates a half-long sound, as in **vacation** [veˈke·ʃən].

ˈ indicates a full or main stress on the following syllable, as in **about** [əˈbɑʊt].

ˎ indicates a secondary or half stress on the following syllable, as in **bookshelf** [ˈbʊkˎʃɛlf].

# I

## THE MECHANISM OF SPEECH

**1.** Before it is possible to discuss intelligently or intelligibly the sounds of any speech, it is necessary to know by just what activities of the speech organs the sounds are formed, and to have some means of symbolizing the several sounds with approximate precision, that is, a phonetic alphabet. In this book all phonetic representations of sounds will be enclosed within square brackets and will immediately follow the conventional spelling when the two are employed together. The phonetic alphabet is that of the International Phonetic Association, with several slight modifications.

**2.** Though there is a very high degree of similarity in the way in which different persons form the various sounds of speech, all speakers do not necessarily produce what seems to be acoustically the same sound by exactly the same formations of the organs of speech. The prime reason for this is that the physical equipment, for example the number and arrangement of teeth or the angle of the jaws, is not the same in all persons. An experimental method, applied by each person upon himself, is therefore a necessity in the study of speech. In the end all organic analysis of speech must be an analysis of individual speech, and one must always make a certain amount of allowance for personal peculiarities, both in one's own speech and in that of others. Extended observation, however, enables one to make generalizations which hold for a very considerable majority of cases.

**3.** All speech sounds in English are made by air as it is expelled through the confining walls of the larynx, the mouth and the nose, the specific character of the sound being determined in each case by the special organ or group of organs which function most actively in shaping or obstructing the air passage. English has no indrawing sounds in articulate speech.

**4.** When all the speech organs are relaxed and the breath is allowed to issue without any constraint, it normally produces no sound, though it may sometimes be heard as breathing or 'heavy breathing,' especially when one breathes with the mouth open or when the nasal passages are abnormally obstructed. When the lips are closed and the breath is expelled forcibly through the nose, it produces the familiar sniff of scorn or contempt, which is of course not an articulate speech sound. Articulate speech sounds are only those sounds which are articulated, or joined, to other sounds in the formation of sound groups or words. The articulate speech sounds of one language are not the same as those of another. French and English, for example, have some sounds which are alike, but in the main, each has its own system of sounds, specially selected from the practically limitless number of sounds which the human organs of speech are capable of producing.

**5.** *Voiced and Voiceless Sounds.* When the rift between the vocal chords is so narrowed by the muscles which control the tightening and loosing of the chords that the air from the lungs as it is driven through this rift, known as the glottis, sets the edges of the chords into vibration, the result is what is technically known as *Voice* or *Voiced sounds* (sometimes called *Sonants*). When the air issuing from the lungs produces a sound without setting the vocal chords in vibration, the sound is *Voiceless* (also called *Breathed* or *Surd*). The difference between voiced and voiceless sounds is plainly audible to the observing ear, and may be further tested by placing the finger on the Adam's apple, when the vibrations will be distinctly felt in the case of the voiced sounds. In testing consonants in this way, the consonant proper should be distinguished from the vowel that accompanies it in the conventional names of the letters of the alphabet. All vowels are voiced, but some consonants are accompanied by voice, e.g., **b** [b] in **be**, **d** [d] in **do**, **g** [g] in **go**, **th** [ð] in **father**, **z**, **s** [z] in **prize**, **rise**, while others are voiceless, e.g., **p** [p] in **pay**, **t** [t] in **tea**, **k** [k] in **key**, **th** [θ] in **thin**, **c**, **s** [s] in **rice**, **sing**. Voiced and voiceless consonants usually go in pairs, that is, [b] represents a voiced sound of which [p] is the voiceless equivalent; so also [d] is voiced, [t] is voiceless; [g] is voiced, [k] is voiceless; [v] is voiced, [f] is voiceless; the medial consonant of **pleasure** [ˈplɛʒəɹ] is voiced, and its voiceless equivalent is the final consonant of **wish** [wɪʃ]; **th** is voiced [ð] in **then**, but voiceless [θ] in **thin**. It is advisable for students to train themselves carefully in observing the difference between voiced and voiceless sounds so that the distinction becomes immediately clear with reference to any particular sound as soon as it is heard.

**6.** Consonants are often written in the conventional spelling with the symbol which ordinarily represents a voiced sound, but the sounds so written are pronounced voiceless when they are assimilated to other voiceless sounds in their vicinity, as the final consonant in **walked** [wɔːkt], **stripped** [strɪpt]; or they are written with the symbol for a voiceless consonant which is assimilated to a neighboring voiced sound, as in **eggs** [ɛgz]; **paths** [paːðz]; **tags** [tægz] as compared with **tacks** [tæks]; **gooseberry** [ˈguːzˌbɛri], in which [s] of **goose** becomes [z] by assimilation to the voiced consonant [b].

**7.** Frequently also a consonant which is under a stress and voiceless, becomes voiced when not under the stress, as in **exhibition** [ˌɛksɪˈbɪʃən], but **exhibit** [ɛgˈzɪbɪt]. It may be stated as a general rule that stress tends to preserve voiceless consonants as such, but lack of stress, or relatively light stress, tends to permit them to become voiced. This applies not only to stress within the word, but also to stress in the word group or phrase. Thus **of** is usually a lightly stressed word in its group, e.g., **a man of ability**, and its phonetic value is [əv], as in [ə ˈmæn əv əˈbɪlɪtɪ]. The adverb **off** [ɔːf] is etymologically the same word, but is stressed and consequently retains its voiceless consonant, as in **it fell off** [ɪt ˈfɛl ˈɔːf].

**8.** The symbol **x** of the ordinary spelling represents **a** double consonant sound [ks] as in **tax** [tæks]; **j**, also sometimes **g**, represents [dʒ] as in **jug** [dʒʌg], **gem** [dʒɛm]; **ch** stands for [tʃ] as in **chin** [tʃɪn]. On the other hand, two symbols are used in the ordinary spelling for [ð] [θ], as in **then** [ðɛn], **thin** [θɪn], where the consonant is but a simple sound. The spelling **q** followed by **u** stands for [kw] as in **quick** [kwɪk].

**9.** *The Mouth.* Besides the vocal chords, the organs most actively concerned in the production of speech sounds are the tongue, the palate, the teeth, the gums (alveoli), the lips and the nose. The tongue, an extremely flexible combination of muscles, may be moved as a whole, and at the same time one part of it is commonly much more active than the rest. It is necessary to distinguish at least four main surface regions of the tongue, the back, which we may observe as being elevated to form the stoppage producing the initial consonant, a voiceless stop consonant, in **call** [kɔːl]; the front (sometimes also called the middle) which is the region immediately in front of the back and which may be observed as forming the stoppage producing the voiceless stop consonant in **kill** [kɪl]; the blade of the tongue, which is the surface just forward of the front, readily observed as functioning in the production of the vowel sound of **seat** [siːt]; and finally the point or tip of the tongue, which plays the most considerable part in the production of the sound of **d** [d], **t** [t], **th** [θ] [ð]. In the analysis of some of the vowels, it is necessary to divide further the surface regions of the tongue between front and back. The term half-front means a position between front and back but nearer front than back, and half-back means a position between the two but nearer back than front.

**10.** The vertical position of the tongue as a whole may also be varied, and it is important to distinguish at least three vertical positions, high, mid and low. When the tongue is in high position, the body of it is raised so that it is felt along the roof of the mouth and against the upper teeth, as in the vowel of **he** [hiː]; when it is in the mid position, as in the stressed vowel of **fetter** [ˈfɛtəɹ], it extends along the middle of the mouth and the point rests against the roots of the lower front teeth; when it is in low position, as in the vowel of **haul** [hɔːl], the tongue rests on the floor of the mouth and the point touches the lower gums. The surface divisions and the vertical positions of the tongue are important in analyzing both vowel and consonant sounds, but more important for vowels than consonants. A looking-glass should be used as an aid in studying the movements and positions of the tongue. For a more exact analysis of the vertical positions of the tongue, one might consider five positions, as follows, high, high-mid, mid, low-mid, low.

**11.** *Tense and Slack Sounds.* One other distinction with respect to the tongue is significant, especially in the study of vowel sounds, that is, the degree of its muscular tension. It may be slack (or relaxed), as in the vowel of **sit** [sɪt], or tense (or flexed), as in the vowel of **he** [hiː]. When the vowel is slack its vertical position is slightly lower than when tense, but not so much so as would follow a general shifting of the body of the tongue. The vowels of **he** and **sit** are both high vowels, the former being high blade tense, the latter high blade slack. The sides of the mouth and the lips generally are also likely to be held more firmly in pronouncing a tense than in pronouncing a slack sound. All long and stressed vowels are relatively tenser than short or unstressed vowels. A phonetic alphabet of high precision should have a means for indicating degrees of tenseness, but for practical purposes perhaps these general remarks and those to be found under the discussion of the separate sounds will prove as useful as an elaborate system of representation, and less distracting. Speakers differ widely in the degree of tenseness and slackness of their sounds, a slow and lazy speaker often having none of the tense vowel sounds which are characteristic of a cultivated and vigorous enunciation. The only way of testing the organic difference between tense and slack sounds is by observing the difference in muscular sensation which attends the production of them. By focusing attention upon these sensations, one may become as clearly conscious of muscular tension in the tongue as of muscular tension in the arms or legs.

**12.** *Stops and Continuants.* The column of air as it issues may be completely stopped by the organs of speech, with a sudden release or explosion, or only partially stopped, with a gradual emission of the breath. When it is completely stopped, the sounds produced are stop consonants (also called explosives, or plosives), e.g., **d** in **did** [dɪd], **p** in **pip** [pɪp], **b** in **bib** [bɪb]. When the air passage is only partly obstructed, the sound produced is a continuant consonant, e.g., the sounds represented in the conventional alphabet by **r**, **l**, **m**, **n**, **th**, **f**, **v**, **s**, **z**, **h**, **ch**, **sh**, **y**. Stop consonants are instantaneous, but continuants share with vowels the possibility of being lengthened indefinitely. The difference between vowel and consonant is largely one of degree, a vowel being a sound produced without any notable obstruction of the vocal passage, a consonant, one in which the air current is definitely obstructed, either wholly or partially. Certain vowels, such as the vowel [iː] when pronounced very tensely, or the vowel [u] pronounced with excessive rounding, shade imperceptibly into the continuant consonants [j], [w]. Normally, however, the distinction between vowel and consonant is quite clear. The continuant consonants **r**, **l**, **m**, **n** are sometimes called semivowels, and they may constitute syllables by themselves without an accompanying vowel, as in **winter** [ˈwɪntɹ], **table** [ˈteːbl], **heaven** [ˈhɛvn]. Words of this type may, of course, be pronounced with a vowel before the final consonant, that is, [ˈwɪntəɹ], [ˈteːbəl], [ˈhɛvən], but these would be very formal pronunciations. When a consonant is syllabic, a dot may be placed under it to indicate this fact. This is not necessary, however, since a consonant which is syllabic will naturally be pronounced so without special direction.

**13.** Stop consonants, both voiced and voiceless, though especially the latter, are pronounced in English with such a violent explosion of the breath, that they are mechanically followed by a slight, but distinctly audible breath continuant, [h]. A more exact representation of the consonants in **dig**, **toy**, etc., would therefore be [dʰɪgʰ], [tʰɔɪ], etc. This slight after-sound will not be indicated in the phonetic transcriptions of the present volume, the general statement here made being intended to cover all instances, but the phenomena should be carefully studied. Note that there is a greater aspiration after an initial than after a final consonant, as in **pop**; or when a consonant stands alone, as in **pool**, than when in close combination with another consonant, as in **spool**, cf. also **tin**, **sting**, **peach**, **speech**, etc.; or when a consonant bears a relatively heavy stress, than when lightly stressed, as in the two stop consonants of **paper**, the two [t] sounds of **potato**, the two [k] sounds of **cocoa**; or after a voiceless than after a voiced stop, cf. **toe** and **dough**. The extent to which the aspiration is present thus seems to depend upon the degree of intensity or energy with which the explosions are made. With some speakers the aspiration is scarcely audible at all, though such speakers are rare and are usually of a somewhat listless habit in speech. On the other hand, an extreme of aspiration is present in some forms of dialect speech, see below, p. 202.

**14.** In words like **better, winter, putty,** and in general in words in which a stressed stop is followed by an unstressed **-er**, or an unstressed vowel, the stop is sometimes pronounced without aspiration, the final syllable **-er** being ordinarily represented merely by a syllabic **r**, i.e., [ˈbɛtɹ], [ˈwɪntɹ]. But the pronunciation with the stop consonant aspirated is to be preferred. When a voiceless stop is not aspirated, it commonly sounds like a voiced stop, as in pronunciations like [ˈwɪndɹ], [ˈbɛdɹ], [ˈwɔdɹ], [ˈlɛdɹ], [ˈpʌdɪ], for **winter, better, water, letter, putty.** See § 240.

**15.** When two stop consonants come together, the first of the two is usually pronounced with an incomplete explosion of the breath. Thus words like **looked** or **befogged** are not pronounced with a fully formed [k] as in **look**, or a fully formed [g] as in **fog**, followed in the former case by [t], in the latter by [d]. If they were, the complete phonetic form of such words would be something like [lʊkʰtʰ], [bɪˈfɔgʰdʰ]. What happens is that the organic position for [k] or [g] is assumed, is then held for a moment, the organic position for the following stop being arrived at before any explosion takes place. In consequence, there is only one complete explosion in **looked befogged,** and many similar consonant combinations. There is, however, a very slight fricative consonant sound, a kind of [h], which is heard after the vowel and before the pause. Analytically, a word like **looked** would consist of the initial consonant, the vowel, the slight frictional glide before the stop position for [k] is completely assumed, a pause, and finally the explosion which produces [t]. See § 346.

16. *Palate and Nose.* The palate may be considered as composed of two parts, the soft-palate (or velum), at the back of the mouth, and the hard-palate, which forms the concave roof of the mouth. In front of the hard-palate lies the bony ridge of the alveoli or gums. The hard-palate is immovable, but the soft-palate is subject to muscular control and can be raised or lowered at will. When it is raised, as for the most part it is in speaking, it closes the entrance to the nasal canals, hence the name **velum**, 'veil.' When it is lowered, the air is permitted to pass through the nose, as in breathing or in the production of the nasal consonants **n** [n] as in **sin** [sɪn], **m** [m] as in **him** [hɪm], **ng** [ŋ] as in **song, sing** [sɔŋ], [sɪŋ]. In pronouncing a nasal consonant, no breath is permitted to escape through the mouth, but the current is stopped either at the lips, as in [m], or within the mouth by the pressure of the tongue against the front of the roof of the mouth, as in [n], or further back, as in [ŋ].

17. *Nasal Vowels.* English has no nasal vowels in recognized good use, though with many speakers in America, almost all the vowels, but especially the low and mid slack vowels, are nasalized, and at the same time are lengthened or 'drawled,' see §§ 80–82, 128. The nasal pronunciation of vowels is usually the result of a lazy and unenergetic enunciation. It is by no means peculiar to American speech, but is heard in England, if not as generally, often quite as markedly as in America. Since nasal vowels result from lowering the velum and thus permitting air to issue through the nose as well as the mouth, a good way to test their presence in one's

speech is to hold the nostrils shut while pronouncing the vowels. If one finds that one's vowels are the same, whether one holds the nostrils shut or does not, there can be no nasalization in the sounds. But if one finds that one produces a different vowel sound when one holds the nostrils shut from that which is produced when one does not, this means that the vowels are nasalized, the peculiar quality of the sounds in the first case being due to the fact that the air which normally escapes through the nose in pronouncing a nasal vowel is obstructed artificially by the pressure of the fingers on the nostrils. This produces the peculiar 'twang' described in the next paragraph. The fault of nasalization is one merely of habit and can be corrected by practice. It is most likely to occur in vowels which precede or follow a nasal consonant, whether [m], [n] or [ŋ], but with many speakers it is heard also in vowels not in nasal surroundings. Nasalization of vowels is so general in American speech that it often passes unnoticed, and is often present in the speech of persons who are quite unaware of the fact and who can be made to realize it only after much patient observation. Some speakers who do not ordinarily nasalize vowels are inclined to do so when they are tired.

**18.** Another kind of faulty nasal speech is sometimes heard in speakers who pinch together the walls of the nose at its outlet, raising the upper lip and tightening all the muscles of that region of the face, the result being a peculiar 'twang' or resonance which is immediately corrected by relaxing these muscles and allowing the breath to issue freely from the nose in pronouncing nasal consonants, and in the case of vowels, by raising the velum so that the air does not enter the nasal canals at all. This kind of nasalization is less common than that described in the preceding paragraph, though it is marked in some types of American dialect speech.

**19.** The 'talking through the nose' of a person with a cold in the head is not truly described by this phrase, for one of the main characteristics of this supposed talking through the nose is that the velum and the nasal passages being inflamed and swollen, the nasal channels are obstructed mechanically, and the escape of the breath through the nose, which takes place when the velum is lowered in pronouncing a nasal consonant, or when it relaxes normally after the pronunciation of other consonants or a vowel, is prevented. The result is that instead of **n** [n], one with a cold will pronounce something like [d], and for **m** will pronounce [b], and for [ŋ] will pronounce [g], as in [gʊd ˈbɔːdɪg] for **good morning**; [sprɪg, ˈdʒɛdtl sprɪg] for **spring, gentle spring**; [ə koːld ɪd baɪ doːz] for **a cold in my nose.**

**20.** *The Lips.* The form of the lips is also to be noted, especially in studying vowel sounds, and is easily observed. They may be drawn back (wide or spread) as they are in pronouncing the vowel of **he**, **see**, **tea**, etc., or they may be rounded (protruded or pouted) as they are in pronouncing the vowel of **too**, **do**, **blue**, etc. When they are neither wide nor rounded, but are in the normal position of rest, as in the first vowel of **father**, or the first vowel of **about**, they are said to be neutral. Various stages of widening are to be observed between neutral position and the extreme wide position of **tea**, and likewise various degrees of rounding between neutral position and the extreme rounding of **too**. Even a slight shift from one position to another may modify the quality of a vowel. Many speakers tend to move their lips very little, and almost all English sounds can be made audibly, though monotonously and not clearly, with practically no motion of the lips. A clear and distinct enunciation, however, demands an active muscular control of the lips.

## II

## DESCRIPTION OF SOUNDS

**21.** *Voiced Stops.* The phonetic symbols for the voiced stops are [b], [d], [g]. The first of these is a voiced bilabial stop, as in **beet** [biːt], **baby** ['beːbɪ], **bib** [bɪb]; the second is a voiced point alveolar stop, as in **do** [duː], **shady** ['ʃeːdɪ], **did** [dɪd]. The character of the sound represented by [g] varies considerably according to the quality of the vowel sounds with which it is combined. With a back vowel, as in the word **gong** [gɔŋ], the sound is a voiced back soft-palate stop. When the vocalic surrounding is front, as in **geese** [giːs], **fatigue** [fæ'tiːg], the consonant is a voiced front hard-palate stop. The shading from the extreme of the back sound to the extreme of the front sound is gradual in differing combinations. As the front or back quality of this sound is dependent upon the vowel with which it is combined and is necessarily determined by it, in the interest of economy in the alphabet one symbol, [g], will be used in this book for all shades of the sound.

**22.** *Voiceless Stops.* The phonetic symbols for the voiceless stops are [p], [t], [k]. They are the voiceless equivalents of [b], [d], [g], the first being a voiceless bilabial stop, as in **pay** [peɪ], **pope** [poːp]; the second a voiceless point alveolar stop, as in **hit** [hɪt], **debtor** ['dɛtəɹ]. As with [g], the character of the sound represented by [k] is determined by vocalic surrounding. In

**call** [kɔːl], the initial consonant is a voiceless back soft-palate stop, but in **keel** [kiːl] it is a voiceless front hard-palate stop.

23. *Fricative Continuants.* The term 'fricative continuants' designates those consonants which produce an acoustic effect of whistling, hissing, puffing, 'rolling,' or merely 'rough breathing.' They are of several varieties and must be described separately.

24. [h] represents the voiceless glottal fricative and the voiceless front fricative. As a voiceless glottal fricative, [h] is produced with the tongue lying neutral on the floor of the mouth, as it does in normal breathing, but with the glottis so narrowed by a partial closure of the vocal chords that the air in passing between them causes an audible friction. If the vocal chords were drawn close together and the glottis quite closed, the air forcing its way through would set the chords vibrating and thus produce a vowel sound. Thus in the exclamation **Ha!** [hɑː], the only change which takes place in the transition from the consonant to the vowel is a change at the glottis, which changes from half-closed in [h] to closed in [ɑː]. When [h] precedes a vowel the formation of which requires a departure of the tongue from that position of almost complete rest which it occupies in [ɑ], the tongue position is assumed for the vowel even while the consonant is being pronounced, as in **hat** [hæt]. And in general one may say that there are as many varieties of [h] as there are varieties of vowels before which it may stand. Before the high vowels, however, the glottal friction tends to be replaced by a friction made in the mouth, and [h] standing before a strongly stressed [iː], as in **heed** [hiːd], becomes a voiceless front fricative, formed by

pressing the front of the tongue so hard against the palate that the air in escaping produces a consonantal noise. The main differences between [iː] and [h] in **heed** are that in the consonant the tongue is pressed closer to the palate, therefore forms more of an obstruction to the current of air, and that the consonant is voiceless, the vowel voiced. The voiceless front fricative is still more unmistakeably heard in words like **hue, hew, Hugh** [hjuː], **huge** [hjuːdʒ], **humor** [ˈhjuːməɹ]. It is both unnecessary and impracticable to record all shades of [h], and the one symbol will be here used to cover all varieties of the sound.

**25.** [j] represents the voiced front fricative, formed with the front of the tongue raised close to the hard-palate, the sound made by the breath escaping through the narrow opening being accompanied by vibration of the vocal chords. Before a back vowel, as in **yawl** [jɔːl], the [j] is formed slightly farther back than it is before a front vowel, as in **yield** [jiːld], but the difference is not great. This sound is not strongly consonantal in English. The tongue position for it is almost the same as for [i], and this vowel slightly raised and intensified passes over into [j]. It is the first element in the so-called 'long **u**' sound, as in **music** [ˈmjuːzɪk], **pure** [pjuːɹ], etc. It is commonly represented in the ordinary spelling by **y**.

**26.** [ʍ] may be described as a voiceless, back, lip-rounded fricative. The tongue is raised at the back, the lips are rounded so as to reduce the opening of the mouth, thus causing a friction that produces a slight whistling sound. Its corresponding voiced form is [w], though [ʍ] is slightly more whistling than [w], the lips being more pursed and the breath expelled more energetically. The usual spelling for [ʍ] is **wh**, as in **whit**

[ʍɪt], **which** [ʍɪtʃ], **while** [ʍaɪl], etc. Many speakers have only [w] for both [w] and [ʍ], see §§ 27, 372.

**27.** [w] is the voiced, back, lip-rounded fricative. The distinction between the voiced and voiceless sound will be apparent to some speakers only after close observation and experiment. Speakers who have no [ʍ] are advised to study carefully the pronunciation of such pairs of words as **whit, wit, whet, wet, when, wen, which, witch**, etc. The ordinary spelling for the sound is **w**, but also **u** after **q**, **g**, as in **quit** [kwɪt], **language** ['læŋgwɪdʒ], after **s** in **persuade, dissuade**, etc., and the sound appears also in several words, e.g., **one** [wʌn], **choir** ['kwaɪəɹ], the spelling of which is exceptional.

**28.** [f], the voiceless upper-teeth lower-lip fricative, as in **fit** [fɪt], **stiff** [stɪf], **famish** ['fæmɪʃ], **rough** [rʌf], **philosophy** [fɪ'lɑsəfɪ]. The sound is caused by the escape of the breath as it is forced through the openings between the upper teeth. With some speakers whose teeth are set very close together, the breath is allowed to escape between the edges of the upper teeth and the lower lip. In general it should be said that owing to the great difference which exists among individuals in the formation of their teeth, all sounds in the production of which the teeth are a prominent factor can be and are produced in a variety of ways.

**29.** [v], the voiced upper-teeth lower-lip fricative, as in **live** [lɪv], [laɪv], **vat** [væt], **vision** ['vɪʒn], ['vɪʒən], **heavy** ['hɛvɪ]. Foreign speakers sometimes pronounce [v] for [w], in learning English, but the error is easily corrected by observing the manner in which the sounds are produced. In pronouncing [w], the upper teeth never touch the lower lip, but both upper and lower lip are protruded. In pronouncing [v] the lips are drawn back or widened.

**30.** [θ] is a voiceless point inter-dental fricative. The point of the tongue is between the upper and lower teeth, the breath escaping mainly between the middle upper teeth. Some speakers extend the point of the tongue between and slightly beyond the teeth, but with others the tongue is placed merely on the edge of the upper teeth. The acoustic effect is the same. Examples of words in which [θ] occurs are **thing** [θɪŋ], **breath** [brɛθ], **hath** [hæθ], **myth** [mɪθ], **wrath** [ræθ].

**31.** [ð] is the voiced equivalent of [θ], being a voiced point inter-dental fricative, as in **that** [ðæt], **thus** [ðʌs], **father** [ˈfɑːðəɹ], **feather** [ˈfɛðəɹ], **baths** (*noun*) [bæːðz], **with** [wɪð]. When strongly stressed, as in the adverbial position at the end of a sentence, **with** may have a voiceless consonant, [wɪθ].

**32.** Many foreigners, for example Frenchmen and Germans, have difficulty with the sounds [θ], [ð] in speaking English, not because the sounds are hard in themselves, but because they do not occur in the native language of the speakers, and being unfamiliar, are pronounced like sounds that are familiar, usually [f], [s] or [v], [z]. Any one who understands the way in which the sounds are made can readily produce them.

**33.** [s], a sound of somewhat complicated formation. The point of the tongue is pressed lightly against the upper teeth, the blade lightly against the gums, the front teeth are loosely closed, and the breath is sent forth in a narrow stream over the tongue and between the teeth. It may be described, therefore, as a voiceless, blade-alveolar point post-dental fricative. It appears in words like **sin** [sɪn], **sieve** [sɪv], **cell** [sɛl], **psalm** [sɑːm], **receive** [rɪˈsiːv], **fancy** [ˈfænsɪ].

**34.** The difference between normal [s] and a sharp, hissing sound sometimes heard for **s** is that in the latter the teeth are tightly closed, the tongue tense, and the breath sent forth with greater force than it is in [s]. In cultivated speech, [s] is a gentle rather than an energetic sound.

**35.** [z] is formed in the same way as [s], with the addition of voicing. The tongue may be very slightly lower and more relaxed in pronouncing [z] than it is in pronouncing [s]. The sound is commonly written as **z** or **s**, as in **zinc** [zɪŋk], **zealous** [ˈzɛləs], **dizzy** [ˈdɪzɪ], **his** [hɪz], **beds** [bɛdz], **music** [ˈmjuːzɪk].

**36.** When [z] occurs at the end of a word, the sound is really composed of two parts. The main part is the voiced continuant represented by the symbol [z], but at its conclusion the sound changes from voiced to voiceless, from [z] to [s]. In their treatment of [z], some speakers, usually those of foreign tradition, have a very 'buzzing' kind of pronunciation, due to the fact that their final [z] is pronounced voiced throughout. This makes the sound seem unusually long, though its peculiarity lies not in its length, but in the lack of the voiceless ending which is present in standard speech.

**37.** [ʃ], as in **ship** [ʃɪp], **wish** [wɪʃ], **chip** [tʃɪp], **shawl** [ʃɔːl], **bush** [bʊʃ], **mission** [ˈmɪʃn], [ˈmɪʃən], may be described as a voiceless, blade-dental point-alveolar fricative. The blade of the tongue presses against the sides of the middle upper teeth, closing the openings there, the point almost touches the upper gums, the teeth are closed, and the breath issues along the channel between the tongue and the roof of the mouth through the openings between the upper front teeth. The channel through which the breath issues is broader than it is in pronouncing [s]. The sound is represented in a great variety of ways in conventional spelling, see § 327.

**38.** [ʒ], as in **pleasure** [ˈplɛʒəɹ], **decision** [dɪˈsɪʒn], **judge** [dʒʌdʒ], is the voiced equivalent of [ʃ]. It has no letter of its own in the conventional alphabet and is indicated in spelling in various ways, see §§ 328 ff.

**39.** [r] is produced by raising the body of the tongue so that the sides of it press against the upper teeth, tilting the point of the tongue so that it just barely touches the bony ridge of the gums, and allowing the breath to escape with a distinctly audible friction over the point of the tongue and between the teeth, which are slightly open. It may be described, therefore, as an alveolar **r**, with reference to the position of the tongue. The vocal chords are in vibration and the lips are slightly drawn back. The breath escapes with considerable force between the up-tilted point of the tongue and the alveoli, and it is here that the consonantal friction in [r] is produced, not as the air passes between the teeth. The tongue positions for [r] are somewhat similar to those for [ʃ], [ʒ], but in [r] the teeth are open, in [ʃ], [ʒ] the upper and lower teeth are generally in close contact.

**40.** This is the sound commonly heard in American speech for **r** initially, as in **red** [rɛd], between vowels, as in **very** [ˈvɛrɪ], and after consonants, as in **dress** [drɛs]. Before proceeding further with the consideration of various other kinds of **r**, the student is advised to observe extensively the occurrence of [r] in the three positions just mentioned in different words, and to study the sound itself so as to be able to distinguish the consonantal from the vocalic element in it. A voiceless **r**, which is merely frictional, should be compared with the voiced fricative [r], as for example the **tr** of **tread** pronounced separately without voicing as compared with **red, read** (preterite of the verb), pronounced [rɛd] with voicing.

**41.** A trilled or rolled **r**, though not very common in American speech, is sometimes heard, especially for **r** between vowels, as in **very, hurry**, etc. It is commonly cultivated in stage pronunciation on the ground that it carries better than the fricative **r**. It is also cultivated by telephone operators in the pronunciation of **three.** It is formed by causing the point of the tongue to tap or vibrate against the gums, once or more, and in highly-developed forms of trilled **r**, a considerable number of times. This sound is so rare in American speech that it has not seemed necessary to provide a special symbol for it. It may be regarded as a variant form of [r].

**42.** [ɹ] is also a voiced sound, but the friction accompanying the vocalic element is so slight that one might hesitate to group it with the fricatives, or with the consonants at all. Its orthographic representation, however, is **r**, and it is commonly thought of as being a variety of this sound.

In pronouncing [ɹ] the point of the tongue is not tilted as high as in [r], but if it were permitted to touch the roof of the mouth, which it does not do, it would strike the region just back of the upper teeth and in front of the place where the concavity of the roof of the mouth begins. It is commonly heard in American speech before consonants and finally, as in **part** [pɑːɹt], **hard** [hɑːɹd], **heard** [həɹd], **cord** [kɔɹd], **fir, fur** [fəɹ], **demur** [dɪˈməɹ], **car** [kɑːɹ], **dinner** [ˈdɪnəɹ], **color** [ˈkʌləɹ], **never** [ˈnɛvəɹ], etc. There is less friction in the pronunciation of [ɹ] than of [r], the space between the tongue and the roof of the mouth being greater, and some phoneticians do not recognize any consonantal value for orthographic **r** before consonants and finally. It is true that [ɹ] is regularly omitted by some speakers, especially in the East and South in America, when it is final or stands before another consonant, the difference between **taw** and **tore**, **pot** and **part**, so far as there is one with such speakers, being altogether a difference of vowel quality or length. In unstressed position, as in **never**, the word ends, in this manner of speech, with the vowel [ə], as in [ˈnɛvə]. A word like **part** consists, in this pronunciation, of only three elements, [p], [ɑː] and [t], giving [pɑːt]. But in all regions of the United States, especially away from the Atlantic seaboard, an orthographic **r** commonly has phonetic value before consonants and when final. Whether one calls this sound which is heard a consonant or not is of little importance, provided the existence and quality of the sound itself are recognized. Its presence can be easily demonstrated by observing the tongue positions in pronouncing a word like **part**. This word, in American pronunciation which is not typically Eastern, contains four elements, the first and last being stop consonants, the second and third resulting from a shifting of the tongue from mid to high position accompanied by curving or tilting of the point. In **never**, when the word ends only in a vowel, as in Eastern American pronunciation, the tongue position at the conclusion of the word is that of [ə], that is mid position, with the point of the tongue touching or on a level with the lower front teeth. With those, however, who are said to pronounce their **r's**, the word ends with the tongue in high position and the tip of the tongue on a level with the roots of the upper teeth, giving ['nɛvəɹ]. The difference between [r] and [ɹ] may be tested by pronouncing the word **never** by itself, and then by letting it be followed by **rains**, as in **it never rains.** Of course if one has no final **r**, this would be simply [ɪt 'nɛvə reɪnz]. But if one pronounces final **r's**, the final consonant of **never** cannot simply be carried over, like a long consonant (see § 83), to satisfy the demand for the initial consonant of **rains**. A slight modification in articulation is observable in pronouncing the two **r's**, which is adequately represented, however it be named, by the two phonetic symbols [ɹ] and [r].

**43.** Some speakers, especially those of an unenergetic habit of enunciation, pronounce [ɹ] for [r] even in the stressed initial position, between vowels, and after consonants. The pronunciation of [r] for [ɹ], that is a strongly fricative consonant finally and before other consonants, as in ['nɛvər], [pɑːrt], etc., is current in localities, but is not general in standard American English.

**44.** Another variety of **r** is heard, especially in the North Central states and in the Middle West, which is produced by bending back the point of the tongue so far that if it actually came into contact with the roof of the mouth, it would strike about the middle of the hard-palate. This is often spoken of popularly as 'guttural **r**,' though it would be truer to the facts to call it a hard-palate **r**, or simply, back **r**. Dialect story writers usually represent it by doubling the spelling, as in **corrn, farrm,** etc. The sound is often so marked in the regions in which it occurs as to constitute as distinct a dialect feature as the loss of [ɹ] before consonants and finally is for the Atlantic seaboard. Speakers who have this back [r] are often said to 'roll their **r**'s,' though as a matter of fact there is no more rolling or tapping of any of the organs of speech in pronouncing this **r** than there is in pronouncing the common [r], [ɹ]. It is, however, sometimes prolonged. Englishmen and Eastern Americans often find this sound offensive.[1]

**45.** *Lateral Continuants.* Lateral or side continuants are represented in standard English only by **l** [l], as in **land** [lænd], **million** [ˈmɪljən], **all** [ɔːl]. In forming this sound the point of the tongue is placed against the roots of the upper teeth, and the blade against the gums, which means that the whole body of the tongue lies in high position; the sides of the tongue are free and the air issues through the narrow channels at the sides of the mouth between the tongue and the cheeks. Normally the breath issues through both sides of the mouth, but the sound may be produced with the channel open only on one side of the mouth. Some speakers curve back the point of the tongue in producing this sound, so that the point

[1] "She [one of the characters in a Mississippi Valley story who has returned home after having been 'cultured up' in the East] did not say 'charrmed' like an alarm clock breaking out. She did not trundle his name [Orson Carver] like a wheelbarrow. Tudie rolled the 'r' on his eardrums as with a drumstick, and by contrast the sound came to him as: 'Misterr Carrverr comes from Harrvarrd. He calls it Havvad.'" — From "A as in Father," by Rupert Hughes, *In a Little Town*, p. 364.

presses against the front part of the hard-palate. It makes little difference in acoustic effect whether the breath issues through only one or through both sides of the mouth, but the curving back of the point of the tongue so that it presses against the hard-palate produces a variety of [l] which is not current in standard speech. This [l] is particularly noticeable when it is preceded by **i** or **e**, as in **hilly**, **sell** and similar words, the curving of the tongue for **l** affecting also the vowels and producing pronunciations somewhat like [ˈhəlɪ], [səl]. It is noticeable also in final unstressed syllables, as in **table**, **moral**, **feeble**, **people**, and it is this 'dark' or 'thick' **l**, as it may be described, which writers of the popular dialect sometimes indicate by a spelling like **peepul** for **people**. It is a sound to be avoided in cultivated speech.

**46.** The quality of [l] in standard speech is not quite the same when it stands in the neighborhood of a front sound, as in **lit** [lɪt], **ill** [ɪl], as when it stands in the neighborhood of a back sound, as in **law** [lɔː], **all** [ɔːl]. The consonant takes color to some extent from its vocalic surrounding, and one may speak of a front and a back [l]. The difference is not so important, however, as to call for separate symbols for the two qualities. The sound is usually voiced, though it may sometimes be voiceless when it follows a voiceless consonant in an unstressed position, as in **hospital** [ˈhɑspɪtl], [ˈhɔspɪtl].

**47.** Because of its vocalic character, [l] sometimes constitutes a syllable without any accompanying vowel, as in **middle** [ˈmɪdl], **table** [ˈteːbl], **battle** [ˈbætl], **special** [ˈspɛʃl], not [ˈmɪdəl], [ˈteːbəl], [ˈbætəl], [ˈspɛʃəl], except in a very formal pronunciation.

**48.** *Nasal Continuants.* The nasal continuants are [m], [n], [ŋ], as exemplified respectively in **may, no, song** and **sing.** In [m] the lips are closed, the tongue is quiescent, the velum lowered, and the vocal chords in vibration, producing a bilabial nasal voiced continuant. In [n] the stoppage in the oral passage is made by the point of the tongue pressing against the upper gums, as in [d], the velum is lowered, allowing the air to pass through the nose, and the vocal chords vibrate, producing a point alveolar nasal voiced continuant. In [ŋ], as in **song** [sɔŋ], the back of the tongue presses against the forward part of the soft-palate, forming a back soft-palate voiced nasal continuant. In **sing** [sɪŋ] the front of the tongue presses against the hard-palate, forming a front hard-palate voiced nasal continuant. The grades of [ŋ] correspond in formation to [g], with the addition of nasalization, and as in the case of [g], [k], [h], only one symbol, [ŋ], will be used for all shades of this sound.

**49.** *Compound Consonants.* The initial and final consonants in **church**, **judge**, call for no special symbols, since **ch** is a combination of [t] and [ʃ], and may therefore be written [tʃ], and **j, dg**, is a combination of [d] and [ʒ], therefore written [dʒ]. It should be observed that **th** of the ordinary spelling does not stand for a double consonant, but for a sound which is as single as the sound of [s] or [f] or [z], and is therefore represented by a simple symbol, [ð] or [θ]. See § 8.

**50.** *Vowels.* In analyzing the vowels, one must consider (1) the vertical position of the tongue, whether high, mid, or low; (2) the region of the tongue which is most elevated in producing the several vowels, whether the back, the front, a region between the back and front, the blade, or point, though the point is rarely of significance in vowel formation; (3) the degree of tenseness of the tongue, whether tense (flexed), or slack (relaxed); (4) the presence or lack of rounding of the lips. The tongue may lie also in altogether neutral position, with no part particularly active, in which case it is said to be flat. In describing the vowels it will be clearest to start with the high front vowels as the ones whose method of formation is most easily observed. It is easy to analyze the vowels at the extremes, like [iː] in **see** [siː], which is the highest and farthest front of all vowels, or [ɔː] in **saw** [sɔː], which is the lowest and farthest back of all English vowels. As one approaches the mid and front positions of the tongue, however, the analysis becomes increasingly difficult, and vowels like [ɛ] in **set** [sɛt], [ɛː] in **there** [ðɛːɹ], [ʌ] in **hut** [hʌt], [ʌː] in **hurt** [hʌːt], with the **r** silent, [æ] in **hat** [hæt], [aː] in **fast** [faːst], [ɑ] in **hot** [hɑt] differ from each other very slightly both in acoustic effect and in organic method of formation. Even slight variations, however, are often sufficient to draw attention to differing manners of pronunciation.

**51.** [i]. *High blade tense wide.* The body of the tongue is raised as high as it can be in the production of any English vowel sound. The blade and front are pressed up close to the hard-palate, the muscles of the tongue and the cheeks are tense or flexed, and the sides of the mouth are drawn back, making the lips wide. The point of the tongue rests against the backs of the lower teeth, as it does in almost all English vowel sounds. The mouth is open and the teeth apart about the space of the thickness of the tip of the little finger. This vowel may be short or half-long, as in **completely** [kəm'pli·tlɪ], **deify** ['di·ɪˌfaɪ], **beatific** [ˌbiə'tɪfɪk], **seasonable** ['si·zənəbl], or long, as in **seed** [siːd], **see, sea** [siː], **deceive** [dɪ'siːv], **seethe** [siːð]. There is no difference in quality between [i] and [iː], though when final, [iː] may become somewhat diphthongal, see § 76.

**52.** [ɪ]. *High blade slack neutral.* This vowel is formed exactly like [i], except that the muscles of the tongue and cheek are relaxed, and the lips are allowed to fall into neutral position. It is always a short vowel, and examples of it are found in **sit** [sɪt], **city** ['sɪtɪ], **finish** ['fɪnɪʃ], **cylinder** ['sɪləndəɹ]. When the tongue is relaxed in [ɪ], it becomes slightly lower than it is in pronouncing [i].

In the two syllables of a word like **city**, the vowel is represented by the same symbol, though as a matter of fact, [ɪ] in unstressed position is slightly lower than [ɪ] in the stressed position. Separate symbols might be used to indicate this, or one may speak descriptively of [ɪ] in unstressed syllables as being more open or lower than [ɪ] in stressed syllables. It is the open [ɪ] which is frequently heard in unstressed initial and final syllables, as in **decide** [dɪ'saɪd], **begin** [bɪ'gɪn], **added** ['ædɪd], **basket** ['bæskɪt].

The vowel [ɪ] also appears as the second element in diphthongs, see §§ 71, 72, 75.

**53.** [e]. *Mid front tense wide.* The whole body of the tongue falls a little into mid position in passing from the two preceding sounds to this sound. The point of the tongue touches the bases of the lower teeth, but the front is arched so that it touches the sides of the upper teeth. The tongue and cheek muscles are flexed, and the lips are wide, though not so wide as in [iː]. The jaw drops a little from the position for [i], so that the distance between the teeth is about the thickness of the index finger. This vowel may be short or half-long, as in **vacation** [ve-ˈke·ʃən], **patriot** [ˈpe·trɪət], **fatally** [ˈfe·təlɪ], **complacent** [kəmˈple·sənt], or long, as in **raid** [reːd], **fade** [feːd], **place** [pleːs]. There is not usually any difference of quality between [e] and [eː], though the latter tends to become diphthongal when final or before voiced consonants and under full stress, see §§ 71, 207.

**54.** [ɛ]. *Mid front slack neutral.* This sound occupies the same position relative to [e] that [ɪ] does to [i]. It is always a short vowel in English, as in **set** [sɛt], **said** [sɛd], **medicine** [ˈmɛdɪsɪn], **debt** [dɛt], **perish** [ˈpɛrɪʃ], **ferry** [ˈfɛrɪ], **guess** [gɛs], **led, lead** (*noun*) [lɛd], **dense** [dɛns], **trench** [trɛntʃ].

**55.** [ɛː]. *Mid half-front slack neutral.* This is a long vowel which occurs only before **r** in stressed syllables, and is represented in spelling by **e, ei, ea, a, ai**, as in **there, their** [ðɛːɹ], **pare, pair, pear** [pɛːɹ], **fair, fare** [fɛːɹ], **lair** [lɛːɹ], **tear** (*verb*), **tare** [tɛːɹ], **fairy** [ˈfɛːrɪ], **Mary** [ˈmɛːrɪ], **chary** [ˈtʃɛːrɪ], **wary** [ˈwɛːrɪ]. The vowel is really slightly lower than [ɛ] and is formed slightly farther back, that is, it is a half-front vowel, but it is represented here by the same symbol, with the mark of length added, to avoid increasing the number of symbols. As [ɛ] is never long, and [ɛː] occurs only in the position before **r** in stressed syllables, no confusion between the two sounds is likely to occur. Instead of [ðɛːɹ], [pɛːɹ], etc., those speakers who do not pronounce their final **r**'s have [ðɛːə], [pɛːə], etc.

**56.** [æ]. *Low front slack wide,* as in **hat** [hæt], **has** [hæz], **fashion** [ˈfæʃn], **laggard** [ˈlægəɹd], and very common in American pronunciation in words like **path** [pæθ], **fast** [fæst], **dance** [dæns], etc., see §§ 124–130. In words of this latter type, the vowel sometimes becomes long, but ordinarily in standard pronunciation it is short. The tongue is in slightly lower position than it is for [ɛː], but is not as low as it can be made to be. To be more exact, one might describe its position as low-mid. The point of the tongue rests against the lower gums, but the front is raised and is felt lightly touching the lower edges of the upper teeth. The muscles of the tongue are relaxed, but the sides of the mouth are slightly drawn back, producing a very slightly wide lip formation. The mouth is open wide enough to enable one to insert the tips of the little and ring fingers.

**57.** [ɑ]. *Low half-back slack neutral*, as in **father** [ˈfɑːðəɹ], **palm** [pɑːm], and, in the pronunciation of some Americans, **fast** [fɑːst], **dance** [dɑːnts], [dɑːns], **calf** [kɑːf], etc. In these words the vowel is long, but the short vowel, with a difference only in quantity from the long, is commonly heard in America in words of the type of **hot** [hɑt], **not** [nɑt], **pod** [pɑd], **stop** [stɑp], etc. The tongue is low in the mouth, though not quite so low as in [ɔː], and the tip touches the lower gums. The part of the tongue which is raised is back, but not so far back as in sounds like [o], [ɔ], [ɔː], with which [ɑ] should be compared. It lies between the back and front surfaces of the tongue, but a little closer to back than to front and is therefore described as half-back. The tongue muscles are relaxed, and the lips are at rest or neutral. The space between the teeth is sufficiently wide to enable one to insert the index and middle fingers. The teeth are farther apart and the mouth more open in pronouncing this vowel than they are in uttering any other English vowel.

**58.** [a]. *Low half-front slack slightly wide.* This sound is widely current, especially in artificial speech in America, as a compromise vowel between [ɑː] and [æ] in words of the type of **fast**, **calf**, **dance**, **grass**, etc., which are pronounced as [fɑːst], [kɑːf], [dɑːnts], [dɑːns], [grɑːs], or [fæst], [kæf], [dænts], [dæns], [græs], or [faːst], [kaːf], [daːnts], [daːns], [graːs], etc. In these and similar words the vowel is commonly long. As a short vowel the sound occurs only as the first element in the diphthong [aɪ], see §§ 72, 209. The tongue position is the same as for [ɑ], except that the part which is elevated is slightly more forward than for [ɑ]; it is not a front sound, but is nearer to front than back position and is therefore described as half-front. The lips are slightly retracted or widened, and with some speakers, especially those who use the sound consciously, the muscles of the tongue and cheek are likely to be somewhat tense. The sound has acquired unusual importance in the discussion of American usage because it is so often cultivated as an artificial refinement in certain words which in natural, unconscious use have [ɑː] or [æ].

**59.** [u]. *High back tense rounded,* as in **mood** [muːd], **tube** [tjuːb], **juice** [dʒuːs], where it is long, or **musician** [mju'zɪʃn], **ludicrous** ['ludɪkrəs], where it is short or half-long. There is no difference in quality between the long and the short vowel, though the long vowel sometimes tends to become diphthongal, see § 76. The tongue is raised high, with the back part of it touching the soft-palate. From the back forward the tongue slopes down until the point touches the lower gums. The muscles of the tongue are moderately tense. The lips are protruded and distinctly pouted or rounded. The teeth are about as far apart as they are for [i], perhaps a little farther.

**60.** [ʊ]. *High back slack rounded,* as in **bush** [bʊʃ], **full** [fʊl], **book** [bʊk], **good** [gʊd]. The positions of the vocal organs are the same as for [u] except that the muscles are relaxed and the vowel is therefore slightly lower. It is normally only a short vowel, though some speakers might pronounce it long before [ɹ], in words like **poor, moor, lure,** etc.

**61.** [o]. *Mid back tense rounded,* as in **notable** [ˈno·təbl], **notation** [noˈte·ʃən], **devotional** [dɪˈvo·ʃənl], where it is short or half-long, or **note** [noːt], **spoke** [spoːk], **rode, road** [roːd], where it is long. There is commonly little difference in quality between [o] and [oː] in American speech, though [oː] tends to become diphthongal under certain conditions, see § 74. The tongue is in mid position in producing this vowel, the back elevated towards the soft-palate, the forward surface sloping down until the point touches the lower gums. The muscles of the tongue are moderately tense, and the lips are rounded slightly less than for [u]. This sound should be compared with [ʌ], [ʌː].

**62.** [ɔ]. *Mid back slack rounded,* as in **authority** [ɔˈθɔrɪtɪ], **long** [lɔŋ], **song** [sɔŋ], and in many words in which usage varies between [ɔ] and [ɑ], as in **positive** [ˈpɔzɪtɪv] or [ˈpɑzɪtɪv], **hot** [hɔt] or [hɑt], **dog** [dɔg] or [dɑg], etc. It is normally a short vowel in standard pronunciation, and its method of formation is the same as that of [o] except that the sound is slack, therefore slightly lower than [o]. The lips are also slightly less rounded.

**63.** [ɔː]. *Low back tense rounded,* as in **law** [lɔː], **awe** [ɔː], **thought** [θɔːt], **caught** [kɔːt]. The tongue is in the lowest possible position, the extreme back of it is elevated towards the soft-palate, the point touches the floor of the mouth beneath the lower gums, and the muscles of the tongue are somewhat tense. The lips are rounded, and the teeth far enough apart to enable one to insert the thickness of the thumb between them. This vowel is normally only a long vowel and occurs only in stressed syllables. In dialect pronunciation it appears in some words which in standard speech have [ɔ] or [ɑ], as in **dog** [dɔːg], **God** [gɔːd], **long** [lɔːŋ], **frost** [frɔːst], see § 111.

Though the same symbol is used for [ɔ] and [ɔː], the organic difference between the two vowels should not be overlooked. The vowel [ɔ] is not merely a shortened [ɔː], but acoustically and organically it is a recognizably different vowel. As the difference in quantity implies also this difference in quality, it has not seemed necessary to provide [ɔː] with a separate symbol.

**64.** [ʌ]. *Mid half-back slack slightly wide,* as in **cut** [kʌt], **up** [ʌp], **butter** [ˈbʌtəɹ], **hurry** [ˈhʌrɪ], **son, sun** [sʌn], **some** [sʌm]. This sound should be compared with [ɔ] the tongue positions for which are the same, except that in [ʌ] the part of the tongue elevated lies a little in front of back position, best described as half-back. The lips also instead of being rounded are slightly wide. Compare this sound likewise with [ɛː]. The vowel [ʌ] is normally only a short vowel.

**65.** [ʌː]. *Mid half-back tense slightly wide.* This vowel occurs only as a long vowel, and only before **r** followed by a consonant, or before **r** final, according to the ordinary spelling, in the speech of those persons who pronounce no **r** in these combinations. Examples would be: **curse** [kʌːs], **hurt** [hʌːt], **fur, fir** [fʌː], **church** [tʃʌːtʃ], **dirt** [dʌːt], **person** [ˈpʌːsən]. The sound should be clearly distinguished from [ʌ]. It is much more tense than [ʌ], therefore appreciably higher and more front, and the lips are slightly more retracted. The point of the tongue touches the lower teeth. The mouth is open, as in [ʌ], sufficiently wide to enable one to insert the ring finger between the teeth. The sound should also be distinguished from [ə] and [ə], both of which, besides being different in quality, are always short.

**66.** [ə]. *Mid flat slack neutral.* This is the so-called obscure vowel, which appears only as a short sound in unstressed syllables, as in **about** [əˈbaʊt], **nation** [ˈneːʃən], **national** [ˈnæʃənəl]. The method of formation of this sound is very similar to that of [ɑ], the main difference being that in [ɑ] the tongue is in low position, in [ə] it is in mid or perhaps low-mid position. The tongue lies almost level in the mouth in pronouncing [ə], the point touches the lower teeth, the muscles are very slack, as they naturally would be in an unstressed syllable, and the lips are at rest in neutral position. The positions of the organs of speech are very much as they are in normal breathing. Vowels which ordinarily have distinct values when they stand in stressed position may all of them become this vowel in the unstressed position (see § 94), especially in popular speech, as in the popular pronunciations **fellow** [ˈfɛlə], **yellow** [ˈjɛlə], **piano** [pɪˈænə] for standard [ˈfɛlo], [ˈjɛlo], [pɪˈæno].

**67.** [ə]. *Mid inverted tense neutral.* This vowel occurs normally only as a short sound, before **r** [ɹ] followed by a consonant or before **r** [ɹ] final, in the speech of those

Americans who sound this [ɹ]. It is considerably tenser than [ə], therefore slightly higher and the middle parts of the tongue are somewhat more elevated. But the most characteristic quality of this vowel is due to the fact that the point of the tongue is lifted up and slightly inverted so that it is directed towards the roof of the mouth. In other words, the tongue position for [ɹ] is practically taken even while the vowel is being pronounced. This is the only vowel in English in the formation of which the point of the tongue rises above the level of the lower teeth, and the only one in which the tongue is hollowed or curved up. For this reason it is called an inverted vowel. The lips are neutral, and the teeth, as in [ə], are open wide enough to enable one to insert the ring finger. Examples of the occurrence of this sound are found in words like **clerk** [kləɹk], **mercy** [ˈməɹsɪ], **pert** [pəɹt], **dirt** [dəɹt], **shirt** [ʃəɹt], **hurt** [həɹt], **spurt** [spəɹt], **dearth** [dəɹθ], **worth** [wəɹθ], **fur, fir** [fəɹ], **her** [həɹ], **sir** [səɹ], **murmur** [ˈməɹməɹ], **infer** [ɪnˈfəɹ], **purr** [pəɹ], **slur** [sləɹ], **stir** [stəɹ].

**68.** In unstressed final syllables, the **r** [ɹ] may be syllabic or may be preceded by [ə] as in **winter** [ˈwɪntɹ] or [ˈwɪntəɹ], **supper** [ˈsʌpɹ] or [ˈsʌpəɹ], **stronger** [ˈstrɔŋgɹ] or [ˈstrɔŋgəɹ]. The second of these would be rather marked formal pronunciations.

**69.** In segregating this sound from surrounding sounds in words, the student is advised to begin with the simplest possible combination, as in **err** [əɹ]. The double spelling **rr** in this word signifies nothing, as the word has phonetically only one consonant. The vowel preceding the consonant should be distinguished first from the vowel of a word like **ere** [ɛːɹ], which has the same vowel as **there, pair, bear,** etc. Those speakers who do not sound [ɹ] in

**err** have only a simple vowel in this word, commonly the vowel [ʌː]. Those speakers who do pronounce the final consonant have a short [ə] followed by the slight frictional **r** which is designated by [ɹ]. It may be helpful to practice pronouncing **err** with an alveolar **r** [r], or a trilled or back **r**, proceeding then to the slighter consonantal sound in [əɹ]. In passing from [ə] to [ɹ] the only change in the organs of speech is the increased raising or tilting of the point of the tongue which brings it into a position close to the roots of the upper teeth and which causes the slight frictional element in [ɹ]. Next one may proceed to the analysis of complexer groups of sounds, like **fir, fur** [fəɹ], **person** [ˈpəɹsən], **heard** [həɹd], **dirt** [dəɹt], **hurt** [həɹt], which should be clearly distinguished both from [fər], [ˈpərsən], [hərd], [dərt], [hərt], and from [fʌː], [ˈpʌːsən], [hʌːd], [dʌːt], [hʌːt]. The organic differences between [ʌ], [ʌː], [ə], [ə] are at first not easy to analyze, but the acoustic distinctions intended by the several symbols are apparent to a sensitive ear and often constitute quite noticeable differences in pronunciation.

**70.** *Diphthongs.* A diphthong is a vowel combination which starts with one tongue position and glides to another before the sound closes. There is no articulatory break between the two elements of a diphthong, as there is, for example, when the first two vowels of a word like **pre-eminent** [priˈɛmənənt] are pronounced. A typical diphthong would be the vowel of **ride** [raɪd]. Diphthongs are sometimes written in the conventional spelling with two letters, as in **house** [hɑʊs], **boil** [bɔɪl], but sometimes also they are written with a single vowel.

In general long vowels tend to become diphthongal. Some of the long vowels, however, as [ɑː], [ɛː], are very rarely diphthongal. The vowel [ɔː] sometimes becomes [ɔɪə], the glide [ə] being caused by the instinctive raising of the tongue from the very low position of [ɔː] to the more normal mid position of [ə]. With inversion of the point of the tongue, this [ə] becomes [ɹ], see § 305. The commonest diphthongs in American English are [eɪ], [aɪ], [ɑʊ], [oʊ], [ɔɪ].

**71.** [eɪ]. This diphthong may be described as a diphthongal variant of [eː]. In a word like **fate** [feːt], there is generally no diphthongal quality present in the American pronunciation of the vowel. It is a simple long vowel. When fully stressed before voiced consonants and at the end of stressed syllables, however, it tends to become more or less markedly diphthongal, as in **fade** [feɪd], **pay** [peɪ], **strayed** [streɪd] as compared with **straight** [streːt].

**72.** [aɪ]. This is the common sound of words like **ride** [raɪd], **tie** [taɪ], **sigh** [saɪ], **sight, site, cite** [saɪt], **buy, by** [baɪ].

**73.** [ɑʊ]. An obvious diphthong, which appears in words like **house** [hɑʊs], **cow** [kɑʊ], **trowel** [ˈtrɑʊəl], **frown** [frɑʊn].

**74.** [oʊ]. Like [eɪ], this sound may be described as the diphthongal quality of a long vowel, in this case [oː]. In words like **note** [noːt], **boat** [boːt], where the vowel stands before a voiceless consonant, it commonly has no diphthongal value. Before voiced consonants and finally, it tends to become more or less markedly diphthongal, as in **rose** [roʊz], **bowl** [boʊl], **road, rode** [roʊd], **tow, toe** [toʊ], **no, know** [noʊ], **though** [ðoʊ]. But see §§ 218–220.

**75.** [ɔɪ]. This is the clear diphthong of words like **boil** [bɔɪl], **boy** [bɔɪ], **void** [vɔɪd], **annoy** [əˈnɔɪ], **coign, coin** [kɔɪn]. With this last example compare **coincidence** [koˈɪnsɪdəns], where **oi** is of course not diphthongal.

**76.** The vowels [i] and [u] are rarely diphthongal, even when fully stressed and long. When [i] becomes diphthongal, it starts on [ɪ] and closes with [i], as in **sea** [sɪi]. Ordinarily, however, American speakers would pronounce the vowel in this and similar words merely as [iː], making no qualitative but only a quantitative difference between the vowel of **see, sea** and the first vowel of **seasonable** [ˈsizənəbl]. In the same way the vowel of **two, too** may be pronounced as a diphthong, composed first of a slack followed by a tense element, that is [tʊu], but it is more likely to be heard merely as [uː]. The difference between the vowel of **tooth** [tuːθ] and the first vowel of **toothsomeness** [ˈtuθsəmˌnɪs] is only one of quantity.

**77.** The diphthongal character of a prolonged [i] and a prolonged [u] may best be observed when these words are under an exceptionally heavy stress. For example, in **I didn't say key, I said tea**, the antithesis calls for a phonetic representation as follows: [aɪ dɪdnt se· ˈkɪiː, aɪ sɛd ˈtɪiː]. So also the vowel of **true** is likely to be noticeably diphthongal in the following phrase, **It may be interesting, but is it true?** [ɪt me· bɪ ˈɪntərɪstɪŋ, bət ɪz ɪt ˈtrʊuː?]. The words **say** and **may** in the above sentences are only slightly stressed and the vowel is short or half-long, not diphthongal.

**78.** [ju]. The so-called 'long **u**' of words like **mute** [mjuːt] is not, strictly speaking, diphthongal, since the sound which precedes [u] is consonantal and not vocalic.

It should be observed, however, that [j] in English is never a strongly consonantal sound; the close relation between [i] and [j] has been pointed out above, see § 25. One may occasionally hear this sound pronounced as [iu], but in standard speech its form is [ju]. It is grouped here with the diphthongs merely for practical convenience.

**79.** The two elements of a diphthong are commonly not equal in stress or length, but one is more prominent than the other. In [eɪ], [oʊ], [ɑʊ], [ɔɪ] the first element is the more prominent, in [ɪi], [ʊu], [ju] it is the second, and in [aɪ] it is mainly the second, though with many speakers the two elements of this diphthong are about equal in stress and length.

**80.** *Quantity.* As the term is used in phonetics, the word quantity refers primarily to duration, not to the difference of quality in sounds. Sounds may be long or short, the long sound being indicated by the sign [ː] placed after it. When it is necessary to indicate a degree between long and short, that is a half-long, which implies of course that one is uncertain whether the sound is long or short and that it may be either, the sign [·] is used. When not marked as long or half-long, sounds are to be considered short. It should be understood that the terms long and short are used not to designate absolute quantity, that a long sound is not always so many seconds or fractions of a second long. The vowel of **awe** [ɔː] is long, but so also is the vowel of **awful** [ˈɔːfəl], though not absolutely so long as the vowel of **awe**. The length of a vowel depends very much upon the number of syllables in the word containing it, the position of the word in context, and also upon the amount of stress the syllable containing the vowel receives. Unstressed vowels are very seldom long. Moreover, all vowels are appreciably longer before voiced than before voiceless consonants; cf. **bead** [biːd] and **beet, beat** [biːt], **feed** [fiːd] and **feet, feat** [fiːt], **league** [liːg] and **leek, leak** [liːk], **peas** [piːz] and **peace** [piːs]; or compare **loaf** with **loaves, life** with **lives, half** with the verb **halve**, etc. In the following words the vowels are all short, but not equally short: **let** [lɛt], **led** [lɛd]; **debt** [dɛt], **dead** [dɛd]; **hit** [hɪt], **hid** [hɪd]; **rot** [rɑt], **rod** [rɑd]; **hook** [hʊk], **hood** [hʊd], etc.

**81.** In a prolonged diphthong it is the first element of [eɪ], [oʊ], [ɑʊ], [ɔɪ] which is lengthened, the second element in [ɪi], [ʊu], [ju], and both in about equal proportions in [aɪ]. Examples of some of these prolonged diphthongs may be observed in a declamatory pronunciation of the first line of the *Star Spangled Banner*, **O say, can you see by the dawn's early light** [ˈoːʊ ˈseːɪ, kæn ju ˈsɪiː baɪ ðə ˈdɔːnz əɹlɪ ˈlaɪt]. Ordinarily, however, it is not necessary to indicate the length of the elements of a diphthong, except [ju].

**82.** Many speakers in America have a slow and unenergetic manner of enunciation, which results in a dragging or 'drawling' of the vowel sounds, so that normally short vowels become long and long vowels become over-long. Thus **hat** [hæt] becomes [hæːt], **pitch** [pɪtʃ] becomes [pɪːtʃ], **well** [wɛl] becomes [wɛːl], etc., this last illustration being one of the conventional marks of Brother Jonathan's English on the stage and in fiction. This statement applies to diphthongs as well as simple vowels. The manner of speech is characteristic of provincial and rustic, not cultivated American English.

**83.** The distinction between long and short applies to consonants as well as vowels. Long consonants occur in English only when two consonants of the same kind come together in compound words or in close syntactical phrases with a main and secondary stress. Compare **pen-knife** [ˈpɛnːˋaɪf] with **penny** [ˈpɛnɪ], **mad dog** [ˈmædːˋɔg] with **mattock** [ˈmætək], **lessee** [ˈlɛsːˋi] with **dressy** [ˈdrɛsɪ]. In rapid pronunciation a word like **pen-knife** may have only a short consonant, just as the phrase **a good deal** may be [əˋgʊdːˈiːl] or [ə gʊˈdiːl], though never [əˈgʊd ˈdiːl], except in artificial pronunciation. Note that long consonants are not double consonants, pronounced with two separate articulations. Spellings such as **occur**, **add**, **egg**, etc., are of course no indication that the consonants written **cc**, **dd**, **gg** are long. The consonant of **egg** [ɛg] is short, but in **egg-glass** [ˈɛgːˋlæs] it is long. Stop consonants are made long by assuming the stop position and holding it for a moment before the explosion is allowed to occur. A long stop consonant cannot be called a double consonant because a double consonant would call for two distinct explosions. A long continuant is merely the ordinary continuant prolonged.

**84.** *Stress.* Syllables are stressed, unstressed, or secondarily stressed (half stressed). Unstressed syllables are not marked, but stress is indicated by the acute accent before the syllable affected, secondary or half stress, by the grave accent, as in **inkwell** [ˈɪŋkˋwɛl]. Stress like length is to be understood as a term of relative, not absolute significance. In a group of words like **A black bird is not necessarily a blackbird** [ə ˈblæk ˈbəɹd ɪz nɑt nɛsəˈsɛrɪlɪ ə ˈblækˋbəɹd], the third syllable of **necessarily** is marked as a stressed syllable, and it is stressed relative to its surroundings, that is, it is the stressed syllable of its word, though not so strongly stressed as the second syllable or third of the phrase or either of the syllables of the last. And though the second and third words of the phrase are both stressed, they are not equally stressed, one or the other being made the more emphatic according as the logic of the phrase appeals to the speaker.

85. The stressing of syllables in words of two or more syllables is fixed with considerable exactness by convention, but the stressing of words in the word group varies with circumstances, logically emphatic words usually receiving relatively heavy stress. Sometimes the conventional stress of words is altered for the sake of emphasis, as when an antithesis is made prominent, e.g., **Thousands for defense, not a man for offense** [ˈθɑʊzəndz fɔɹ ˈdiːfɛns, nɑt ə mæn fɔr ˈɔfɛns]; or in a very emphatic or exclamatory word, e.g., **delighted** [ˈdiːˋlaɪtɪd], **absolutely** [æbsəˈljutlɪ], **exactly** [ˈɛgˋzæktlɪ], **exquisite** [ɛksˈkwɪzɪt], etc. Sometimes in the word group, even a word logically very unimportant is stressed for emphasis, especially in colloquial style, e.g., **"What did he say?" "He didn't have anything to say"** [ˈʍɑt dɪd hɪ ˈseɪ? hɪ ˈdɪdnt hæv ˈɛnɪθɪŋ ˈtu ˋseɪ].

86. The second element of compound words, so long as it bears a fairly clear logical content, carries a secondary stress, as in **book-shelf** [ˈbʊk-ˋʃɛlf], **butter-knife** [ˈbʌtəɹ-ˋnaɪf], etc., but when the second element no longer has a separate logical value, it loses its stress, as in **husband** [ˈhʌzbənd], **cupboard** [ˈkʌbəɹd], etc. Sometimes the two elements of a compound are pronounced with practically equal or level stress, as in **beef-steak** [ˈbiːf-ˈsteɪk], **ax-handle** [ˈæks-ˈhændl], **Broadway** [ˈbrɔːd-ˈweɪ], etc.,

but usually such words, when they appear in context, carry only a secondary stress on the second element, as in **beefsteak and potatoes** [ˈbiːf-ˌsteɪk n pəˈteɪtoz], unless a special need for emphasizing both logical elements in the compound is present.

**87.** Syllabic accent in words is fixed more or less exactly by convention, and especially in words of native origin, little variation in usage occurs. In some words of Latin origin, however, several ways of stressing the same word are current. In dissyllables compounded of a prefix plus a root, it is a fairly general rule that verbs stress the root, as in **perfume** [pəɹˈfjuːm], **refuse** [rɪˈfjuːz], **proceed** [proˈsiːd], **combine** [kəmˈbaɪn], **protest** [proˈtɛst], **transfer** [trænsˈfəɹ], **absent** [æbˈsɛnt], **premise** [prɪˈmaɪz], **annex** [æˈnɛks], **abstract** [æbˈstrækt], **address** [æˈdrɛs], etc.; whereas substantives stress the prefix, [ˈpəɹfjum], [ˈrɛfjuz], [ˈpro·sidz], [ˈkɑmbaɪn], [ˈpro·tɛst], [ˈtrænsfəɹ], [ˈæbsənt], [ˈprɛmɪs], spelled **premise** or **premiss**, [ˈænɛks], [ˈæbstrækt], [ˈædrɛs], etc. But the rule is not infallible, and some noun compounds of this type are stressed sometimes on the first and sometimes on the second syllable, e.g., **address**, **annex**, **ally**, **allies**, **alloy**, **access**, **excess**, **recess** (but only **success** [səkˈsɛs]). Academic authority sometimes prescribes a single pronunciation, e.g., [æˈlaɪ], [æˈlaɪz] for **ally**, **allies**, or [rɪˈsɛs] for **recess**, in spite of the fact of divided practice in usage.

**88.** In **cement** a distinction was formerly made between the noun [ˈsɛmənt] and the verb [sɪˈmɛnt], but now both noun and verb are stressed on the second syllable. The word is not etymologically a compound but seems to have been assimilated in feeling to verb compounds.

**89.** Sometimes stress determines meaning, as in **accent** [ˈæksɛnt], 'to stress or emphasize in speech,' but [ækˈsɛnt], 'to emphasize particularly a thought or distinction.' The stressing of certain words also may change with their syntactical position. Thus **abject, adult, adverse, excess, occult**, and a great many other compounds of like kind used as adjectives, for which the dictionaries usually record only one form, with stress on the second syllable, may be stressed according to rule when the adjective stands in absolute position, e.g., **He was most abject** [æbˈdʒɛkt] **in his behavior**, but when the adjective stands in regular adjective position before the modified word, the stress is likely to shift to the first syllable, e.g., **The most abject** [ˈæbdʒɛkt] **creature I ever saw.** Compare the phrase **a complex argument** [ə ˈkampleks ˈɑɹgjumənt] with **his argument was very complex** [hɪz ˈɑɹgjumənt wəz ˈvɛrɪ kamˈplɛks], or **occult sciences** [ˈɑkʌlt ˈsaɪənsɪz] with **in the regions of the occult** [ɪn ðə ˈriːdʒənz əv ðɪ ɑˈkʌlt]. In instances of this sort, accent seems to be determined by the rhythm of the phrase, and rhythm undoubtedly plays a large part in all variabilities of stressing in English. The statement of these rhythmical rules would be very complex, and the dictionaries, being under the necessity of speaking briefly and dogmatically, do not give a faithful or detailed picture of usage in these respects. Those speakers who follow the dictionary rules as to stressing are frequently compelled to substitute a mechanical rule in place of a natural practice. It is impossible to formulate any simple practical rules of certain guidance in the stressing of these variable dissyllables and polysyllables in English, since the words do not fall into clearly maintained categories. Under the circumstances, the most economical and practical method is to learn the stressing of such words by observing and following usage.

**90.** The word **program, programme**, is pronounced [ˈproˌgræm], though a popular pronunciation [ˈprogrəm] is also heard and seems to be growing in use. In **acorn** standard American pronunciation is [ˈeɪˌkɔɹn], but in some regions of the South and West an earlier pronunciation [ˈeɪkəɹn] survives in local use. For **frontier** the usual American pronunciation is [frʌnˈtɪəɹ], but in England [ˈfrʌntɪə]. For **quinine** a number of pronunciations occur (see § 213), the most common being [ˈkwaɪˌnaɪn].

**91.** In words of three syllables an uncertainty in usage with respect to the stressing of the first or second syllable affects a number of words, of which a few typical examples may be cited. Words ending in **–ate** are commonly stressed on the first syllable, as in **acclimate, compensate, concentrate, confiscate, contemplate, demonstrate, illustrate**, though some speakers cultivate a pronunciation with stress on the second syllable.[1] For **remonstrate,** however, the stress is more commonly on the second syllable. The word **consummate** as a verb is stressed on the first syllable, as an adjective on the second.

**92.** Other instances of trisyllabic words in which usage is unsettled are **albumen, armistice, aspirant, combatant, combative, opponent, vagary**, the prevailing usage having stress on the first syllable of all these words except the last two. For **deficit** only a pronunciation with stress on the first syllable is current in America, but [dɪˈfɪsɪt] is general in England. For **envelope** (*noun*) the pronunciation is often [ɛnˈvɛləp], but more commonly

[1] See New English Dictionary, under **contemplate.**

[ˈɛnvəˌlo·p] or [ˈɑnvəˌlo·p], [ˈɔnvəˌlo·p]. For **eczema** the professional and formal pronunciation is [ˈɛkzɪmə] or [ˈɛksɪmə], but popularly the word is often pronounced [ɛkˈziːmə]. The word **plebiscite** is a somewhat learned word with no definitely fixed popular pronunciation. It is most commonly pronounced [ˈplɛbɪˌsaɪt], [ˈplɛbɪsɪt], and less frequently [plɛˈbɪsɪt]. For **gondola**, a somewhat learned word, the conventional pronunciation is [ˈgɑndələ], but in popular speech often [gɑnˈdoːlə]. For **vehement** the standard pronunciation is [ˈvɪəmənt], but [vɪˈhiːmənt] is heard in popular speech. For **inquiry** a pronunciation with stress on the first syllable is sometimes heard, but the common standard pronunciation is [ɪnˈkwaɪrɪ]. For **idea** the standard pronunciation is [aɪˈdiə], but one frequently hears, especially in the South, [ˈaɪdɪə]. A pronunciation [ˈaɪˈdiː], with both syllables about equally stressed, is popular and illiterate.

**93.** Under the head of words of three syllables may be considered words ending in -**able**, since the **l** in this ending is very lightly syllabic. The general tendency is to stress these words on the first syllable, unless the influence of another form, like **deny**, **rely**, **comply**, preserves the stress on the second syllable, as in **deniable** [dɪˈnaɪəbl], **reliable** [rɪˈlaɪəbl], **compliable** [kəmˈplaɪəbl]. But **referable**, **preferable** are always [ˈrɛfərəbl], [ˈprɛfərəbl], in spite of **refer**, **prefer**, [rɪˈfəɹ], [prɪˈfəɹ]. In **applicable**, **despicable**, **disreputable**, **formidable**, **hospitable**, the stress is commonly on the first syllable, but not infrequently the second syllable is stressed by cultivated speakers. In **admirable**, **dissoluble**, **lamentable**, **refutable**, **revocable**, the stress is very rarely on the second, though this pronunciation for **admirable** is frequent in popular English, and may sometimes be heard in the other words, perhaps through the influence of head forms like **dissolve** [dɪ'zɔːlv], **lament** [lə'mɛnt], **refute** [rɪ'fjuːt], **revoke** [rɪ'voːk].

**94.** An instance of unexpected stress in a trisyllabic word is **Willamette** [wɪ'læmət], town and river in Oregon.

**95.** In words of four syllables the question is again one of stressing either the first or the second syllable, though when the first syllable is stressed, there is usually more or less secondary stress on the third. Thus for **contemplative** the most general pronunciation is [kən'tɛmplətɪv], but also ['kɑntəm'ple·tɪv]; for **aristocrat** both [ə'rɪstəkræt] and ['ærɪstə'kræt]; for **fragmentary** the general pronunciation ['frægmən'tɛrɪ], but sometimes [fræg'mɛntərɪ]. For **difficulty** the only current pronunciation in America is ['dɪfɪkəltɪ]. For **diocesan** the analogy of **diocese** ['daɪəsɪs] sometimes produces a pronunciation ['daɪə'siːsən] for standard [daɪ'ɔsɪsən]. But the word is learned and has no general currency.

**96.** For **advertisement** both ['ædvəɹ'taɪzmənt] and [æd'vəɹtɪzmənt] are in current use; for **obligatory** both [ə'blɪgə'tɔrɪ] and ['ɑblɪgə'tɔrɪ]; for **peremptory** both ['pɛrəm'tɔrɪ] and [pər'ɛmptərɪ]. The standard pronunciation of **municipal** is [mju'nɪsəpl], but a popular form ['mjunə'sɪpl] is sometimes heard. For **capillary** both ['kæpə'lɛrɪ] and [kə'pɪlərɪ] are current, the former being the more general. For **celibacy** the current pronunciation in America is ['sɛləbɪsɪ], but in England both ['sɛləbɪsɪ] and [sə'lɪbəsɪ] are in standard use.

**97.** In general, American speech makes a much greater use of secondary stress in polysyllables than British speech. Words like **declamatory**, **dignitary**, **derogatory**, **dysentery**, **extraordinary**, **sedentary**, **temporary**, many place names, such as **Birmingham**, **Bradbury**, etc., commonly receive in England only one stress, [dɪˈklæmɪtrɪ], [ˈdɪgnɪtrɪ], [dɪˈrɔgətrɪ], [ˈdɪsəntrɪ], [ɪkˈstrɔːdnrɪ], [ˈsɛdəntrɪ], [ˈtɛmprɛrɪ], [ˈbʌːmɪŋəm], [ˈbrædbrɪ]; but in America such words almost universally bear a strong secondary stress besides the main stress, as in [dɪˈklæməˌtɔrɪ], [ˈdɪgnəˌtɛrɪ], [dɪˈrɔgəˌtɔrɪ], [ˈdɪsənˌtɛrɪ], [ɪkˈstrɔːɹdɪˌnɛrɪ], [ˈsɛdənˌtɛrɪ], [ˈtɛmpəˌrɛrɪ], [ˈbəɹmɪŋˌhæm], [ˈbrædˌbɛrɪ].

**98.** In some words, however, secondary stress, though heard in popular speech, has been discarded in cultivated pronunciation, e.g., **interest**, **interesting**, [ˈɪntərɪst], [ˈɪntərɪstɪŋ], popularly pronounced [ˈɪntərˌɛst], [ˈɪntərˌɛstɪŋ] or [ˌɪntərˈɛstɪŋ]; **cemetery** [ˈsɛmɪtrɪ], popularly [ˈsɛməˌtɛrɪ]; **favorite** [ˈfeːvrɪt], **genuine** [ˈdʒɛnjuɪn], popularly [ˈfeːvəˌraɪt], [ˈdʒɛnjuˌaɪn].

**99.** *Vowels in Unstressed Syllables.* The general tendency of vowels in unstressed syllables, especially in informal colloquial speech, is to weaken and to become the vowel [ə], or in certain endings, [ɪ], see §§ 146, 173. Sometimes, however, in more formal speech, a vowel is used in unstressed syllables which has not the full and clear value which one ordinarily gives to the vowel in stressed position, nor yet the weakened sound of [ə] or [ɪ], but a sound intermediate between the two. Thus the word **oblige** in informal speech would be [əˈblaɪdʒ], and in very formal speech, a kind of spelling-pronunciation, it might be [oˈblaɪdʒ]. But the initial vowel is more likely to be a compromise between [ə] and [o], and if it is desirable to indicate this orthographically, it is suggested that this be done by placing two dots over the [o], giving [ö'blaɪdʒ]. The same device can be applied to the other vowels. Thus the word **violet** may be transcribed as normally ['vaɪəlɪt], but formally as ['vaɪölĕt]; **attack** as normally [ə'tæk], but formally [ǣ'tæk]; **fashion** as normally ['fæʃn] or ['fæʃən], but formally ['fæʃŏn]. It has not been deemed necessary to indicate these distinctions in the transcriptions of the present volume.

**100.** *Sound groups.* The division of speech into detached words, as in conventional printing and writing, does not usually correspond to the actual sound groupings of the language as spoken. In the phrase **Life like a dome of many colored glass** ['laɪf laɪkə'doɪm əv'mɛnɪ'kʌləɹd'glæs], there are only three sound groups, the last being as much a single sound group as the word **incomprehensibility** [ɪn'kɑmprɪ'hɛnsɪ'bɪlɪtɪ]. In phonetic transcriptions, however, it seems more convenient to follow the traditional division into words, except when for special reasons it is advisable to indicate the real phonetic groupings.

**101.** In some few words like **don't, hasn't, isn't, won't,** this fusing of words into sound groups is represented in the conventional spelling, and writers of dialect stories often indicate them by spelling, as in "I gotta go" for "I've got to go." But what is thus made a humorous dialect characteristic is humorous only because of the unconventional spelling. All current colloquial speech in some degree makes such combinations and 'telescopings' of words which are syntactically closely related, e.g., **I used to think** [aɪ 'justə θɪŋk]; **Don't you want to come?** ['doɪntʃu 'wɔntə kʌm?]; **It wasn't your turn** ['twʌzən'tʃʊɹ 'təɹn]; **Did you get it?** [dɪdʒə 'gɛt ɪt?] or [dʒə 'gɛt ɪt?].

**102.** *Pitch.* It is impossible to indicate by any simple mechanical means which are adequate the rising and falling intonations of the voice in speech. Three degrees of pitch are readily observable, which may be designated as high, level and low, and one may construct intonation curves which will correspond to these more obvious changes of pitch in connected speech. It is doubtful, however, if these curves will convey to any one not already familiar with the speech a satisfactory realization of its cadences. The intonations of a speech are very important for its idiomatic use, but they are too subtle and varied for simple description, and must therefore be learned by direct observation and experience. Perhaps the most apparent general characteristic of American speech, so far as cadence is concerned, is its levelness of tone. The voice rises and falls within a relatively narrow range, and with few abrupt transitions from high to low or low to high. To British ears American speech often sounds hesitating, monotonous and indecisive, and British speech, on the other hand, is likely to seem to Americans abrupt, explosive and manneristic. Both habits of speech, it need scarcely be said, are established by convention, and one is not more conscious or affected than the other.

One reason for the relative levelness in pitch of American speech may be that the American voice in general starts on a higher plane, is normally pitched higher than the British voice. If it is true, as is often said, that American life is more intense, more highly keyed nervously, than life in England, the high pitch of the American voice may reasonably be regarded as a natural consequence of this state of affairs. There is likely to be less range of cadence in a tense than in a relaxed manner of speech. If one ventured to give any general advice to American speakers, it would be therefore to cultivate repose and ease of utterance. From this will result naturally the variety in cadence and the flexibility which give to speech its characteristic melodic qualities. The relatively dry climate of America may have something to do also with the high pitch of the American voice. It is a fact easy of verification that the pitch of one's voice is considerably lower in soft foggy weather than it is on a dry clear day.

**103.** *Speed.* The rate of speed in utterance varies widely with the emotional quality of the content of speech, and also with the temperament of individuals. Some people talk like greased lightning, others are as slow as molasses. American speech as compared with British is commonly said to be slow and 'drawling.' The effect of 'drawling' is partly produced by the levelness of intonation in American speech, partly by the retention of secondary stresses in polysyllables (see § 97), though partly also by a distinctly slow tempo in the utterance of many speakers. The habit of slow tempo in speech is usually regarded in America, however, as a mark of rustic speech, or of somewhat humorous Brother Jonathan speech, and it is doubtful if on the whole American cultivated speech is any slower than British speech. Even if it were, however, this could not be said to constitute a very serious charge against the language.

**104.** *Timbre.* The timbre, or characteristic quality of the speaking voice, is something over which the individual has very little control. It is determined by nature through the special character and shape of each person's vocal apparatus, including of course the vocal chords, just as the characteristic sound of a fife or flute or other instrument is determined by its physical structure. Since probably no two persons have exactly the same physical equipment of speech, the timbre of no two voices can be exactly alike. Timbre is therefore the most individual and personal of all the elements of speech. A keen ear can readily distinguish several different voices and assign them definitely to their owners, even when the voices pronounce what we commonly call the same sound. From its nature timbre does not enter into the discussion of practice in pronunciation. Training may, of course, accomplish much in enabling one to realize the possibilities of one's 'organ,' as for example by correcting defects and developing the various muscles controlling the production of speech, but training cannot alter its essential character.

**105.** *Proper Names.* The pronunciation of proper names, both place names and personal names, is in general subject to the same rules as the pronunciation of the other words of the language. A traditional spelling is more likely to be retained in proper names, however, long after the pronunciation has changed. This is especially true in family names, in which conservative family tradition often preserves a spelling which corresponds very inadequately to the current pronunciation of the names. In England this peculiarity is more marked than in America, and spellings and pronunciations like **Colquhoun** [kə'huːn], **Claverhouse** ['klævəz], **Cockburn** ['koʊbən], **Marjoribanks** ['mɑːʃ–, 'mɑːtʃbæŋks], **Meagher** ['mɑːə], **Rivaulx** ['rɪvəz], to mention but a few among many, are likely to seem grotesque to the American eye and ear. In America the general tendency is to bring about a closer agreement between spelling and pronunciation, and for **Colquhoun** we commonly have **Calhoun**, for **Cockburn** either **Coburn** or a pronunciation which corresponds to the spelling **Cockburn**, for **Meagher** a spelling **Maher**, or a spelling **Meeker** with corresponding pronunciation, or **Meagher** is pronounced [ˈmiːgəɹ].

**106.** Some American place names are direct borrowings from England, such as **Leominster** [ˈlɛmɪnstəɹ], **Gloucester** [ˈglɔstəɹ], **Worcester** [ˈwuːstəɹ], in Massachusetts, and have retained an archaic spelling. But the name of the town in Ohio named after the town in Massachusetts is **Wooster**, and many other proper names in America have undergone a similar rationalizing modification. Since proper names are always the personal possessions, so to speak, either of families, or of localities in which they are current, their pronunciations and spellings must be accepted in the form which their possessors wish them to have.

**107.** Many names of foreign origin have been Americanized, French **Du Bois** being pronounced [duˈbɔɪz], German **Koch** pronounced [kɑtʃ], Dutch **Schurman**, in which **sch** was [sk], as it still is in **Schuylkill** [ˈskuːlkɪl], **Schuyler** [ˈskaɪləɹ], etc., being pronounced as though it were the same as **Sherman**. One cannot make a general rule as to the pronunciation of such names of foreign origin, though it may be said that in the main any efforts which individuals may make to preserve the pronunciation of their names in accordance with their original phonetic forms are likely to prove unavailing in view of the strong general tendency to follow native analogies in pronunciation. Change in pronunciation may of course be held in check by changing spelling, as was done in the name **Knickerbocker**, originally spelled with **a** in the next to last syllable, pronounced [ɑ], but changed to **o** to avoid the common tendency to pronounce **a** as [æ] or [e]. Incidentally this change throws light on the American pronunciation of **o**, see §§ 110–111. It may be added that in thus Americanizing names of foreign origin, American speakers have done no more than English-speaking peoples have always done, as, for example, in what, from the Gallic point of view, must seem outrageous Anglicizations of **Bourchier** into [ˈbɑʊtʃə], of **Belvoir** into [ˈbiːvə], of **Beaulieu** into [ˈbjuːlɪ]. The French even the account, however, by Gallicizing English names, and any foreign words which pass current among a people are almost sure to suffer a sea-change in the course of time.

**108.** A somewhat noticeable feature in the American as well as British pronunciation of proper names is the tendency to stress dissyllabic family names on the second syllable, especially when in spelling the second syllable is written with a double consonant, as in the pronunciations **Birrell** [bɪˈrɛl], **Bithell** [bɪˈθɛl], **Cornell** [kɔɹˈnɛl], **Burnett** [bəɹˈnɛt], **Bennett**, **Bennet** [bɛˈnɛt], **Gillett** [dʒɪˈlɛt], **Furness** [fəɹˈnɛs], **Purcell** [pəɹˈsɛl], **Purnell** [pəɹˈnɛl], etc., but also even **Farrar** [fəˈrɑːɹ], **Millard** [mɪˈlɑːɹd], etc. In older usage these names were commonly all stressed on the first syllable, and in some instances the pronunciation with stress on the second syllable is quite recent and consciously assumed.

**109.** *Levels of Speech.* It is extremely important in the study of speech to be able to observe with detachment speech habits which in the main are quite unconscious. Though conscious speech habits are by no means unimportant, they constitute but a small part of the whole complex of a language and rarely indicate the direction of development which the language is taking. The student must cultivate the ability to observe the activities of natural speech, which is normal speech, utilized for the purposes of communication with very little thought as to its formal character. Natural or normal speech thus differs from precise speech, which is largely self-conscious and theoretical, and it differs also from slovenly speech with which the precise speaker is inclined to confuse it. A speech may be fairly characterized as slovenly only when its articulations are habitually muddy and indistinct, when its general effect is such as to indicate a laxness of speech activities parallel to what untidiness and uncleanliness would be in other personal habits. Ungrammatical or dialect speech is not necessarily slovenly, and in fact it is often the reverse, being frequently very crisp and energetic. On the other hand, one may find slovenly speakers even among those who pass as highly cultivated. The natural level, between precise and slovenly speech, may best be observed in the familiar conversation of educated persons whose habits of speech are not finical or affected.

The appeal in testing natural speech must always be to the ear. No one 'speaks as he writes' in English, and the attempt to regulate speech by the visible word lands one in countless absurdities. The precise speaker, however, will often do violence to the natural form of a word in order to make it over according to the pattern of the visible word. No one in natural speech pronounces two **g**'s in **suggest** [səˈdʒɛst], and it is a purist affectation to attempt to do so. In **asked** no one pronounces a final [d], the sound being always [t], and in current speech, no one pronounces both a clear [k] and a clear [t]. One may pronounce a very slight [k]-sound, though most speakers have no [k] at all, but simply a long [s], e.g., [aːsːt], and some omit the [t] altogether, pronouncing the preterite like the present. This last pronunciation is not prevalent among cultivated speakers, though it represents no greater departure from the written form of the word than the prevalent pronunciation. In any case the natural pronunciation departs from the conventional spelling. In natural speech, unstressed vowels tend to become [ə], as, for example, **about** [əˈbɑʊt], **upon** [əˈpɔn], **amend, emend** [əˈmɛnd], **national** [ˈnæʃənəl], **description** [dɪˈskrɪpʃən], [dəˈskrɪpʃən], and only a conscious desire to reform the natural speech could lead to the attempt to introduce a clear vowel in the unstressed syllable of these words. But it seems safer to follow the normal processes of the language, and in doing so, one cannot do better than direct attention to the unconstrained speech of educated and well-bred persons. The decision who such persons are must naturally be left to individual judgment.

All natural and unconstrained speech is not, however, on the same level. The speech of formal discourse and of the public address, and in general of all expression where exceptional clearness and carrying power are important, differs in many details from the speech of colloquial and familiar conversation. Each is of course appropriate in its own surroundings, and it would be as much an error to speak formally when the situation called for familiar speech as to speak colloquially in a formal situation. If either level of speech be regarded as exceptional, it is obviously the formal speech, as the speech of a special occasion, that must be so regarded. In this volume the unconstrained colloquial speech of educated and well-bred persons has been taken as the norm, and deviations from it have been characterized as formal or precise or dialectal (provincial, local, or popular), or slovenly.

## III

## SOUNDS AND THEIR OCCURRENCE

### [ɑ]

**110.** A short vowel [ɑ] is general in America, with local exceptions in New England, in **fop** [fɑp], **got** [gɑt], **hot** [hɑt], **lot** [lɑt], **not** [nɑt], **stock** [stɑk], **chocolate** [ˈtʃɑklɪt], and many other words written with **o** before a voiceless stop. In sections of New England, as in British pronunciation, such words have a sound which closely approximates [ɔ], that is, [fɔp], [hɔt], [lɔt], [nɔt], [stɔk], [ˈtʃɔklɪt], etc., and this pronunciation may also be heard, especially in certain words, for example **chocolate**, elsewhere, though exceptionally, in America.

**111.** In many other words commonly written **o**, usage varies widely throughout America between [ɔ] and [ɑ], the length of these vowels also varying from short to half-long or long, and even at times to over-long. The quantities are so unstable that it is difficult to indicate them with certainty:

(*a*) Before a voiced stop, both pronunciations occur in **dog** [dɔg] or [dɑg], **log** [lɔg] or [lɑg], **hog** [hɔg] or [hɑg], etc.; in **God** [gɔd] or [gɑd], **sod** [sɔd] or [sɑd], etc. Before [b], however, the preponderance of usage seems to be markedly in favor of [ɑ], as in **rob** [rɑb], **sob** [sɑb], **nobby** [ˈnɑbɪ], etc. The pronunciation of **daub** [dɔːb] as [dɑb] is popular and dialectal.

(*b*) Before the continuant consonants the same variation occurs:

(1) before [l] or [r]: **doll** [dɔl] or [dɑl], **follow** ['fɔlo] or ['fɑlo], **hollow** ['hɔlo] or ['hɑlo], **pollen** ['pɔlən] or ['pɑlən], etc.

**coroner** ['kɔrənəɹ] or ['kɑrənəɹ], **forest** ['fɔrɪst] or ['fɑrɪst], **foreign** ['fɔrɪn] or ['fɑrɪn], **forehead** ['fɔrɪd] or ['fɑrɪd], **horrid** ['hɔrɪd] or ['hɑrɪd], **orange** ['ɔrɪndʒ] or ['ɑrɪndʒ], **torrid** ['tɔrɪd] or ['tɑrɪd].

(2) before nasal continuants: **John** [dʒɔn] or [dʒɑn], **on** [ɔn] or [ɑn], **strong** [strɔŋ] or [strɑŋ], **pomp** [pɔmp] or [pɑmp], **romp** [rɔmp] or [rɑmp], etc.

The pronunciations [stɔmp] for **stamp** (*verb*) [stæmp] and [trɔmp] for **tramp** (*verb*) [træmp] are dialectal.

For **bomb** the current pronunciations in America are [bɑm] and [bɔm], and [bʌm] is also heard, though probably less commonly in America than in England. The influence of the spelling favors [bɔm], and for this reason many speakers incline to regard [bʌm] as a popular and dialectal pronunciation. See § 204. The pronunciation [bʊm] is not general.

(3) before other continuants:

**coffee** ['kɔfɪ] or ['kɑfɪ], **off** [ɔf] or [ɑf], **often** ['ɔfn] or ['ɑfn], **soft** [sɔft] or [sɑft], **cough** [kɔf] or [kɑf].

**cost** [kɔst] or [kɑst], **docile** ['dɔsɪl] or ['dɑsɪl], **hospital** ['hɔspɪtl] or ['hɑspɪtl], **ostrich** ['ɔstrɪtʃ] or ['ɑstrɪtʃ], **Boswell** ['bɔzwɛl] or ['bɑzwɛl], **rosin** ['rɔzɪn] or ['rɑzɪn].

**broth** [brɔθ] or [brɑθ], **Gothic** ['gɔθɪk] or ['gɑθɪk], **moth** [mɔθ] or [mɑθ], **bother** ['bɔðəɹ] or ['bɑðəɹ].

**grovel** ['grɔvəl] or ['grɑvəl], also ['grʌvəl], **novel** ['nɔvəl] or ['nɑvəl]; **hovel** is ['hɑvəl] or ['hʌvəl], never ['hɔvəl]; so also **hover** [ˈhɑvəɹ] or [ˈhʌvəɹ]. For **shovel** the only pronunciation is [ˈʃʌvəl], [ˈʃʌvl].

(*c*) After [w], the sounds in question occur in words usually written **a**, but with a similar variation in usage, though the preference here seems to be clearly in favor of [ɔ], as in **quarrel** [ˈkwɔrəl], **swamp** [swɔmp], **swan** [swɔn], **want** [wɔnt], **wash** [wɔʃ], **wasp** [wɔsp], **water** [ˈwɔtəɹ]. But the preference is by no means consistent, and [ˈswɑlo], [ˈwɑbl] seem to be more common for **swallow**, noun and verb, and **wabble**, than [ˈswɔlo], [ˈwɔbl]; and in individual usage, many speakers who say **wash** [wɔʃ], **Washington** [ˈwɔʃɪŋtən] will also pronounce **watch** as [wɑtʃ] and **squab** as [skwɑb]. This inconsistency extends through the whole group of words, and the same speaker who says **God** [gɑd] will say **dog** [dɔg], and so with many other words. In such a state of affairs, all that can be said with respect to these usages is that they vary according to habit or preference. One caution may be entered, however, against making the vowel [ɔ] too long, as in the pronunciations commonly indicated in dialect stories by the spellings *dawg* and *Gawd*, that is, [dɔːg], [gɔːd].

On the dialectal pronunciation of [ɔː] as [ɑ] or [ɑː], see § 187.

**112.** The colloquial contraction **aren't** [ˈɑrənt], or with omission of the **r** [ɑːnt], often becomes [eːnt], [eɪnt], but only in very familiar colloquial or dialect pronunciation. The pronunciation [eːnt], [eɪnt] is also extended to the singular in dialect speech. In the first person singular, interrogative, one occasionally hears [ˈɑrənt aɪ], or sometimes [ænt aɪ] from cultivated speakers, who use this form to avoid the somewhat awkward "am not I," but the usage is not general.

**113.** The pronunciation of **was** is [wɑz] or [wɔz], or in rapid speech and when the word is lightly stressed, [wəz]. The pronunciation [wʌz] when the word is stressed is scarcely cultivated usage.

For [ɑ] in the diphthong [ɑʊ], see § 222.

### [ɑː]

**114.** This sound occurs in **father** [ˈfɑːðəɹ], where it is practically universal in American speech, the pronunciations [ˈfæːðəɹ] and [ˈfɔːðəɹ] being only occasional and dialectal. But in no other word of the same type does this uniformity in usage obtain. In **rather** standard usage varies between [ˈrɑːðəɹ], [ˈraːðəɹ] and [ˈræðəɹ], with the preponderance in favor of [ˈræðəɹ]. [ˈrʌðəɹ] is illiterate and dialectal. In other words, like **gather, lather, slather, blather**(**skite**), **Mather**, the vowel is prevailingly [æ], or [æ·], with local exceptions in New England in favor of [ɑː], see § 125. [ɑ·] or [ɑ] occurs also in **bother**, which forms a fairly satisfactory ear-rime with **father**, though it offends the eye. Beside [ˈbɑ·ðəɹ], or [ˈbɑðəɹ], much less commonly [ˈbɔðəɹ] also occurs, see § 111, (3).

**115.** [ɑː] occurs regularly in words where **a** is written before **lm**, the **l** being silent, in **psalm** [sɑːm], **palm** [pɑːm], **balm** [bɑːm], **calm** [kɑːm], **alms** [ɑːmz], see §§ 274–276. In **salmon, almond** both [ˈsæmən], [ˈæmənd] and [ˈsɑːmən], [ˈɑːmənd] occur. A spelling-pronunciation, with the **l** sounded, is sometimes heard in these two words, but is not general. Before **f, s, th, nce, nch, nt, lf, lv,** [ɑː] occurs locally in some regions of the East, but generally the sound varies between [aː], [æ], [æ·], and in some words [ɔː], see §§ 124, 128. For **au** pronounced [ɑː], see § 186.

**116.** Before [ɹ] final or preceding a consonant, **a**, often also **ea**, of the conventional spelling, is [ɑː], as **hart**, **heart** [hɑːɹt], **star** [stɑːɹ], **marred** [mɑːɹd], **Clark(e)** [klɑːɹk], etc., **hearth** [hɑːɹθ], **large** [lɑːɹdʒ].

**117.** In British English certain words spelled **e** before **r** and a consonant are pronounced [ɑː], with the **r** silent, as in **clerk** [klɑːk], **Hertford** [ˈhɑːtfəd], **Derby** [ˈdɑːbɪ], but in America words which are so written are pronounced with [ə], and when they are pronounced with [ɑː], as in the proper name **Clark(e)**, they are written with **a.** An exception in American speech is **sergeant**, which is commonly pronounced [ˈsɑːɹdʒənt], like the proper name **Sargent.**

**118.** The standard pronunciation of **hearth** is [hɑːɹθ], but [həɹθ] is also heard as an old-fashioned or dialectal pronunciation.

**119.** Those speakers who have no [ɹ] before consonants and finally, have [ɑː] in words like **hard** [hɑːd], **part** [pɑːt], **harp** [hɑːp], **hearth** [hɑːθ], **marred** [mɑːd], **tar** [tɑː], **car** [kɑː]. But some speakers in New England have a vowel in these words which closely approximates [aː], and even at times [æː], e.g., **Harvard** [ˈhaːvəd], **part** [paːt], etc., see § 45, note, where this sound is indicated by the spelling **Havvad.**

For the pronunciations **tar** [tɑːə], **car** [kɑːə], etc., see § 301.

**120.** [ɑː], sometimes shortened to [ɑ], occurs in some words of foreign origin, as in **lava** [ˈlɑːvə], **data** [ˈdɑːtə], **errata** [ɛˈrɑːtə], **bas-relief** [ˌbɑːrɪˈliːf], **spa** [spɑː], **mirage** [mɪˈrɑːʒ], **garage** [gəˈrɑːʒ], popularly often [ˈgærɪdʒ], though some of these also have Anglicized pronunciations with [æ], e.g., [ˈlævə], [ˈdætə], etc. The word **vase** is either [vɑːz] or [veːs], [veːz], the last being much the most general pronunciation. The pronunciation of **tomato** is commonly [təˈme·to], but [təˈmɑːto] is also in fairly general use, especially as a consciously cultivated pronunciation. The form [təˈmæto] is relatively rare. In **piano**, the form [pɪˈæno] is general, [pɪˈɑːno] exceptional. For **drama** three pronunciations are current, [ˈdrɑːmə], [ˈdræmə] and [ˈdreːmə], though the first is the only one widely used. For **suave** the usual American pronunciation is [swɑːv], but in England [sweɪv].

**121.** In American place names, like **Alabama**, **Colorado**, **Nevada**, **Nebraska**, **Montana**, a pronunciation with [ɑː] in the stressed syllable is sometimes heard, especially in the East, but in the states themselves and in America generally, the words are pronounced [æləˈbæmə], [kɑlə-ˈrædə], [nəˈvædə], [nəˈbræskə], [mɔnˈtænə].

**122.** Where cultivated speech regularly has [ɔː], as in **caught** [kɔːt], **bought** [bɔːt], **haughty** [ˈhɔːtɪ], **naughty** [ˈnɔːtɪ], etc., a dialect pronunciation [kɑːt], [bɑːt], [ˈhɑːtɪ], [ˈnɑːtɪ], etc., prevails in some regions.

**123.** In several regions of the Atlantic seaboard a glide vowel is introduced between a preceding [k], [g] and [ɑː], as in the Virginia pronunciation of **carter** [kɪˈɑːtə], **garden** [gɪˈɑːdən], but this pronunciation is distinctly local or dialectal. See § 217.

[aɪ]

**124.** This sound occurs as a simple vowel normally only as a long or half-long vowel, though the short of it appears as the first element in the diphthong [aɪ], see § 209. It is heard in certain positions, chiefly in somewhat conscious and academic speech, as a compromise sound between [ɑː], which is rejected as being too 'broad,' and [æ] or [æ·], a popular sound widely distributed over the whole country, which is rejected as being too 'narrow' or 'flat.' It is cultivated in words written **a**, sometimes **au**, before a voiceless continuant, or before a nasal followed by a voiceless stop or continuant, as in **grass**, **half**, **laugh**, **path** (also before a voiced continuant, as in **paths**, **calves**, **halves**, **baths**, when the voiced form is a variant, usually the plural, of a head form with a voiceless sound), **aunt**, **branch**, **can't**, **dance**, **fancy**, **France**, **shan't**, etc.

**125.** Before a voiced continuant and before a nasal followed by a voiced stop or continuant, **a** is usually pronounced [æ], as in **flange** [flændʒ], **grand** [grænd], **has** [hæz], **have** [hæv], **lather** [ˈlæðəɹ], **rather** [ˈræðəɹ], **pansy** [ˈpænzɪ], though speakers who acquire the pronunciation [a] consciously and attempt to carry it through consistently sometimes indulge in pronunciations like [ˈpanzɪ], [haz], etc.

**126.** Some exceptions to the above groupings may be noted: **cant** (*noun*) is always [kænt], and **pant**, **pantry**, **panther** are scarcely ever heard except as [pænt], [ˈpæntrɪ], [ˈpænθəɹ]. Some speakers who pronounce **aunt** as [aːnt], say [ænt] for **ant**. The word **gas** is almost universally [gæs], and **hath** (perhaps because of **have** and **has**, with voiced consonants) is always [hæθ]. Before [ʃ] **a** is never [aː], but [æ], as in **dash** [dæʃ], **fashion** [ˈfæʃən], **rational** [ˈræʃənəl], etc.

**127.** When it comes to a question of choice among the several possible pronunciations of **dance**, **laugh**, **branch**, etc., the decision usually rests between [aː] and [æ], [ɑː] being ruled out as too 'broad' and as somewhat 'la-di-da.' And when it comes to a question of choice between these two the purist tendency has been to condemn the pronunciation [æ], although this is by far the more common sound in all the words in point in American speech. The result has been to give to [aː] extraordinary dictionary and academic prestige in the face of a strongly opposing popular usage. The reasons for this are several: first, that standard British speech and some forms of New England speech have [ɑː] in the words in question; second, that New England has exerted, and to some extent continues to exert, a strong influence upon formal instruction and upon notions of cultivation and refinement throughout the country; and third, that the pronunciation [æ] is often prolonged, or drawled, and nasalized in a way that makes it seem not merely American, but provincially American. To steer between the Scylla of provincialism, [æː], and the Charybdis of affectation and snobbishness, [ɑː], many conscientious speakers in America cultivate [aː]. The writer has tested this sound on many different groups of speakers from various sections of the country, and has never found one who used the sound who did not do so with a certain degree of self-consciousness. If the cult of this sound continues long enough, it may in time come to be a natural and established sound in the language. In the meantime, it seems a pity that so much effort and so much time in instruction should be given to changing a natural habit of speech which is inherently just as good as the one by which the purist would supplant it. Especially in public school instruction it would seem to be wiser to spend time on more important matters in speech than the difference between [hæf] and [haːf].

[æ], [æː]

**128.** This is the sound, usually a short vowel, universally current in **hat** [hæt], **cab** [kæb], **bad** [bæd], **patter** [ˈpætəɹ], **grand** [grænd], **fashion** [ˈfæʃən], and a large number of other words. It is also the natural pronunciation of the majority of American speakers in words written **a** before a voiced or voiceless continuant and before **n** followed by a voiced or voiceless continuant or stop, as in **glass** [glæs], **bath** [bæθ], **dance** [dænts] or [dæns], **can't** [kænt], **branch** [bræntʃ], etc. The vowel tends to become long in words of this type, and locally and dialectally to become over-long, see §§ 82, 127. It is especially likely to be long before a voiced sound, for example, **path** [pæθ], but **paths** [pæːðz].

**129.** Before **r, rr** followed by a vowel, orthographic **a** is usually [æ], as in **carry** [ˈkærɪ], **carriage** [ˈkærɪdʒ], **Clara** [ˈklærə], **caret** [ˈkærɪt], **claret** [ˈklærɪt], **parent** [ˈpærənt], **Paris** [ˈpærɪs], **parish** [ˈpærɪʃ], **marry** [ˈmærɪ], **tarry** (*verb*) [ˈtærɪ]. As an adjective **tarry** [ˈtɑːrɪ] retains the vowel of the simple word **tar** [tɑːɹ]. Some speakers, however, pronounce [ɛ] for **a** before **r** and a vowel, not distinguishing **parish** and **perish**, **marry** and **merry**. The pronunciation with [æ] is to be preferred. A special grouping must be made for words like **chary, fairy, Mary, vary, wary,** for which see §§ 133, 141.

**130.** For **radish** [ˈrædɪʃ], the popular dialects often have [ˈrɛdɪʃ]. The pronunciation of **plait**, 'to braid,' is [plæt], but the common form of the word in the sense 'to fold,' 'to make folds,' is **pleat** [pliːt]. Etymologically the words have the same origin and are sometimes confused. For **apricot** both [ˈæprɪˌkɑt] and [ˈeːprɪˌkɑt] are in general use. The final syllable may be light, [-kət]. For **bade**, past tense of **bid**, the standard pronunciation is [bæd], as in **I bade him goodbye** [aɪ ˈbæd hɪm ˈgʊdˌbaɪ], though a spelling-pronunciation [beːd] or [beɪd] is occasionally heard, especially when the word occurs in phrases which have passed out of colloquial use. For **banal** the common pronunciation is [bæˈnæl] or [ˈbænəl], less frequently [ˈbeːnəl]. Two pronunciations are current for **halibut**, [ˈhæləbət] or [ˈhɑləbət]. For **raillery** both [ˈreːlərɪ] and [ˈrælərɪ] are heard, with academic authority in favor of the former; but so far as the word is popular at all, common usage favors the second. Two forms, [ˈreːʃənz] and [ˈræʃənz], for **rations** are in use, the second being the more general. For **asphalt** the common British pronunciation is [æsˈfælt] or [ˈæsˌfælt], but in America nearly always the word is [ˈæsˌfɔlt]. The proper name **Spokane** is locally [spoˈkæn], and [spoˈkeːn] is heard from speakers who know the word only as an eye-word.

### [e], [e·], [eː]

**131.** The sound represented by [e] can best be observed in words like **chaotic** [keˈɑtɪk], **archa-ic** [ɑɹˈke-ɪk], or in polysyllables like **vacation** [veˈke·ʃən] where the first vowel is short, the second half-long, **Baconian** [beˈko·njən], **fatally** [ˈfe·təlɪ], **bakery** [ˈbe·kərɪ], **bay-berry** [ˈbe·ˌbɛrɪ], **pay-roll** [ˈpe·ˌro·l], etc. In some of these words the quantity varies from short to half-long according to the degree of stress. High vowels like [e] and [i] are less likely to be obviously prolonged than mid or low vowels, and one is consequently often in doubt whether to take them as long or short.

**132.** In monosyllables with a full stress, the vowel lengthens and frequently becomes diphthongal. This is especially apparent when the vowel is final, as in **day** [deɪ], **they** [ðeɪ], **whey** [ʍeɪ], etc., and before voiced consonants, as in **fade** [feɪd], **grave** [greɪv], **haze** [heɪz], etc., see § 207. Before voiceless consonants, however, even in stressed monosyllables, the diphthongal quality is very slight, and often not audibly present at all. Compare, for example, **rate** with **raid** (the spelling of **raid** is not significant), or **face** with **phase**, or **waif** with **wave, waive.** If the vowel is diphthongized at all, it is more likely to be diphthongal in **raid, phase, wave, waive**, than in **rate, face, waif.** But with many speakers the diphthongal quality, if present at all, is so slight as not to be appreciated by the ear. For such speakers the sound is to be recorded simply as [eː]. No questions of propriety in usage are raised by the variation between [eː] and [eɪ], the difference being so slight that it does not attract attention to itself.

**133.** A clear [e]-vowel rarely occurs before [r], but is sometimes heard in formal speech in **vary** (to distinguish the word from **very**), **Mary** (as distinguished from **merry**), **chary** (as distinguished from **cherry**), **parent, vagary** [vəˈge·rɪ], **wary**, etc., where the spelling exerts an influence on the pronunciation, see § 129.

**134.** For **patent** both [ˈpeːtənt] and [ˈpætənt] occur, the former when the word has the sense 'obvious,' 'apparent.' But **latent** is always [ˈleːtənt]. For **quoit** the common popular pronunciation is [kweːt], but the cultivated and dictionary pronunciation is [kwɔɪt] or [kɔɪt]. The common standard pronunciation for **patriot, patriotism, patriotic**, in America is [ˈpe·trɪət], [ˈpe·trɪəˌtɪzm], [pe·trɪˈɑtɪk], but [pætr–] is also heard, more frequently in **patriotism, patriotic**, than in **patriot.** For **Danish** the standard pronunciation is [ˈdeːnɪʃ], the long vowel being maintained by the analogy of **Dane**. In popular speech, however, the vowel is often shortened, as in ['dænɪʃ], and as it is in both popular and cultivated speech in **Spanish** ['spænɪʃ] as compared with **Spain** [speːn]. Cf. **Polish** and **polish**, § 179. For **glacier** American speech has ['gleːʃɪəɹ], ['gleːʃəɹ], but ['glæsjə] only as a Briticism. A pronunciation ['gleːsɪəɹ] may be heard occasionally in formal speech. The pronunciation of **aye**, 'ever', is [eː], [eɪ], as distinguished from **ay**, 'yes', which is [aɪ]. The plural of **ay** is spelled **ayes** but pronounced [aɪz]. For **again**, **against**, the usual pronunciations are [ə'gɛn], [ə'gɛnst], though [ə'geːn], [ə'geːnst] are occasionally heard, probably because of the spelling. For **always** the standard pronunciation is ['ɔlˌweːz] or ['ɔlˌwe·z], but in popular speech the word often becomes ['ɔlwəz], ['ɔlwɪz], and sometimes ['ɔləz]. For **Isaiah** both [aɪ'zeːə] and [ɪ'zaɪə] are in current use, the former being the more general.

[ɛ]

**135.** This is the common sound of English **e** in **get** [gɛt], **ten** [tɛn], **bend** [bɛnd], **lense** [lɛnz], **tread** [trɛd], **breath** [brɛθ], **meadow** ['mɛdo], **educate** ['ɛdʒuˌke·t], and hosts of other words. The current pronunciation of **again, against**, [ə'gɛn], [ə'gɛnst], is occasionally changed under the influence of spelling to [ə'ge·n], [ə'ge·nst] or [ə'geɪn], [ə'geɪnst]. Before [r] followed by a vowel, **e** is commonly [ɛ], as in **very** ['vɛrɪ], **perish** ['pɛrɪʃ], **terrible** ['tɛrɪbl], **ferry** ['fɛrɪ], **merit** ['mɛrɪt]. For [ɛ] in words of this type pronounced [ʌ], see § 201. For **hero, zero, Nero**, etc., see § 168.

**136.** In a few learned words, like **serum**, **Ceres**, **series**, **e** before **r** is [i] or [ɪ], likewise **cereal**, **serial** ['sɪrɪəl], **serious** ['sɪrɪəs], **period** ['pɪrɪəd]. The spelling of **bury** ['bɛrɪ] is exceptional. As the name of a town in England, **Bury** is pronounced [ˈbjuərɪ]. A variant form **yelk** [jɛlk] exists by the side of **yolk** [joːk].

**137.** The preterite of the verb **eat** is always spelled **ate** and almost universally pronounced [eːt] in America, but occasionally [ɛt], this being a generally current British pronunciation, see *New English Dictionary,* and Michaelis-Jones, *Phonetic Dictionary,* under this word. Most Americans regard [ɛt] as dialectal. The proper name, as well as the common noun, **Jenny, jenny,** is always [ˈdʒɛnɪ] in cultivated American speech, but [ˈdʒɪnɪ] for **Jenny** is good British usage. So also [ˈkɪmɪst] for **chemist** and derivatives is good British usage, but in America the word is always [ˈkɛmɪst].

**138.** In **epoch** the stressed vowel is usually short, giving [ˈɛpək], but sometimes in very formal pronunciation the word becomes [ˈiːpɑk]. For **tenet, tenable** the usual pronunciation is [ˈtɛnɪt], [ˈtɛnəbl], occasionally [ˈtiːnɪt], [ˈtiːnəbl]. For **deaf** the standard pronunciation is [dɛf], but [diːf], which is an older historical survival, is often heard in the popular dialects. In Webster's day, [diːf] was the general pronunciation, see *Dissertations,* p. 128. As an adjective **cleanly** is pronounced [ˈklɛnlɪ], as an adverb, [ˈkliːnlɪ]. In **pretty, England, English,** the standard pronunciation is [ˈprɪtɪ], [ˈɪŋglənd], [ˈɪŋglɪʃ], the occasional pronunciation with [ɛ] being artificial and due to the spelling.

**139.** For **get** [gɛt] and derivatives popular English frequently has [gɪt]; so also [tʃɪst] for **chest** [tʃɛst], [jɪt] for **yet** [jɛt], [ɪnˈstɪd] for **instead** [ɪnˈstɛd], and similarly with other words.

Before [g], in the popular dialects, [eɪ] is often heard for standard [ɛ], as in the pronunciations [eɪg], [beɪg], [leɪg], [ˈnʌtˌmeɪg] for standard **egg** [ɛg], **beg** [bɛg], **leg** [lɛg], **nutmeg** [ˈnʌtˌmɛg], etc.

For **keg** [kɛg] a frequent dialect form is [kæg]. So also **yes** [jɛs] is very often [jæs] in popular pronunciation.

[ɛː]

**140.** This symbol represents the long vowel commonly heard before **r** in such words as **there** [ðɛːɹ], **where** [ʍɛːɹ], **dare** [dɛːɹ], **fair** [fɛːɹ], **hare, hair** [hɛːɹ], **pare, pair, pear** [pɛːɹ], **lair** [lɛːɹ]. These words may also be heard with a glide vowel before [ɹ], [ðɛːəɹ], [ʍɛːəɹ], [dɛːəɹ], etc., or with loss of the final consonant, [ðɛːə], [ʍɛːə], [dɛːə], etc.

On the organic difference between [ɛ] and [ɛː], see above, §§ 54, 55.

**141.** The pronunciation of **chary, fairy, hairy, Mary, vary, wary** is [ˈtʃɛːrɪ], [ˈfɛːrɪ], [hɛːrɪ], [ˈmɛːrɪ], [ˈvɛːrɪ], [ˈwɛːrɪ], which distinguishes **chary** from **cherry, fairy** from **ferry, hairy** from **Harry** [hærɪ], **Mary** from **merry, marry, vary** from **very, wary** from **wherry**. On words of this type pronounced with [e], see § 133.

**142.** There is considerable variation among cultivated speakers in the quality of the vowel in words of the type of **there, where**, etc., degrees being present all the way from [ɛː] to [æː], or when the vowel is short as in **berry, very**, etc., from [ɛ] to [æ]. But pronunciations like **there** [ðæːɹ], **hair** [hæːɹ], **stair** [stæːɹ], or **very** [ˈværɪ], **terrible** [ˈtærɪbl] are scarcely to be recommended for imitation.

**143.** The slight glide vowel inserted before the [ɹ] in **fair** [fɛːəɹ], **hair** [hɛːəɹ], **there** [ðɛːəɹ], etc., when the [ɹ] is not pronounced is often prolonged and even becomes [ɑ], e.g., **fair** [ˈfɛːə] or [ˈfɛːɑ], **hair** [ˈhɛːə] or [hˈɛːɑ], **there** [ˈðɛːə] or [ˈðɛːɑ]. The vowel [ɑ] in such pronunciations often receives a fairly heavy stress. These latter usages are nowhere general in America, though sometimes cultivated in imitation of what is taken to be Eastern American or British usage.

**144.** In words compounded with **aero–**, as in **aeroplane, aeronaut, aerostat**, etc., the standard formal pronunciation of the first syllable is [ˈeːərə–] or [ˈɛːərə–]. But [ˈɛːrə–] is quite generally used. The final vowel of the syllable may also be heard as [o] in careful speech. The pronunciation [ˈɛrɪə–] is popular and dialectal.

**145.** In **were** the common pronunciation is [wəɹ] or [wʌːr], though the pronunciation [wɛːɹ], also [wæːɹ], is sometimes cultivated in precise speech.

[ə]

**146.** The vowel [ə] is a sound of wide occurrence in unstressed position, and is the sound which vowels in general tend to become when, as in rapid speech, they are somewhat obscured. It occurs in all positions in the word, initially, medially and finally, e.g., **about** [əˈbɑʊt], **finally** [ˈfɑɪnəlɪ], **zebra** [ˈzibrə], **Cuba** [kjʊbə], **sofa** [ˈsofə], **a man** [əˈmæn], **Iceland** [ˈaislənd], etc. Certain words in which standard speech retains a relatively clear vowel in final unstressed syllables, occur with this obscure vowel in dialect speech, e.g., dialect **yellow** [ˈjɛlə], **potato** [pəˈteːtə], **tomato** [təˈmeːtə], **piano** [pɪˈænə], **window** [ˈwɪndə], **fellow** [ˈfɛlə], **thorough** [ˈθʌrə], **always** [ˈɔlwəz].

**147.** In careless and rapid speech some speakers have a tendency to omit [ə] where cultivated speech retains it.

This is especially noticeable when [ə] is preceded by a vowel or [r], as in **poem**, in popular pronunciation [poːm], in standard speech [ˈpoːɛm], or [ˈpoːəm] or [ˈpoːɪm], see § 173; **moral**, popularly [ˈmɔɹl], in standard speech [ˈmɔrəl]; **towel**, popularly [tɑʊl], in standard speech [ˈtɑʊəl]; **quarrel**, popularly [ˈkwɔɹl], in standard speech [ˈkwɔrəl]; **diary**, popularly [ˈdaɪrɪ], in standard speech [ˈdaɪərɪ]; **diamond**, popularly [ˈdaɪmənd], in standard speech [ˈdaɪəmənd]; **real**, **really**, popularly [riːl], [ˈriːlɪ], in standard speech [ˈriːəl], [ˈriːəlɪ], sometimes also [ˈrɪəl], [ˈrɪəlɪ]; **cruel**, popularly [kruːl], in standard speech [ˈkruːəl]; **violet**, popularly [ˈvaɪlət], [ˈvɑːlət], in standard speech [ˈvaɪəlɪt], very formally [ˈvaɪolɛt].

The pronunciation of **deal**, **seal**, **peal**, etc., as [diːl], [siːl], [piːl] is standard, the spelling **ea** in these words being a representation of what is historically a simple vowel, whereas in **real** the spelling **ea**, which looks the same, is of entirely different origin. It is derived from an originally dissyllabic word, with the syllabic break between the two vowels, and standard speech continues to maintain the word as a dissyllable.

**148.** The final unstressed syllable of words ending in **a** is pronounced [ə] in standard speech, but frequently [ɪ] in popular speech, as in **opera** [ˈɑpərə], **era** [ˈiːrə] or [ˈɪrə], **extra** [ˈɛkstrə], **America** [əˈmɛrɪkə], **Noah** [ˈnoːə], **Martha** [ˈmɑːɹθə], etc., pronounced [ˈɑprɪ], [ˈɪrɪ], [ˈɛkstrɪ], [əˈmɛrɪkɪ], [ˈnoːɪ], [ˈmɑːɹθɪ], etc. For **Iowa** the common pronunciation is [ˈaɪəwə], dialectally sometimes [ˈaɪəwɪ].

**149.** For **cupola** [ˈkjupələ], popular pronunciation frequently has a transposition of the unstressed vowels, giving [ˈkjupəˌlo]. In **cocoa** [ˈkoːko] the final vowel is silent; the word is a metathesized form of **cacao**, but this original form of the word is now used only in scientific writing. When compounded with **-nut**, the word is frequently spelled **coco-**, as in **coco-nut** [ˈkoːko-ˌnʌt]. The word **curaçao** [ˌkjurəˈsɑːo], derived from the name of a Dutch island in the Carribean, is commonly metathesized into **curaçoa** [ˌkjurəˈsoːə] or [ˌkjurəˈsoʊ].

**150.** As an inflectional ending, **e** in the ending **-es** is always silent when the **s** is voiceless, as in **rites**, **writes** (third singular of the verb) [raɪts], **likes** [laɪks], **rates** [reːts], etc., and it is silent also when the **s** is voiced, except when the syllable **-es** is preceded by [s], [z], [ʃ] or [ʒ], in which case **e** [ə] is pronounced, as in **pieces** [piːsəz], **prizes** [praɪzəz], **wishes** [ˈwɪʃəz], **stages** [steːdʒəz].

**151.** Between [l] and a succeeding [m] a vowel [ə] is sometimes present in popular speech which does not appear in standard speech, as in **elm** [ɛlm], **film** [fɪlm], **realm** [rɛlm], etc., pronounced [ˈɛləm], [ˈfɪləm], [ˈrɛləm], etc. So also [ˈæθəˌlit], [æθəˈlɛtɪk] for **athlete** [ˈæθˌlit], **athletic** [æθˈlɛtɪk].

**152.** Before [l] or [ɹ], and after a vowel, a slight glide [ə], [ə] is sometimes present, as in such pronunciations as **stole** [ˈstoːəl], **four** [fɔːəɹ], **milk** [mɪəlk], **dart** [dɑːəɹt], etc., but this sound is so slight in standard pronunciation that it does not seem necessary to represent it phonetically, see §§ 160, 167. It is often exaggerated in the speech of young children, who prolong also the preceding vowel.

**153.** Before [r], intervocalic, a very distinct [ə] is present in British speech, especially noticeable to American ears when the vowel preceding [r] is [ɪ], [ɛ] or [aɪ], as in **period** [ˈpɪərɪəd], **peeress** [ˈpɪərɪs], **parent** [ˈpɛərənt], **miry** [ˈmaɪərɪ], **Byron** [ˈbaɪərən]; but this [ə] is scarcely ever heard in America, the words cited being pronounced ['pɪrɪəd], ['pɪrɪs] or ['pɪrɛs], ['pærənt] or ['pɛrənt], ['maɪrɪ], ['baɪrən]. In the adjective form of **fire** [faɪəɹ], which is spelled **fiery**, a pronunciation ['faɪərɪ] may be heard, but also ['faɪrɪ]. But **wiry** from **wire** ['waɪəɹ] is always ['waɪrɪ].

[ə]

**154.** This symbol stands for the short inverted vowel sound, which is to be clearly distinguished from [ə]. The sound appears in stressed and unstressed syllables, and is represented in conventional spelling by various vowel letters before **r** final or followed by a consonant, as in **bird** [bəɹd], **burr** [bəɹ], **sir** [səɹ], **fir**, **fur** [fəɹ], **heard** [həɹd], **person** ['pəɹsən], **serpent** ['səɹpənt], **worthy** ['wəɹðɪ], **myrtle** ['məɹtl], etc. The vowel is normally short, but may be prolonged in exceptional instances, as in the somewhat exotic word **myrrh** [məɹ] or [məːɹ]. For **iron**, **tired**, **hired**, etc., see § 304.

**155.** When [ɹ] is not pronounced before the consonant in **bird**, **heard**, **person**, etc., the vowel is usually [ʌː]. When final [ɹ] is not pronounced, it often leaves a weak [ə] as its survival, **burr** [bʌːə], **fir**, **fur** [fʌːə], etc. Final **r** in unstressed syllables when not pronounced is preceded by [ə], as in **never** ['nɛvə], **feather** ['fɛðə], etc. In affected speech this vowel sometimes becomes [ɑ], see § 143.

**156.** For **girl** the current pronunciation is [gəɹl] or [gʌːl], but [gɛːɹl], [gæɹl], [gɪɹl] are sometimes heard and are often cultivated as refined pronunciations.

**157.** For **courteous**, **courtezan** the usual pronunciation is ['kəɹtɪəs], ['kəɹtəzən], but for **courtier**, ['kɔɹtɪəɹ], ['kɔɹtʃəɹ] are more general.

**158.** For [ə] of the standard speech in words containing [ɹ] followed by a consonant, in New York and its vicinity a diphthong is heard, commonly represented in dialect stories by the spelling **oi**, e.g., *thoid*, 'third,' *foist*, 'first,' *boid*, 'bird.' The phonetic elements of this diphthong are usually [ə] followed by [ɪ]. This pronunciation has not made its way into cultivated usage.[1]

**159.** For **very, terrible, syrup**, etc., pronounced ['vəɹɪ], ['təɹɪbl], ['sərəp], etc., see § 201. The pronunciation of [ə] for [ə] before [r] followed by a vowel in unstressed syllables is to be avoided, e.g., **history** ['hɪstərɪ] pronounced ['hɪstərɪ].

**160.** Between [aɪ], [ɑʊ] and a succeeding final [ɹ], a vowel [ə] is regularly present in accented words, **hire** and **higher** ['haɪəɹ] being homonyms; so also **flour, flower** ['flɑʊəɹ] are homonymous. Not infrequently a slovenly kind of pronunciation is heard in which this [ə] is omitted and the preceding diphthong is reduced to [ɑː], **flower, flour** being pronounced [flɑːɹ], **fire** pronounced [fɑːɹ], as though it were the same as **far, our, hour** pronounced [ɑːɹ]. The word **our** in unstressed position in colloquial speech is very commonly [ɑːɹ], so commonly that perhaps one cannot characterize it as slovenly. But its phonetic form is due entirely to the fact that it is slightly stressed. In stressed position the diphthong [ɑʊ] is never [ɑː] in standard speech.

[i], [i·], [iː]

**161.** The vowel [i] is heard only in polysyllables, like **expediency** [ɛks'pidɪənsɪ], where the stress on the accented syllable is comparatively light, or in unstressed syllables,

[1] See Babbitt, *Dialect Notes*, I, 463.

as in **eternal** [i'təɹnəl], **economy** [i'kɑnəmi], **œsophagus** [i'sɑfəgəs]. The half-long vowel may be recognized in compounds, like **tea-table** ['ti·ˌte·bl], and the long vowel in words containing full stress, as in **tea** [tiː], **he** [hiː], **key, quay** [kiː], **deed** [diːd], **bean** [biːn], **priest** [priːst], **convene** [kən'vɪːn], **eagle** ['iːgl], **Egypt** ['iːdʒɪpt].

**162.** For **sleek, creek, clique** the standard pronunciations are [sliːk], [kriːk], [kliːk], though [slɪk], [krɪk], [klɪk] are widely current in familiar colloquial use, and [slɪk], in the sense 'cunning,' 'sly,' may be said to have passed into general use. The pronunciation [fə'tɪg] for **fatigue** [fə'tiːg] is not cultivated usage. For **amenable** the standard pronunciation is [ə'miːnəbl], but for **amenity** almost always [ə'mɛnɪtɪ], though sometimes [ə'miːnɪtɪ].

**163.** In words of Greek origin commonly spelled **æ**, as in **Æschylus, Æsculapius, æsthetic, anapæst**, the usual pronunciation in America is ['ɛskɪləs], [ɛskju'leːpɪəs], [ɛs'θɛtɪk], ['ænəpɛst], but [iːs–] in England and not infrequently also in America. **Æsop** is always ['iːˌsɑp], and the spelling **œ** is usually [i] or [iː], as in **œsophagus** [i'sɑfəgəs], **Œnone** [i'noːnɪ], **œcumenical** [ikju'mɛnɪkl], **Œdipus** ['iːdɪpəs], though pronunciations with [ɛ], as in ['ɛdɪpəs], [ɛkju'mɛnɪkl], are also heard.

**164.** For **Elizabethan** both [əlɪzə'biːθən] and [əlɪzə'bɛθən] occur. For **scenic** the common pronunciation is ['sɛnɪk], though ['siːnɪk], which is the more usual British pronunciation, and is of course supported by the analogy of **scene** [siːn], is sometimes heard. For **fetid, fetish** both ['fiːtɪd], ['fiːtɪʃ] and ['fɛtɪd], ['fɛtɪʃ] are current, and for **leisure** both ['liːʒəɹ] and ['lɛʒəɹ]. For **either, neither** the general pronunciation is ['iːðəɹ], ['niːðəɹ], but occasionally [ˈaɪðəɹ], [ˈnaɪðəɹ] are heard, often as a conscious refined pronunciation. It is popular and general nowhere in America. For **inveigle** the usual pronunciation is [ɪnˈviːgl], but sometimes also [ɪnˈveːgl]. For **penal** the pronunciation is [ˈpiːnəl], for **penalize** either [ˈpiːnəlaɪz] or [ˈpɛnəlaɪz], for **penalty** always [ˈpɛnəltɪ].

**165.** Words containing the prefix **pre–** as a stressed syllable usually have the pronunciation [pri–] when the syllable is logically important, as in clear compounds like **prehistoric** [ˈprihɪsˈtɔrɪk], **predigested** [ˈpridaɪˈdʒɛstɪd], **prefix** [ˈprifɪks], **prepay** [ˋpriˈpeɪ], also in a few somewhat learned words, the etymological origins of which are still felt, as in **precinct** [ˈpriˋsɪŋkt], **prefect** [ˈpriˋfɛkt], **prelude** [ˈpriˋluːd], also sometimes [ˈprɛlˋuːd]. Otherwise the syllable is usually pronounced [prɛ–], though custom is not completely uniform, some words like **predecessor, predilection, premature, presentation** being pronounced either [prɛ–] or [pri–]. The pronunciation with [prɛ–] is the more common, and in some words, e.g., **predicate, preference, prejudice, preparation, preposition, preterite,** it is the only one in good use.

**166.** In the ending **–itis**, as in **appendicitis, neuritis, phlebitis, meningitis,** etc., both [–iːtəs] and [–aɪtəs] occur; also **angina** [ænˈdʒiːnə], [ænˈdʒaɪnə], better [ˈændʒɪnə], **Argentine** [ˈɑɹdʒənˋtiːn] or [ˈɑɹdʒənˋtaɪn], **adamantine** [ædəˈmænˋtiːn] or [ædəˈmænˋtaɪn]. For **oblique** the more usual pronunciation is [oˈbliːk], but also, less frequently, [oˈblaɪk].

**167.** Before [r], [ɹ], [i] is commonly lowered to [ɪ] and a glide vowel sometimes inserted between [ɪ] and [r], [ɹ], as in **cereal, serial** [ˈsɪərɪəl], **hear** [hɪəɹ], **hearing** [ˈhɪərɪŋ],

**pier, peer** [pɪəɹ], **tier, tear** [tɪəɹ]; but some speakers tend to preserve a clear [i]-sound in a few words, usually of learned character, as in **eery** [ˈiərɪ], **era** [ˈiərə], **query** [ˈkwiərɪ], **series** [ˈsiərɪz] or [ˈsiəriz]. So also **dreary, weary** are sometimes pronounced [ˈdriərɪ], [ˈwiərɪ]. This glide vowel before [r], [ɹ] is often not present at all in American speech, and is in general much less marked as a characteristic of American than of British speech.

**168.** In **hero, Nero, zero** a clear [i]-vowel is generally maintained, giving [ˈhiːˌro], [ˈniːˌro], [ˈziːˌro], but many speakers lower the vowel to [ɪ], as in [ˈhɪˌro], [ˈnɪˌro], [ˈzɪˌro].

[ɪ]

**169.** This is the short sound commonly current in **sit** [sɪt], **mission** [ˈmɪʃən], **timid** [ˈtɪmɪd], **ink** [ɪŋk], **rich** [rɪtʃ], etc. In stressed syllables it is generally written **i**, though also **y** in **lyric** [ˈlɪrɪk], **syllable** [ˈsɪləbl], **synagogue** [ˈsɪnəgɔg], and some others.

**170.** For **i, y** followed by **r** and a vowel, the standard pronunciation is [ɪ], as in **dirigible** [ˈdɪrɪdʒɪbl], **miracle** [ˈmɪrəkl], **mirror** [ˈmɪrəɹ], **sirup, syrup** [ˈsɪrəp], **syringe** [ˈsɪrɪndʒ], also [sɪˈrɪndʒ], **tyranny** [ˈtɪrənɪ], **virile** [ˈvɪrɪl], also [ˈvaɪrɪl], exceptions to this rule being cases in which **i, y** is pronounced [aɪ], as in **gyrate, pirate, siren, tirade, tyrant, virile, virus.** On **i, y** followed by **r** and a vowel pronounced [ʌ], [ə] in popular speech, see § 201.

**171.** For **been** the normal pronunciation is [bɪn], though [biːn] is sometimes heard as a precise or consciously cultivated pronunciation. For **breeches, breeching** the usual pronunciation is [ˈbrɪtʃəz], [ˈbrɪtʃɪŋ], but a spelling-pronunciation [ˈbriːtʃəz], [ˈbriːtʃɪŋ] is sometimes cultivated. In **busy** [ˈbɪzɪ], **business** [ˈbɪznɪs], the spelling **u** is exceptional for [ɪ].

**172.** There is a distinctly audible difference between stressed and unstressed [ɪ], as, for example, in the two syllables of **pity, city**, which for lack of a separate symbol for each sound, we represent by [ˈpɪtɪ], [ˈsɪtɪ]. The same applies to initial unstressed syllables, as in **desist** [dɪˈzɪst], **begin** [bɪˈgɪn], **initial** [ɪˈnɪʃəl], etc. The unstressed [ɪ] is more relaxed, as one would expect it to be, than stressed [ɪ], and in a phonetic transcription of greater precision than the one here employed, each sound would have its own symbol.

**173.** In unstressed syllables, this sound occurs for **a, e, i** and **u** of the conventional spelling, though usage in many words varies widely, some speakers pronouncing [ɪ], some [ɛ] and some the obscure vowel [ə]:

(1) before the stressed syllable, as in **begin** [bɪˈgɪn] or [bəˈgɪn], **debate** [dɪˈbeːt] or [dəˈbeːt], **decide** [dɪˈsaɪd] or [dəˈsaɪd], **engage** [ɪnˈgeːdʒ] or [ɛnˈgeːdʒ], **except** [ɪkˈsɛpt] or [ɛkˈsɛpt], **elect** [ɪˈlɛkt], [ɛˈlɛkt] or [əˈlɛkt].

(2) after the stressed syllable, as in the preterites of verbs, **added** [ˈædɪd], [ˈædɛd] or [ˈædəd]; **disgusted** [dɪs-ˈgʌstɪd], [dɪsˈgʌstɛd] or [dɪsˈgʌstəd]; in a variety of nouns and adjectives of different endings, as in **naked** [ˈneːkɪd], [ˈneːkɛd] or [ˈneːkəd]; **sonnet** [ˈsɑnɪt], [ˈsɑnɛt] or [ˈsɑnət]; **rabbit** [ˈræbɪt], [ˈræbɛt] or [ˈræbət]; **prelate** [ˈprɛlɪt] (very formally [ˈprɛlet]), [ˈprɛlɛt] or [ˈprɛlət]; **minute** (*noun*) [ˈmɪnɪt], [ˈmɪnɛt] or [ˈmɪnət]; **honest** [ˈɑnɪst], [ˈɑnɛst] or [ˈɑnəst]; **lettuce** [ˈlɛtɪs], [ˈlɛtɛs] or [ˈlɛtəs]; **palace** [ˈpælɪs], [ˈpælɛs] or [pæləs]; **goodness** [ˈgʊdnɪs], [ˈgʊdnɛs] or

['gʊdnəs]; **riches** ['rɪtʃɪz], ['rɪtʃɛz] or ['rɪtʃəz]; **poem** ['poːɪm], ['poːɛm] or ['poːəm]; **vowel** ['vaʊɪl], ['vaʊɛl] or ['vaʊəl]; **college** ['kalɪdʒ], ['kalɛdʒ] (very formally ['kaledʒ]); **courage** ['kʌrɪdʒ], ['kʌrɛdʒ]; **usage** ['juːsɪdʒ], ['juːsɛdʒ]; **damage** ['dæmɪdʒ], ['dæmɛdʒ]; **manage** ['mænɪdʒ], ['mænɛdʒ]; **orange** ['ɔrɪndʒ], ['ɔrɛndʒ] or ['ɔrəndʒ].

"Philadelphia, New York City, and some parts of the West and South," says Grandgent,[1] often substitute [ə] for [ɪ] in final syllables, as in ['gʊdnəs] for ['gʊdnɪs], ['anəst] for ['anɪst], **I've got it** [aiv 'gat ət] for [aiv 'gat ɪt], ['pæləs] for ['pælɪs], but "in the rest of the country this pronunciation is regarded as extremely vulgar." Tests which the writer has applied to speakers from regions here excepted show that the statement as to the vulgarity of [ə] in final syllables is exaggerated and does not now apply. Such pronunciations as ['pæləs], ['anəst] are current throughout the country, and cannot now be described as extremely vulgar by any standards generally accepted.

**174.** For **adobe**, **prairie** the standard pronunciation is [ə'doːbɪ], ['prɛːrɪ]. For **Cincinnati** both [sɪnsə'nætɪ] and [sɪnsə'nætə] occur, the former being locally and generally the more common pronunciation. For final **a** [ə] pronounced [ɪ] in popular speech, see above, § 148. The desire to avoid this popular pronunciation of final **a** [ə] as [ɪ] at all hazards sometimes leads speakers to pronounce final [ə] when cultivated standard speech has [ɪ], and this probably explains a pronunciation like [sɪnsə'nætə]. So also occasionally [mɪ'zʊrə] for standard **Missouri** [mɪ'zʊrɪ], and even ['prɛːrə] for ['prɛːrɪ] has been observed (Sturte-

[1] *Die Neueren Sprachen*, II, 449 (1895); see also *Dialect Notes*, I, 319–323 (1894).

vant, *Linguistic Change,* p. 83).[1] For **Ypsilanti** [ɪpsɪ'læntɪ] occasionally [ɪpsɪ'læntə] is heard. It may be that the pronunciation of words like **Cincinnati, Missouri, Ypsilanti** has been affected by the analogy of many other place names like **Nebraska, Montana, Nevada,** etc., which regularly have [ə] for the final vowel. Final unstressed **y**, both in common and proper nouns, is always [ɪ], as in **heavy, busy, Albany, Schenectady,** etc.

**175.** For **jaundice** ['dʒɔndɪs] the popular dialects often have ['dʒɔndəɹz], ['dʒændəɹz]. For **Italian** popular speech commonly has ['aɪ'tæljən], but standard speech only [ɪ'tæljən].

[o], [o·], [oː]

**176.** This vowel is heard as a short sound, sometimes as the stressed vowel of polysyllables, as in **locomotive** ['lokə'motɪv], **connotative** [kə'notətɪv], in unstressed syllables, as in **obedient** [o'biːdɪənt], **approbation** [æpro'beːʃən], **yellow** ['jɛlo], **window** ['wɪndo], **piano** [pɪ'æno], and in secondarily stressed syllables when the vowel may be short or half-long, as in the compounds **dough-nut** ['do·'nʌt], **tow-path** ['to·'pæθ], **go-cart** ['go·'kɑɹt], etc. On the weakening of unstressed [o] to [ə], see above, § 146.

**177.** When the sound is fully stressed and long, and especially when it is final, it tends to become diphthongal, starting with [o] and closing with [ʊ], as in **dough, doe** [doʊ], **toe, tow** [toʊ], **flow, floe** [floʊ], **château** [ʃæ'toʊ], etc. Before consonants, as in **rote, rode, roll,** etc., the diphthongal quality of the vowel is always less marked

[1] Though I am informed by Mr. F. L. Mott that ['prɛːrə] is a pioneer pronunciation for **prairie**, in Iowa, in the speech of persons who cannot be supposed to have been influenced by refined analogies.

and often not present at all. This sound is much less diphthongal in American than in British speech. In the latter a great variety of diphthongal shadings occur, some of them familiar in the exaggerated representations of Englishmen and their speech on the American stage. In the speech of many, perhaps of most, Americans there is scarcely any trace of diphthongal quality in the sound, which may in most instances be represented simply as [oː] or [o·]. See § 218.

**178.** In substantive compounds with **pro–**, the prefix, when stressed, in some words is regularly pronounced [ˈpro–], as in **probate, proceeds, profile, programme, prolix** [ˈprolɪks] or [prəˈliks], **prologue, pronoun, protest**; in others, regularly [ɑ], or sometimes [ɔ], as in **problem, project, prophet, prospect, proverb**; and in still others, the pronunciation varies between [o] and [ɑ], the latter being the more general, as in **process, produce, product, progress, provost.**

**179.** For **sloth, slothful** the standard pronunciation is [sloːθ], [ˈsloːθfəl], but a variant pronunciation [slɔːθ], [ˈslɔːθfəl] is not infrequent. The pronunciation of **loam** in standard speech is [loːm], but frequently [luːm] in dialect speech. An archaic spelling **shew, shew-bread** is sometimes met with for [ʃoː], [ˈʃoː-ˌbrɛd]. The proper name **Polish** is [ˈpoːlɪʃ], following the analogy of **Pole** [poːl], but the verb **polish** is [ˈpɑlɪʃ]. For **bowie-** in the compound **bowie-knife** both [ˈboːɪ-] and [ˈbuːɪ-] occur. The usual standard pronunciation for **shone** is [ʃoːn] or [ʃoʊn], but [ʃɔn], [ʃɔːn], even [ʃʌn] are occasionally heard. The pronunciation of **whole** as [hʌl] is dialectal.

**180.** In Eastern New England, a number of words which elsewhere have a long vowel are pronounced with a short [o]-vowel which is slightly more fronted than the ordinary vowel, giving a mid half-front tense rounded vowel. "This vowel is used by educated New England speakers in about fifty common words and their derivatives, and it certainly prevails in the cultivated usage of this region in **Polk, polka, whole,** and probably in **both, folks, Holmes, most, only,** and some others."[1]

[ɔ]

**181.** This sound is a short vowel, and may be best observed in polysyllables, where it may be stressed, as in **auditory** [ˈɔdɪˌtɔrɪ], **Audubon** [ˈɔdʊbən], or in unstressed syllables, as in **audacious** [ɔˈdeːʃəs], **authentic** [ɔˈθɛntɪk], **automatic** [ɔtoˈmætɪk], etc.

**182.** It occurs also with some speakers in many syllables written **o**, as in **hot, not, nod, log, soft, moss, on,** etc., or **a** after **w**, as in **water, watch,** etc., but usage varies in the value which it gives to the vowel in these words, see above, §§ 110, 111, and the vowel also varies in length from short to half-long or long, in some words, as in **soft** [sɔft], **moss** [mɔs], **dog** [dɔg], etc., pronounced also [sɔːft], [mɔːs], [dɔːg], or even dragged out in popular speech until they are over-long.

**183.** In words written **o** before [ŋ], the customary pronunciation is [ɔ], as in **long** [lɔŋ], **song** [sɔŋ], **throng** [θrɔŋ], **wrong** [rɔŋ], but occasional speakers have [ɑ] instead of [ɔ]. The pronunciation [lɔːŋ], [sɔːŋ], [θrɔːŋ], [rɔːŋ], etc., is heard only in dialect speech.

[1] Grandgent, *Publications of the Modern Language Association*, Vol. VII (New Series), p. 217 (1899). This vowel is dialectally common in Eastern New England in many words like **road, coat, boat, colt, post,** etc.

**184.** For **squalor** the usual pronunciation is [ˈskwɔləɹ], though [ˈskweːləɹ] is sometimes heard. For **swollen** the common form is [ˈswɔlən], but very frequently also [ˈswoːlən].

[ɔː]

**185.** This sound occurs in many syllables under full stress, as in **law** [lɔː], **draw** [drɔː], **taut, taught** [tɔːt], **thought** [θɔːt], **talk** [tɔːk], **naught** [nɔːt], **all** [ɔːl], **salt** [sɔːlt], **fault** [fɔːlt], **Paul** [pɔːl], etc.; also in dissyllables like **augur** [ˈɔːgəɹ], **aural** [ˈɔːrəl], **author** [ˈɔːθəɹ], **audit** [ˈɔːdɪt]; and in compounds, like **strawberry** [ˈstrɔ·ˌbɛrɪ], **chalk-line** [ˈtʃɔ·kˌlain], in which the vowel may be long or half-long. On the organic difference between [ɔ] and [ɔː], see above, §§ 62, 63.

For **sauce** (*noun*), **saucy** the standard pronunciation is [sɔːs], [ˈsɔːsɪ], but in the sense 'impertinent speech,' 'impertinent,' popular pronunciation commonly has [sæs], [ˈsæsɪ].

**186.** In words of the type of **daunt, flaunt, gaunt, gauntlet, haunt, launch, taunt,** the common pronunciation is [dɔːnt], [flɔːnt], [gɔːnt], etc., but some speakers say [dɑːnt], [flɑːnt], [gɑːnt], and for some words, as in [hænt], [læntʃ], a pronunciation with [æ] or [æː] is current in dialect speech. For **laundry** the current pronunciation is [ˈlɔːndrɪ], with an occasional variant pronunciation [ˈlɑːndrɪ]. For **Laura** the usual pronunciation is [ˈlɔːrə], but also sometimes [ˈlɑːrə].

**187.** The pronunciation of **caught, bought, talk, taught,** etc., with [ɑ·] or [ɑː], is current in some regions locally, but is not heard in standard cultivated English. So also the pronunciations [ˈdɑːtəɹ], [ˈslɑːtəɹ] for **daughter** [ˈdɔːtəɹ], **slaughter** [ˈslɔːtəɹ] are provincialisms.

**188.** A number of Indian proper names, in secondarily stressed syllables written **aw, ah, a,** have [ɔː], as in **Choctaw** [ˈtʃɑkˌtɔː], **Kenesaw** [ˈkɛnəˌsɔː], **Utah** [ˈjuˌtɔː], **Altamaha** [ˈæltəməˌhɔː], **Omaha** [ˈoməˌhɔː], **Ottawa** [ˈɑtəˌwɔː], etc.

**189.** Before [ɹ] followed by a consonant, when the [ɹ] is not pronounced, **o** is pronounced [ɔː], as in **corn** [kɔːn], **force** [fɔːs], **port** [pɔːt], etc. But the pronunciation [hɔːs] for **horse**, spelled *hoss* in dialect stories, is commonly regarded as illiterate and dialectal, though here, as in many instances, it is really the visual and not the audible form of the word that is objected to. When the [ɹ] is pronounced the preceding vowel is only half-long or short.

**190.** Before [r] followed by a vowel, the usual pronunciation of **o** is [ɔ·] or [ɔː], as in **glory** [ˈglɔ·rɪ], **story** [ˈstɔ·rɪ], **tory** [ˈtɔ·rɪ], **oral** [ˈɔ·rəl], not distinguished in pronunciation from **aural, moral** [ˈmɔ·rəl]. But some speakers, retaining an older pronunciation probably under the influence of spelling, in at least some of these words have [o·] or [oː], as in **glory** [ˈglo·rɪ], **story** [ˈsto·rɪ], **tory** [ˈto·rɪ], **oral** [ˈo·rəl], etc.

**191.** Before [ɹ] final, **o** (**ou, oo, oa**) is pronounced [ɔ·] or [ɔː], as in **store** [stɔ·ɹ], **more** [mɔ·ɹ], **pore, pour** [pɔ·ɹ], **fore, four, for** [fɔ·ɹ], **door** [dɔ·ɹ], **floor** [flɔ·ɹ], **roar** [rɔ·ɹ], **sore, soar** [sɔ·ɹ]. See § 197. These words might be written also [ˈstɔ·əɹ], etc., though with most speakers the glide vowel is very slight.

The preposition **for** is often [fəɹ] in rapid speech, written *fur* in dialect stories.

[u], [uː]

**192.** This sound is of wide occurrence, both as long and short. As a long, it tends to become diphthongal, [ʊu], but this pronunciation for what is commonly [uː] is not general enough in American speech to call for frequent representation. The quantity of the sound varies according to its surrounding from short to half-long and long. Instances of [u] occur in polysyllables like **recrudescence** [rikru′dɛsəns], **altruistic** [æltru′ɪstɪk], **absolutely** [′æbsə‵lutlɪ], also [′æbsə‵ljutlɪ], **Lusitania** [lusɪ′te·njə], etc. When the sound is long it is commonly represented in conventional spelling by **oo**, as in **boot** [buːt], **cool** [kuːl], **soon** [suːn], **spool** [spuːl], but also **ou**, as in **group** [gruːp], **soup** [suːp], **troupe** [truːp]; **u**, as in **dune** [duːn], **lunar** [′luːnəɹ], **rule** [ruːl], **rune** [ruːn]; **o**, as in **do** [duː], **to** [tuː]; **ui** as in **bruit** [bruːt], **fruit** [fruːt], **suit** [suːt], also [sjuːt], etc.

**193.** In some words usage varies widely between [u] and [ʊ], the resulting groups being very unsystematic. All speakers say **goose** [guːs], **mood** [muːd], **moon** [muːn], for example, and all say **book** [bʊk], **foot** [fʊt], **good** [gʊd], **shook** [ʃʊk], **stood** [stʊd]. But in the following words, which is not an exhaustive list, usage varies between [u], long or short, and [ʊ], and in popular use, one or two words have [ʌ]: **aloof, butcher, boot, broom, coop, Cooper, food, groom, hoof, hoop, Hooper, nook, proof, rood, roof, rook, room, rooster, root, soon, soot, spook, spoon, woof.**[1]

Of these words, according to the writer's observation, the following prevailingly have [uː]: **aloof, boot, broom, food, groom, proof, roof, rood, room, rooster, root, soon, spook, spoon, woof**; the following prevailingly have [ʊ]:

[1] The first two words in this list are included on the authority of Grandgent, *Die Neueren Sprachen*, II, 457, but for **aloof** the writer has heard only [ə′luːf], and for **butcher** only [′bʊtʃəɹ], or [′buːtʃəɹ] so rarely that this form of the word seems scarcely to be regarded as a current American pronunciation.

**butcher, coop, Cooper, hoof, hoop, Hooper, nook, rook, soot** (also in popular pronunciation [sʌt]).

The pronunciations **boot** [bʊt], **broom** [brʊm], **food** [fʊd], **soon** [sʊn], **spoon** [spʊn], etc., for words in the first group must be characterized as local or provincial, but **coop** [kuːp], **Cooper** ['kuːpəɹ], **hoof** [huːf], **hoop** [huːp], etc., for words in the second group, are supported by the usage of many cultivated speakers, whose pronunciation is probably influenced to some extent by the spelling.

On the differences of usage between [uː] and [ju], see §§ 229–231.

**194.** For **acoustic** both [ə'kuːstɪk] and [ə'kɑʊstɪk] are in common use, the former being perhaps the more general. For **bouquet** the standard pronunciation is [bu'keɪ], the pronunciation [bo'keɪ] or ['bo·ˋkeɪ] being old-fashioned or rustic. For **brooch** both [bruːtʃ] and [broːtʃ] occur. For **route** [ruːt], **tour** [tuːɹ], [tuːəɹ], **wound** [wuːnd], the popular dialects often have [rɑʊt], [tɑʊəɹ], [wɑʊnd]. The spelling of **zoology**, aided by the abbreviation **Zoo,** results sometimes in a pronunciation [zu'ɑlədʒɪ], the standard pronunciation being [zo'ɑlədʒɪ].

[ʊ]

**195.** This is normally only a short vowel and is commonly written **u** in the conventional alphabet, as in **bull** [bʊl], **bush** [bʊʃ], **cushion** ['kʊʃən], **full** [fʊl], **put** [pʊt], as a term in golf pronounced [pʌt], **tulle** [tʊl], etc. For **supple** the usual pronunciation is ['sʌpl], but ['sʊpl] occurs commonly in dialect speech and occasionally in cultivated speech. For **brusque** both [brʊsk] and [brʌsk] are current, with the preference in favor of [brʊsk]. For **fulsome** the usual pronunciation is ['fʊlsəm], but ['fʌlsəm] is also countenanced by usage.

**196.** This sound appears also in words written **u** before **r**, as in **lure** [lʊɹ] or [lʊəɹ], **sure** [ʃʊɹ] or [ʃʊəɹ], **pure** [pjʊɹ] or [pjʊəɹ], **cure** [kjʊɹ] or [kjʊəɹ], **endure** [ɪn'djʊɹ] or [ɪn'djʊəɹ], **rural** ['rʊrəl], **fury** ['fjʊrɪ], **jury** ['dʒʊrɪ]; written **ou** in **your** [jʊɹ] or [jʊəɹ], when unstressed [jəɹ]; written **oo** in **poor** [pʊɹ] or [pʊəɹ], **moor** [mʊɹ] or [mʊəɹ], **boor** [bʊɹ] or [bʊəɹ].

The glide vowel in these words is always very slight in standard speech, though more apparent before [ɹ] final than before [r] followed by a vowel. Pronunciations like ['rʊərəl], ['fjʊərɪ], ['dʒʊərɪ] are general in British pronunciation but rare in America.

**197.** For **your, poor, moor, boor,** a pronunciation [jɔːəɹ], [pɔːəɹ], [mɔːəɹ], [bɔːəɹ], riming with **yore, pore, more, bore,** with [ɹ] omitted of course in some dialects, is current in localities but not in standard American pronunciation. As a proper name **Moore** is pronounced [mʊəɹ], and when pronounced [mɔːəɹ] it is written **More.** For **door, floor,** however, the only current pronunciations are [dɔ·ɹ], [dɔ·əɹ], [flɔ·ɹ], [flɔ·əɹ]. See § 191.

[ʌ]

**198.** This sound is commonly written **u** in the conventional spelling, as in **but** [bʌt], **buzz** [bʌz], **cunning** ['kʌnɪŋ], **cup** [kʌp], **husband** ['hʌzbənd], etc., but frequently also **o**, as in **come** [kʌm], **done** [dʌn], **money** ['mʌnɪ], **some** [sʌm], and **ou**, as in **couple** ['kʌpl], **cousin** ['kʌzɪn], ['kʌzn], **double** ['dʌbl], **enough** [ɪ'nʌf], **trouble** ['trʌbl], **slough** [slʌf], **tough** [tʌf], etc.

**199.** For **u** before **r** followed by a vowel, the standard pronunciation is [ʌ], as in **burrow** ['bʌro], **hurry** ['hʌrɪ],

**turret** ['tʌrɪt], **scurry** ['skʌrɪ]; also **o** with the value of [ʌ], as in **borough** ['bʌro], **thorough** ['θʌro]; and **ou** with the value of [ʌ], as in **courage** ['kʌrɪdʒ], **nourish** ['nʌrɪʃ], **flourish** ['flʌrɪʃ], etc. With some speakers there is a tendency to pronounce the vowel [ə] in these combinations, that is, to pronounce **burrow, borough, hurry, turret,** etc., as ['bəro], ['hərɪ], ['tərɪt], etc., but this pronunciation is not often heard in cultivated speech. To make the difference clear, pronounce first the monosyllable **her,** then add a second syllable [ɪ] without changing the phonetic form of the first syllable, and finally substitute for [ə] in the stressed syllable the vowel [ʌ] as in **cut**, etc.

**200.** The standard pronunciation of **bury** is ['bɛrɪ], see § 136. For **foreign** ['fɔrɪn], a form ['fʌrɪn] is sometimes heard in dialect pronunciation.

**201.** For **e** [ɛ], **i**, **y** [ɪ] before [r] followed by a vowel, standard English has [ɛ], [ɪ], see §§ 135, 170, but for these vowels dialect pronunciation often has [ʌ], **merry**, **very**, **terrible**, **American**, **bury** being pronounced ['mʌrɪ], ['vʌrɪ], ['tʌrɪbl], [ə'mʌrɪkən], ['bʌrɪ], and **miracle**, **squirrel**, **stirrup**, **syrup**, **Syracuse** being pronounced ['mʌrəkl], ['skwʌrəl], ['stʌrəp], ['sʌrəp], ['sʌrə͵kjus]. But usage in this latter group is not altogether uniform, and though perhaps no cultivated speaker ever says ['mʌrəkl], many cultivated speakers do say ['sʌrəp], ['stʌrəp], ['skwʌrəl]. In words of this type, [ə] may also be heard in the popular dialects.

**202.** In **constable**, **conjure**, **monger**, **mongrel**, and some other words written **o** before **n**, both ['kʌnstəbl], ['kʌndʒəɹ], ['mʌŋgəɹ], ['mʌŋgrəl] and ['kɑnstəbl], ['kɑndʒəɹ], ['mɑŋgəɹ], ['mɑŋgrəl] are in good use, the latter being the more general.

**203.** For **com–** in **combat** and derivatives, American usage almost universally has [kɔm–] or [kɑm–], but occasionally [kʌm–], as in British pronunciation. But **company, compass** are always [ˈkʌmpənɪ], [ˈkʌmpəs].

**204.** For **bombard, bombast**, [ˌbʌmˈbɑːd], [ˈbʌmˌbɑst] are current British pronunciations, but in America the words are commonly [ˌbɔmˈbɑːɹd], [ˈbɔmˌbæst]. The general pronunciation of **bomb** in America is [bɔm], see § 111.

**205.** For **just, such**, [dʒʌst], [sʌtʃ], the popular speech often has [dʒɪst], [dʒɛst], [sɪtʃ], [sɛtʃ].

[ʌː]

**206.** This sound is heard only in the pronunciation of speakers who do not sound [ɹ] in the final position and before consonants. It is heard only in stressed syllables, words like **never** [ˈnɛvə], **better** [ˈbɛtə], **butter** [ˈbʌtə] ending simply in [ə] when the final consonant is not pronounced. It is a normal vowel, formed with the point of the tongue touching the roots of the lower teeth, and it should be clearly distinguished from [ə]. It occurs finally in words like **fur, fir** [fʌː], **infer** [ɪnˈfʌː], **cur** [kʌː], **spur** [spʌː], **purr** [pʌː], **myrrh** [mʌː], and medially in **turn** [tʌːn], **fern** [fʌːn], **furl** [fʌːl], **whirl** [ʍʌːl], **dirt** [dʌːt], **shirt** [ʃʌːt], **worth** [wʌːθ], **certain** [ˈsʌːtn], and similar words. When **r** final is not pronounced, it sometimes leaves a trace of its existence as a weak [ə], as in [fʌːə], [kʌːə], etc. This weak [ə] may be regarded as the survival of a glide vowel before [ɹ], therefore similar in character to the unstressed end vowel of **never** [ˈnɛvə], etc.

Since the vowel [ʌː] occurs only in the speech of persons who do not sound **r** in the final position and before consonants, it does not appear generally in American speech, but only in certain forms of what is called loosely "Eastern pronunciation." To most other speakers, pronunciations like **fur, fir** [fʌː], **cur** [kʌː], etc., seem either local or affected.

[eɪ]

**207.** The vowel [e] when prolonged tends to diphthongize into [eɪ], especially when the vowel is final, as in **hay** [heɪ], **grey, gray** [greɪ], **weigh** [weɪ], etc. In standard American speech the first element of this diphthong is a clear [e]-vowel, but some speakers tend to lower the first element to [ɛ], and this latter seems to be the accepted standard pronunciation in England (see Jones, *Pronunciation of English,* § 117). It follows that the diphthongal quality of the sound is more marked in British than in American pronunciation, since the glide from [ɛ] to [ɪ] is greater than from [e] to [ɪ]. In fact, with many American speakers the sound is not diphthongal at all, being merely [e·] or [eː], except when it is unusually emphatic and long at the end of a word, in which case it becomes [eɪ] with practically all speakers.

[ɪi]

**208.** This diphthong is not general in American speech, but it occurs occasionally in full stressed monosyllables which end with the vowel or in monosyllables in which the vowel stands before a voiced consonant. Thus for **sea, see** [siː] one sometimes hears a diphthongal pronunciation [sɪi], especially when the word is emphatic. Compare also **seat** [siːt] with **seed** [siːd] or [sɪid], **freak** [friːk] with **league** [liːg] or [lɪig], **fleece** [fliːs] with **freeze** [friːz] or [frɪiz]. But the diphthongal quality of this sound is always so slight that it is scarcely worth while to record it.

[aɪ]

**209.** This sound is represented in the conventional spelling in a variety of ways, as in **rite, right, write** [raɪt], **lie, lye** [laɪ], **sky** [skaɪ], **deny** [dɪˈnaɪ], **guy** [gaɪ]. When exceptionally emphatic it may become [ai].

**210.** The pronunciation of **lichen** is [ˈlaɪkən] or [ˈlɪtʃən], most commonly the former. For **sacrifice** the usual pronunciation is [ˈsækrɪˌfaɪs], sometimes [ˈsækrɪˌfaɪz], but only very rarely [ˈsækrɪˌfɪs]. For **bison** the common pronunciation is [ˈbaɪzn], though [ˈbɪsn], [ˈbaɪsn] are current forms in England. For **dynasty** both [ˈdaɪnəstɪ] and [ˈdɪnəstɪ] occur, the former being the more general. The pronunciation [fəˈraɪnə] for **farina** [fəˈriːnə] is British but not American usage.

**211.** The word **roil**, 'to make turbid,' is obsolete in England, but generally current in America. It has two pronunciations, the more familiar being [raɪl], especially in the metaphorical sense of the word, 'to vex,' 'to anger.' In this sense the word may also be spelled **rile**. Popularly **roil** is always pronounced [raɪl], as the diphthong **oi** regularly was in the eighteenth century, and still is by some old-fashioned folk, as in **spoil** [spaɪl], **boil** [baɪl], **join** [dʒaɪn], etc. In conventional cultivated use, however, a spelling pronunciation, [rɔɪl], has largely supplanted the older [raɪl].

**212.** In words ending in –**ile**, as in **servile, febrile, tactile, reptile, hostile**, the general tendency in America is to pronounce the last syllable as [–ɪl], and so always in **agile, fragile**. In England the reverse is true, a pronunciation like [ˈædʒɪl] being characterized by Michaelis-

Jones, *Phonetic Dictionary*, p. 11, as dialectal. Usage is not uniform, however, in America, and some speakers say [ˈsəɹˌvaɪl], [ˈhɑsˌtaɪl], [ˈhɔsˌtaɪl], [ˈrɛpˌtaɪl], etc. The pronunciation of **gentile** is always [ˈdʒɛnˌtaɪl], to keep the word etymologically distinct from **gentle.**

**213.** For **quinine** several pronunciations are current, perhaps the most common being [ˈkwaɪˌnaɪn], but also [kwɪˈnaɪn], [kwɪˈniːn], [kɪˈniːn].

**214.** For **cowardice, favorite, genuine** the standard pronunciation is [ˈkaʊəɹdɪs], [ˈfeːvərɪt], [ˈdʒɛnjuɪn], popularly often [ˈkaʊəɹˌdaɪs], [ˈfeːvəˌraɪt], [ˈdʒɛnjuˌaɪn]; but [ˈkaʊəɹˌdaɪs] the writer has observed occasionally also in cultivated speech.

**215.** Some speakers, especially family groups, have [ɑ] for the first element of this diphthong, giving [ɑɪ], as in **pile** [pɑɪl], **mine** [mɑɪn], **kind** [kɑɪnd], and producing what most persons regard as a rather 'mushy' pronunciation. The second element of the diphthong is likely to become [ə], also, in this pronunciation.

**216.** For [aɪ] sometimes [əɪ] is heard, as in **fine** [fəɪn], **time** [təɪm], but only in dialect and provincial speech. It is probably this sound which writers of dialect stories have in mind when they spell **fine, time** as *foin, toim,* etc.

**217.** Occasionally one hears from the older generation, pronunciation like **kind** [kɪˈaɪnd], **sky** [skɪˈaɪ], with a slight [ɪ] glide vowel between the consonant and the diphthong. This was formerly a fashionable pronunciation (see Webster, *Dissertations,* p. 109), but has now almost completely disappeared. See § 123.

[oʊ]

**218.** For this diphthong, see §§ 74, 177.

Normally in American speech the first element of this diphthong when it occurs is a clear [o]-vowel, but some speakers pronounce a sound very similar to [ʌ], as in **know** [nʌʊ], **go** [gʌʊ], and also prolong the second element of the diphthong. In American speech the diphthongal quality of the sound is likely to be less marked than in British speech. The diphthong also assumes a greater variety of forms in British than in American speech, and Jones records all of the following variants as current in London, [oʊ], [ɔʊ], [ʌʊ], [əʊ], [ɑʊ], [aʊ] (*Pronunciation of English,* § 152). He remarks that "In the best speaking care should be taken to round the lips properly in pronouncing [oʊ], and not to exaggerate the diphthongization," § 154. Neither caution is urgently applicable to American speech.

**219.** Both [o] and [ʊ] are rounded vowels, the former a mid back tense vowel, the latter a high back slack vowel, and the change in organic position in the glide from [o] to [ʊ] is not very great. Examples of words which are likely to be pronounced as diphthongs are **so, sow, sew** [soʊ], **though** [ðoʊ], **know** [noʊ], **roll** [roʊl], **oath** [oʊθ], **rose** [roʊz], etc. But all such words are often pronounced simply with [oː].

**220.** In unstressed or secondarily stressed syllables, as in **thorough** [ˈθʌro], **borough, burrow** [ˈbʌro], **fellow** [ˈfɛlo], **window** [ˈwɪndo], **sorrow** [ˈsɑro], **piano** [pɪˈæno], etc., the vowel is scarcely ever diphthongal, and in popular speech often weakens to [ə]. The pronunciation [ˈbʌro] or [ˈbʌroʊ] for **borough** is marked as dialectal by

Michaelis-Jones, *Phonetic Dictionary*, p. 47, for the British standard form [ˈbʌrə]; so also with **thorough**, see p. 423. But [ˈbʌro], [ˈθʌro] are current cultivated pronunciations in America, as well as [ˈbʌɹə], [ˈbʌrə], the former perhaps even to be preferred.

[ʊu]

**221.** For this diphthong, see § 76.

[ɑʊ]

**222.** This is the common diphthong **ou**, **ow** of **house** [hɑʊs], **cow** [kɑʊ]; **ough** of **slough** [slɑʊ], 'a swamp' (**slough**, 'to cast off,' 'the cast skin of a snake,' is pronounced [slʌf]), **bough** [bɑʊ]; **au** in some words of foreign origin, as in **aurochs** [ˈɑʊəɹˌɔks], **Augean** [ɑʊˈdʒiən], **Faust** [fɑʊst]. For **slough** a spelling **slew**, **slue**, **sloo**, and a corresponding pronunciation [sluː], are current in the Western States.

**223.** In several regions of the Atlantic seaboard, a triphthong appears in this sound when preceded by [k], [g], as in **cow** [kɪˈɑʊ], **count** [kɪˈɑʊnt], **gout** [gɪˈɑʊt], but this pronunciation is distinctly local and dialectal.

**224.** The recognized pronunciation of **jowl** is [dʒɑʊl], but [dʒoːl] is sometimes heard, perhaps on the analogy of the more familiar word **bowl**, though the analogy of **howl** would seem to be just as strong in the other direction. The word **jowl**, however, is not in general popular use, and for that reason has not acquired an established pronunciation.

**225.** The same is true of archaic forms like **enow**, a variant of **enough**, and **trow**, for which both [ɪˈnɑʊ], [trɑʊ] and [ɪˈnoʊ], [troʊ] are found as rimes in verse, where the words chiefly occur. When **enow** appears in the proper name, spelled **Goodnow, Goodenow, Goodenough,** it is pronounced [ˈgʊdˌnoʊ], [ˈgʊdəˌnoʊ].

**226.** For **blouse** the usual pronunciation is [blɑʊz], but a more or less fashionable pronunciation (*milliner's French*), [bluːz], is sometimes affected. The final consonant may also be voiceless, as in [blɑʊs].

**227.** In British pronunciation the first element of this diphthong is very commonly [a], as in **round** [raʊnd], **gown** [gaʊn], **renown** [rɪˈnaʊn], etc., and this pronunciation is sometimes heard in America, though far less frequently than [ɑʊ]. In New England and in the Southern States the first element of the diphthong is often pronounced [æ], as in **hound** [hæʊnd], **out** [æʊt], but this pronunciation is heard in cultivated speech only as a Southernism.

[ɔɪ]

**228.** This diphthong is conventionally written **oi, oy,** as in **boil** [bɔɪl], **toy** [tɔɪ], also **uoy** in **buoy** [bɔɪ], **buoyant** [ˈbɔɪjənt]. A spelling-pronunciation [buɪ], [ˈbuɪjənt] is sometimes heard for **buoy, buoyant,** but is not general. The eighteenth century pronunciation of this diphthong was [aɪ], and this pronunciation still lingers among some old-fashioned and rustic speakers in words like **boil** [baɪl], **join** [dʒaɪn], and persists generally in the somewhat colloquial word **roil, rile** [raɪl], see § 211.

[ju], [juː]

**229.** This is a rising diphthong, the first element being slightly stressed, the second element stressed and usually prolonged. On the consonantal quality of the first element, see §§ 25, 78. The diphthong is the sound commonly known as 'long **u**,' and is written in the ordinary spelling **u**, as in **music** ['mjuːzɪk], **musician** [mju'ziʃən], **use** [juːs], [juːz]; **ew**, as in **few** [fjuː], **new** [njuː]; **eau**, as in **beauty** ['bjuːtɪ]. In the initial position and after lip consonants, usage uniformly has the sound [ju] for orthographic long **u** and its equivalents, as in **use** [juːs], [juːz], **rebuke** [rɪ'bjuːk], **butte** [bjuːt], **fusion** ['fjuːʒən], **mule** [mjuːl], **view** [vjuː], etc. The combination **sp** is followed by [ju] the same as **p**, as in **spurious** ['spjuːrɪəs], **spume** ['spjuːm].

**230.** Before **r**, the second element of the diphthong is likely to be lowered to [ʊ], e.g., **pure**, pronounced [pjuɹ] or [pjʊɹ], **cure** [kjuɹ] or [kjʊɹ], etc. When the **r** is not pronounced, a slight [ə]-vowel may take its place; when it is pronounced, a glide vowel [ə] may be heard before the consonant.

**231.** After [l] and [r] the diphthong is rarely heard except in precise speech, the current pronunciation being [uː], as in **lute** [luːt], **Lucy** ['luːsɪ], **Luke** [luːk], **rule** [ruːl], **rude** [ruːd], **rune** [ruːn], **ruse** [ruːz].

After [d], [t], [θ], [n], [s], usage varies widely, some speakers pronouncing **duty** ['djuːtɪ], **tube** [tjuːb], **enthusiasm** [ɛn'θjuːzɪæzm], **nude** [njuːd], **new** [njuː], **suit** [sjuːt], and others [duːtɪ], [tuːb], etc. The dictionaries generally authorize only the first of these pronunciations after [d], [t], [θ], [n], [s], and academic authority is very likely to condemn the pronunciation [uː] as uncultivated, in spite of the fact that it occurs widely in the speech of educated and informed people. It has long been current in America, as is evident from Noah Webster's defense of [uː] in **duty**, etc., as the best pronunciation.[1]

**232.** After [k], orthographic **u**, representing the long vowel, is regularly [juː], as in **cube** [kjuːb], **cucumber** [ˈkjuːˌkʌmbəɹ], **cuneiform** [ˈkjuːnɪəˌfɔɹm], **acute** [əˈkjuːt], **culinary** [ˈkjuːləˌnɛrɪ], also pronounced [ˈkʌləˌnɛrɪ]. The analogy of these words has affected **coupon** [ˈkuːˌpɔn], which in popular speech is often pronounced [ˈkjuːˌpɔn].

**233.** After [g], the spelling **u** usually indicates merely the quality of the consonant, as in **guard** [gɑːɹd], **guess** [gɛs], and has no phonetic value, or it stands for a short vowel, as in **gun** [gʌn], **gush** [gʌʃ], etc. In **legume**, **leguminous**, **lugubrious**, **gubernatorial**, the vowel after **g** is usually [uː], rarely [juː].

**234.** In unstressed syllables, [ju] of standard pronunciation is sometimes weakened in popular pronunciation, as in **accurate** [ˈækjurɪt], pronounced [ˈækərɪt], **sinew** [ˈsɪnju], pronounced [ˈsɪnu], **argue** [ˈɑːɹgju], pronounced [ˈɑːɹgɪ], **ague** [ˈeːgju], written in dialect stories as *ager*, **value** [ˈvælju], written in dialect as *vally*, etc. The pronunciation [ˈfɪgəɹ] for **figure** is occasionally heard on the lips of cultivated speakers in America for standard [ˈfɪgjuɹ], but much less commonly than in England. Michaelis-Jones, *Phonetic Dictionary*, s. v., describes [ˈfɪgjuɹ] as dialectal in England. In rapid speech [ˈfɪgjuɹ] may become [ˈfɪgjəɹ].

[1] Webster, *Dissertations* (1789), pp. 153 ff. It seems to be less general in the South, than it is in New England, whence it has spread to all sections of the country.

## CONSONANTS

### [b]

**235.** This consonant is pronounced in essentially the same way in all positions. A **b** appears, however, in the conventional spelling of some words which has no phonetic value, (1) before **t**, as in **debt** [dɛt], **doubt** [dɑʊt], **subtle** [ˈsʌtl], **subtly** [ˈsʌtlɪ]; (2) after **m**, as in **bomb** [bɔm] or [bʌm], **dumb** [dʌm], **climb** [klaɪm], **comb** [koːm], **crumb** [krʌm], **jamb** [dʒæm], **lamb** [læm], **lambkin** [ˈlæmkɪn], **numb** [nʌm], comparative degree **number** [ˈnʌməɹ], superlative **numbest** [ˈnʌməst], **aplomb** [əˈplɔm], **plumb** [plʌm], **plumber** [ˈplʌməɹ], **tomb** [tuːm].

**236.** When **m** is followed by **b** and a vowel, the **b** normally goes with the second syllable and is then pronounced, as in **limber** [ˈlɪmbəɹ], **lumber** [ˈlʌmbəɹ], **number** [ˈnʌmbəɹ], **timber** [ˈtɪmbəɹ], etc., except when the influence of a main form, in which the **m** is not pronounced, affects the pronunciation of derivatives, as in **climb** [klaɪm], **climbing** [ˈklaɪmɪŋ], **climber** [ˈklaɪməɹ], **plumb** [plʌm], **plumbing** [ˈplʌmɪŋ], **plumber** [ˈplʌməɹ], etc.

**237.** In the combination **mbl**, [b] is always pronounced, as in **crumble** [ˈkrʌmbl], **humble** [ˈhʌmbl], **nimble** [ˈnɪmbl], **thimble** [ˈθɪmbl], **tremble** [ˈtrɛmbl], etc.

**238.** In **rhomb** [rɔmb] a learned pronunciation with [b] is sometimes heard, due to the influence of spelling, and in **iamb** [ˈaɪˌæmb], also a learned word, the pronunciation with [b] is general. In **cupboard**, **p** has been assimilated to **b** which remains as a short consonant, [ˈkʌbəɹd]. In the proper name **Jacob**, the final consonant very generally becomes voiceless, the word being pronounced [ˈdʒeːkəp]; so also in **Jacobs, Jacobson.**

[d]

**239.** The pronunciation of **d** of the conventional spelling remains uniform, except as the sound is affected by assimilation to neighboring sounds. Immediately after a voiceless consonant, [d] is regularly assimilated, becoming also voiceless, as in **backed** [bækt], **baked** [beːkt], **sniffed** [snɪft], **hissed** [hɪst], **flapped** [flæpt], **wished** [wɪʃt], **frothed** [frɔθt], etc.

**240.** The reverse process may sometimes be observed in relaxed and slovenly speech, that is, a voiceless [t] in voiced surrounding becomes voiced, as in **belated** [bɪˈleːtəd], pronounced [bɪˈleːdəd]; **rated** [ˈreːtəd], scarcely distinguished in pronunciation from **raided** [ˈreːdəd]; **fitted** [ˈfɪtəd], pronounced [ˈfɪdəd]. In popular speech **putty** is frequently pronounced [ˈpʌdɪ], and in some dialects **water** becomes [ˈwɔdə], **letter** becomes [ˈlɛdə], **bitter** becomes [ˈbɪdə], etc., see § 14.

**241.** After [l] and [n], where according to rule one expects to find a voiced [d], in some words forms with both [d] and [t] exist, and the latter pronunciation is sometimes represented by **t** in the conventional spelling, as in **learned, learnt**, [ləɹnd], [ləɹnt], as participial adjective [ˈləɹnəd]; **burned, burnt**, [bəɹnd], [bəɹnt]; **spoiled, spoilt**, [spɔɪld], [spɔɪlt]; **spelled, spelt**, [spɛld], [spɛlt]; **spilled, spilt**, [spɪld], [spɪlt]. Usage is arbitrary in pronunciations of this type. One may say [spɪlt] for **spilled**, but not [kɪlt] for **killed**, except in dialect Irish-English, where pronunciations with [t] are found in many preterites and past participles which have only [d] in standard English.

**242.** For **used**, in the sense of 'employ,' 'make use of,' the common pronunciation is [juːzd], but for **used**, 'to be accustomed to,' a widely current pronunciation is [juːst], when the final consonant [d] is assimilated to the [t] of the sign of the infinitive which in most instances follows the word. In a phrase like **I used to go** [aɪ ˈjuːstə ˈgoʊ], there is of course only one [t], to which the preceding consonant has also been assimilated, [z] becoming [s]. A like assimilation is common in **I had to go** [aɪ ˈhætə ˈgoʊ] or [aɪ ˈhætːə ˈgoʊ].

**243.** After [n], in standard familiar speech [d] before a consonant is frequently omitted, as in **grandmother** [ˈgrænˌmʌðəɹ]; **handkerchief** [ˈhænkəɹˌtʃɪf], or following the general tendency in the pronunciation of [n] before [k], see § 289, [ˈhæŋkəɹˌtʃɪf]; **handsome** [ˈhænsəm]; **Windsor** [ˈwɪnzəɹ]; **brand-new**, also spelled **bran-new** [ˈbrænːˌjuː]. Unemphatic **and** frequently becomes merely [n], as in **time and tide** [taɪm n taɪd], **good and hot** [gʊd n hɑt], etc. These pronunciations may be heard from cultivated speakers, but usage does not countenance this omission in all instances, pronunciations like **band-box** [ˈbænˌbɑks], **landlady** [ˈlænˌleːdɪ], **landlord** [ˈlænˌlɔɹd], being heard only in careless or very rapid speech.

**244.** A similar omission of [d] takes place before [n] in **Wednesday** [ˈwɛnzˌdeɪ], [ˈwɛnzdɪ].

**245.** After [n] in stressed syllables, [d] is sometimes added in popular speech, as in [drɑʊnd] for **drown**, [gɑʊnd] for **gown**.

**246.** In the combination **nge**, a [d] is commonly pronounced after [n], as in **angel** [ˈeːndʒəl], **danger** [ˈdeːndʒəɹ],

**hinge** [hɪndʒ], **impinge** [ɪm'pɪndʒ], **strange** [streɪndʒ], etc., though some speakers pronounce such words without a [d], i.e., ['eɪnʒəl], ['deɪnʒəɹ], etc. The pronunciation with [d] is to be preferred. The same is true of the combination **rge**, as in **barge** [bɑːɹdʒ], **large** [lɑːɹdʒ], **forge** [fɔɹdʒ], **urge** ['əɹdʒ]; and **lge**, as in **bilge** [bɪldʒ], **bulge** [bʌldʒ], **indulge** [ɪn'dʌldʒ], and other words. See § 341.

[g]

**247.** This sound varies considerably according to its vocalic surrounding, as may be observed by comparing **gig** [gɪg] with **gone** [gɔn], see § 21. No questions of propriety are raised by this variation, however, because all speakers instinctively make the adaptation necessary to fit the consonant to its surroundings.

**248.** A **g** of the conventional spelling is silent in a number of words before [m] and [n], as in **paradigm** ['pærədɪm], sometimes ['pærə'daɪm]; **phlegm** [flɛm], but **phlegmatic** always [flɛg'mætɪk]; **condign** [kən'daɪn]; **foreign** ['fɔrɪn]; **impugn** [ɪm'pjuːn]; **reign** [reɪn]; **sovereign** ['sɑvrən]. For **poignant, poignancy** the usual pronunciations are ['pɔɪnənt], ['pɔɪnənsɪ], but through the influence of spelling, ['pɔɪgnənt], ['pɔɪgnənsɪ] are also sometimes heard. An initial **g** is silent in **gnarled** ['nɑːɹld], **gnash** [næʃ], **gnat** [næt], **gnaw** [nɔː], **gnome** [noːm], **gnu** [nuː], **gnostic** ['nɔstɪk]. For **physiognomy** the usual pronunciation is [fɪzɪ'ɔgnəmɪ], but also sometimes [fɪzɪ'ɔnəmɪ].

**249.** The combination **ng** of the conventional spelling represents simply [ŋ] in pronunciation when final, as in **sing** [sɪŋ], **singing** [sɪŋɪŋ], **wrong** [rɔŋ], **tongue** [tʌŋ], **young** [jʌŋ], etc. But in the combination **ngl** [ŋgl], **ngr** [ŋgr] before vowels or when [l], [r] are syllabic, a [g] is retained, as in **angle** [ˈæŋgəl]; **England** [ˈɪŋglənd], **English** [ˈɪŋglɪʃ], though some speakers say [ˈɪŋlənd], [ˈɪŋlɪʃ]; **Inglis** [ˈɪŋglɪs], **Ingalls** [ˈɪŋgəlz]; **single** [ˈsɪŋgl]; **anger** [ˈæŋgəɹ], **angry** [ˈæŋgrɪ]; **finger** [ˈfɪŋgəɹ]; **linger** [ˈlɪŋgəɹ]; **longer** [ˈlɔŋgəɹ]; **stronger** [ˈstrɔŋgəɹ]; **younger** [ˈjʌŋgəɹ], etc. In the superlatives **longest** [ˈlɔŋgəst], **strongest** [ˈstrɔŋgəst], **youngest** [ˈjʌŋgəst], the [g] is retained through the influence of the comparative with [ɹ]. On the other hand, words like **bringer** [ˈbrɪŋəɹ], **hanger** [ˈhæŋəɹ], **ringer** [ˈrɪŋəɹ], **singer** [ˈsɪŋəɹ], **stringer** [ˈstrɪŋəɹ], etc., in which the same combination of letters occurs as in **linger**, etc., have no [g] because the derivative forms are influenced by head forms like **bring** [brɪŋ], **hang** [hæŋ], etc.

**250.** The combination **ngu**, when the **u** has phonetic value and is not silent as in **tongue**, **harangue**, is pronounced [ŋgw], as in **languid** [ˈlæŋgwɪd]; **language** [ˈlæŋgwɪdʒ]; **languish** [ˈlæŋgwɪʃ]; **lingual** [ˈlɪŋgwəl], **linguist** [ˈlɪŋgwɪst], and probably by attraction to **lingual**, etc., [ŋg] in **lingo** [ˈlɪŋgo]. For **languor** all three pronunciations occur, [ˈlæŋəɹ], [ˈlæŋgəɹ] and [ˈlæŋgwəɹ], the first two being more general than the third.

**251.** For **recognizance**, 'a bond or pledge to keep the peace,' etc., the usual pronunciation is [rɪˈkɑgnɪzəns], less often [rɪˈkɑnɪzəns]. As a military term, meaning a preliminary examination of a region, the spelling is **reconnaissance**, pronounced [rɪˈkɑnɪsəns]. For **recognize** the only standard pronunciation is one with [g], as in [ˈrɛkəgˌnɑɪz], though one not infrequently hears [ˈrɛkənɑɪz] in rapid speech and, perhaps even more frequently, **recognition** pronounced [rɛkəˈnɪʃən].

**252.** For **suffragan** the accepted pronunciation is [ˈsʌfrəgən], but the pronunciation of **suffrage** [ˈsʌfrɪdʒ] sometimes produces ['sʌfrɪdʒən] in the speech of persons to whom the word is mainly an eye-word.

**253.** The combination **gh** of the conventional spelling is always silent, as in **right** [raɪt], **freight** [freːt], **sought** [sɔːt], etc., except when it stands for [f], see § 357, or in a few words for [g], as in **ghostly, ghost, ghetto.**

[h]

**254.** The main question that arises in connection with **h** is whether it is pronounced or whether it is silent. In America there is no group of speakers who add and omit [h] before vowels in the manner of the Cockney English, but in general whenever **h** appears in writing in stressed position, American speakers pronounce it. To this rule there are some exceptions, **heir, heiress, honor, honest, hour** never having an initial [h]. In **herb** and the proper names **Humphrey, Humphries**, the initial **h** is sometimes pronounced, sometimes not, the pronunciation without [h] being the more general. In **human, humble, humor** a pronunciation without [h] is almost never heard in America in the speech of cultivated persons, the phonetic forms of these words being ['hjuːmən], ['hʌmbl], ['hjuːməɹ]. But perhaps ['juːməɹ] should be recognized as an occasional cultivated pronunciation. In derivatives from **herb**, such as **herbage, herbalist, herbarium**, the initial consonant is always pronounced.

**255.** In unstressed syllables, initial [h] is sometimes lost. For **shepherd** and **forehead** the usual pronunciations are ['ʃɛpəɹd] and ['fɔrɛd] or ['fɔrɪd], though a spelling-pronunciation ['fɔrˎhɛd] is occasionally heard. For **vehement, vehicle** the standard pronunciations are ['vɪəmɛnt] and [ˈviːkl], though popular forms with [h] are not infrequent. When the [h] is pronounced in **vehement**, the stress is likely to be on the second syllable, [vɪˈhiːmənt].

**256.** In weak syllables [h] is sometimes dropped in standard speech in words which retain it when the syllable is stressed, as in **history** [ˈhɪstərɪ], **an historical novel** [æn ɪsˈtɔrɪkl ˈnɑvl]; **him** [hɪm], but **I saw him** [aɪ sɔː ɪm]; **herald** [ˈhɛrəld], but **an heraldic device** [æn ɛrˈældɪk dɪˈvaɪs].

**257.** In proper names compounded with **-ham**, [h] is sometimes lost, as in **Chatham** [ˈtʃætəm], **Graham** [ˈgreːəm], **Pelham** [ˈpɛləm], **Wyndham** [ˈwɪndəm], **Fordham** [ˈfɔɹdəm], and in a great many other dissyllables like these. But in trisyllables the general tendency of American speech is to put a secondary stress on the third syllable, which thus maintains the full form of **-ham** in words like **Birmingham** [ˈbəɹmɪŋˌhæm], **Buckingham** [ˈbʌkɪŋˌhæm], **Frothingham** [ˈfrɔðɪŋˌhæm], **Wilbraham** [ˈwɪlbrəˌhæm], locally pronounced [ˈwɪlbəɹˌhæm], etc. In **Waltham**, **Wrentham**, names of towns in Massachusetts, the **t** and **h** combine, giving [ˈrɛnθəm], and for **Waltham** [ˈwɔlˌθæm], with a heavy secondary stress. These are the local pronunciations, but persons to whom the words are merely eye-words would probably pronounce them [ˈrɛntəm] and [ˈwɔltəm].

**258.** After **x** [ks], [gz], **h** is normally not pronounced, as in **exhibit** [ɛgˈzɪbɪt], **exhibition** [ɛksɪˈbɪʃən]; **exhaust** [ɪgˈzɔːst]; **exhort** [ɪgˈzɔɹt], etc. Occasionally one hears **exhale** [ɛksˈheːl], **exhume** [ɛksˈhjuːm], where the [h] is pronounced in an effort to make the second elements of the words etymologically prominent.

[j]

**259.** This sound is commonly written **y** in the ordinary alphabet, as in **yawl** [jɔːl], **yes** [jɛs], **yearn** [jəɹn], **youth** [juːθ], etc. Words written with initial **u**, as in **use** [juːs], **union** ['juːnjən], etc., have this sound as the first element of the so-called 'long **u**.' In internal position [j] appears in **companion** [kəm'pænjən], **onion** ['ʌnjən], **carrier** ['kærɪjəɹ]; **collier** ['kɑlɪjəɹ] or ['kɑljəɹ], etc. It is also occasionally heard in the speech of precise persons who try to avoid the sound [tʃ] generally current in words like **feature**, **nature**, etc., which are artificially pronounced ['fiːtjʊɹ], ['neːtjʊɹ], etc.

**260.** The word **yeast** [jiːst] in popular speech often loses the initial consonant, becoming [iːst].

**261.** In illiterate speech, a pronunciation ['kɑljəm] for standard **column** ['kɑləm] is frequent.

**262.** For [j] in French and Italian words written **gn**, see § 285. The word **reveille** is commonly pronounced ['rɛvəlɪ], though occasionally [rə'veːjə]; **surveillance** is either [səɹ'veːləns] or [səɹ'veːljəns]; **cotillon** is either [ko'tɪlən] or [ko'tɪljən], but when the latter pronunciation is intended, the spelling is usually **cotillion**.

[k]

**263.** The ordinary spellings for this sound are **k**, **c**, **ch**, **ck**, **qu** (with the value of [k] or [kw]), and **x** (with the value of [ks]), as in **king** [kɪŋ], **call** [kɔːl], **chemist** ['kɛmɪst], **black** [blæk], **exchequer** [ɛks'tʃɛkəɹ], **tax** [tæks]. In words written **cc** only one [k] is pronounced, as in **account** [ə'kɑʊnt], **accuse** [ə'kjuːz], etc. In **schism** [sɪzm] and derivatives, **ch** is silent. For **schedule** the current pronunciation in America is [ˈskɛdjul], but [ˈʃɛdjul] is the more general pronunciation in England. The pronunciation of **cham** is [kæm], the word being an older variant form of **khan** [kɑːn]. In **flaccid** [ˈflæksɪd], the first **c** represents [k], the second [s].

The spelling **ch** is silent in **drachm** [dræm] and **yacht** [jɑt].

**264.** In the combination **kn, k** is silent, except when preceded by a vowel with which it makes a syllable, as in **knowledge** [ˈnɑlɪdʒ], but **acknowledge** [ækˈnɑlɪdʒ]; **knee** [niː], **knight** [naɪt], etc.

**265.** Before [t], [k] is lost in **victuals** [ˈvɪtlz], **indict** [ɪnˈdaɪt] and derivatives, likewise in **arctic** [ˈɑːɹtɪk] in popular speech and not infrequently also in cultivated speech. The form [ˈɑːɹtɪks] is commonly used as the name of a kind of over-shoes. In most words, however, [k] is regularly pronounced before [t], as in **convict** [ˈkɑnvɪkt], **deduct** [dɪˈdʌkt], **depict** [dɪˈpɪkt], **picked** [pɪkt]. For **Connecticut** the standard pronunciation is [kəˈnɛtɪkət].

**266.** No [k] appears in the combination **scl**, as in **muscle** [ˈmʌsl], **corpuscle** [ˈkɔɹˌpʌsl]. For **corpuscle** a second spelling and pronunciation occur, **corpuscule** [kɔɹˈpʌskjul], hence also **corpuscular** [kɔɹˈpʌskjuləɹ].

**267.** In the combination [ŋk] followed by another consonant, many somewhat careless speakers tend to omit [k], pronouncing **anxious** [ˈæŋkʃəs] as [ˈæŋʃəs]; **injunction** [ɪnˈdʒʌŋktʃən] as [ɪnˈdʒʌŋʃən]; **linked** [lɪŋkt] as [lɪŋt], etc. In the unstressed position this pronunciation is general, as in **anxiety** [æŋˈzaɪɪtɪ]; **punctilious** [pʌŋˈtɪlɪəs], but **punctual** [ˈpʌŋktʃʊəl]; **sanctimonious** [sæŋtɪˈmoːnɪəs], but **sanctify** [ˈsæŋktɪˌfaɪ], etc.

**268.** In **blackguard** [ˈblæˌgɑɹd], **k** is silent, being assimilated to the following **g**.

**269.** The combination [ks], in unstressed position when followed by a voiced consonant or a vowel, generally becomes [gz], as in **exact** [ɛgˈzækt], **exhibit** [ɛgˈzɪbɪt], **exile** (*verb*) [ɛgˈzaɪl], **auxiliary** [ɔgˈzɪlɪɛrɪ], **luxurious** [lʌgˈʒʊrɪəs].

**270.** Analogy operates in words of this type, however, a form like **axiom** [ˈæksɪəm], with [ks] under the stress, retaining this pronunciation in **axiomatic** [æksɪoˈmætɪk], and **vex** [vɛks] preserving a voiceless consonant in **vexation** [vɛksˈeːʃən]. But [vɛgˈzeːʃən] is also heard, and under the influence of **luxurious**, a pronunciation [ˈlʌgʒərɪ] for **luxury** [ˈlʌkʃərɪ]. In the same way **exile** (*noun and adjective*) [ˈɛgzaɪl] is to be accounted for, by the side of [ˈɛksaɪl], the former being now the more common pronunciation of the word.

**271.** Under the stress and before voiceless consonants, [ks] generally remains, as in **exhibition** [ˌɛksɪˈbɪʃən], **exigency** [ˈɛksɪdʒɛnsɪ], **exit** [ˈɛksɪt], **excellent** [ˈɛksɛlənt], **expire** [ɛkˈspaɪəɹ], **extreme** [ɛkˈstriːm], **ecstatic** [ɛkˈstætɪk], etc.

**272.** A [k] is often added in popular speech between [ŋ] and [θ], **length** [lɛŋθ], **strength** [strɛŋθ], and derivatives, being pronounced [lɛŋkθ], [strɛŋkθ], etc.

[l]

**273.** An **l** of the ordinary spelling is silent before [k], as in **talk** [tɔːk], **walk** [wɔːk], **chalk** [tʃɔːk], **caulk** [kɔːk], **Falkland** [ˈfɔklənd], **folk** [foːk], **yolk** [yoːk], when the vowel preceding [k] is [o] or [ɔ]. After other vowels [l] is retained, as in **calculate** [ˈkælkjuˌle·t], in dialect speech also pronounced [ˈkæk–]; **elk** [ɛlk], **milk** [mɪlk], **hulk** [hʌlk]. In **Balkan** [ˈbɔːlkən] the spelling has probably influenced the pronunciation (cf. **balk** [bɔːk], **balky** [ˈbɔːkɪ], where the [l] is not pronounced), or the syllable division, which carries the [l] with the first syllable, causes it to be pronounced. In **falcon**, **falconry**, the l is always pronounced in American speech, probably because this is mainly a literary word and the spelling has thus been unusually influential.

**274.** Before **m** and after **a** [ɑː], [æ], **o** [oː], an **l** of the ordinary spelling is silent, as in **balm** [bɑːm], **calm** [kɑːm], **alms** [ɑːmz], **palm** [pɑːm], **psalm** [sɑːm], **qualm** [kwɑːm], **salmon** [ˈsæmən] or [ˈsɑːmən], **almond** [ˈɑːmənd] or [ˈæmənd], **holm** [hoːm], **Holmes** [hoːmz]. But **l** is pronounced after [ɛ], [ɪ], [ʌ], as in **helm** [hɛlm], **film** [fɪlm], **culm** [kʌlm], **Hulme** [hʌlm], and of course in words in which **m** goes with a succeeding vowel, as in **almanac**, **Palmyra**, **calmative**, a medical term derived from **calm**, etc. In a word like **almond**, which might be written [ˈɑːmnd], the second syllable is apparently so slightly syllabic as not to cause a separation between the preceding **l** and **m**. Yet a pronunciation [ˈælmənd] does occur not infrequently in popular speech, and the local pronunciation of **Salmon**, a frequent proper name in Connecticut, is [ˈsælmən].

**275.** In **psalter**, **psaltery**, [ˈsɔltəɹ], [ˈsɔltərɪ], **l** is always pronounced. In **psalmist** it is usually not pronounced, through force of the analogy of **psalm**. But in **psalmody**, **psalmodic**, pronunciations on the analogy of **psalm** without **l**, and pronunciations with **l**, [ˈsælmədɪ], [sælˈmɑdɪk] are both current, in the latter case the two consonants going with separate syllables.

**276.** After **a** [ɑː], [aː], [æ], **o** [ɔː], **l** is silent before [f], [v], in **calf, half, salve, golf** [gɔːf], but also pronounced [gɔlf], the latter being perhaps the more common pronunciation in America. When the [f] or [v] goes with a succeeding syllable, a preceding [l] is pronounced, as in **palfrey** [ˈpælfrɪ], **salvage** [ˈsælvɪdʒ], **salvation** [sælˈveːʃən], etc. In the proper names **Ralph, Rolfe**, an [l] is always pronounced, probably through the influence of the spelling, though formerly a pronunciation without [l] was also current. The verb **salve**, in the special sense of saving a ship or a ship's cargo, is pronounced [sælv].

**277.** Before [n], [l] is silent in **Lincoln** [ˈlɪŋkən].

**278.** The spelling **colonel** for [ˈkəɹnl], [ˈkʌːnl], is due to the French and Italian form of this word, but the pronunciation is due to the Spanish form, in which **r** appears instead of **l** in the spelling.

**279.** In **solder** [ˈsɑdəɹ], **l** is silent, though otherwise generally pronounced before **d.** Dialectally this word is sometimes pronounced [ˈsɔːdəɹ], written *sawder* in dialect stories. In **could, would, should**, no [l] is present in pronunciation, and historically no **l** should appear in the spelling of **could.** The Middle English form of this word is **coude**, but later the spelling changed to **could** under the influence of the analogy of **would** and **should**, both of which had **l** through etymological origin. But **could** seems to have retained its pronunciation without [l], and even to have attracted **would** and **should** to it. As auxiliaries, these words were all slightly stressed in the word group, and this fact may have contributed to the loss of the [l] in them.

**280.** Words written **ll**, normally have only a single [l]-sound, as in **holly** [ˈhɑlɪ], **fully** [ˈfʊlɪ], etc., except when for the sake of unusual clearness a word like **wholly** is pronounced [ˈhoːllɪ] to distinguish it from **holy** [ˈhoːlɪ], or **solely** is pronounced [ˈsoːllɪ] to keep it etymologically distinct from the word **soul**, or **foully** is pronounced [ˈfɑʊllɪ] to keep it etymologically distinct from **fowl**. Ordinarily, however, **wholly** and **holy** are pronounced exactly alike, [ˈhoːlɪ].

[m]

**281.** The pronunciation of [m] in standard English causes no difficulty. When **m** is written, it is always pronounced, except in **mnemonic** [nɪˈmɑnɪk] and derivative forms of this word, where it is silent, and in **comptroller** [kənˈtroːləɹ], where it is pronounced [n].

**282.** In popular English [m] is sometimes made syllabic after [l], **elm** [ɛlm], **helm** [hɛlm], **film** [fɪlm], etc., being pronounced [ˈɛləm], [ˈhɛləm], [ˈfɪləm], etc.

**283.** For **pumpkin** standard pronunciation has [ˈpʌmp-kɪn], [ˈpʌmkɪn], but dialect speech commonly has [ˈpʌŋ-kɪn], [ˈpʌŋkn].

[n]

**284.** The usual orthographic spelling for [n] is **n**, but also **gn**, **kn**, with **g** and **k** silent, as in **no** [noʊ], **ant** [ænt], **penny** [ˈpɛnɪ], **ton** [tʌn]; **condign** [kənˈdaɪn], **gnaw** [nɔː], **feign** [feɪn], **foreign** [ˈfɔrɪn], **poignant** [ˈpɔɪnənt]; **knee** [niː], **knell** [nɛl], **knock** [nɑk], **knoll** [noːl], **know** [noʊ].

**285.** In words of French and Italian origin written **gn**, as in **cognac, mignonette, vignette, Bologna, Campagna,** and in Spanish words written **ñ**, as in **cañon, señor, piñon,** the sound is [nj], as in [ˈkoːnˌjæk], [ˌmɪnjəˈnɛt], [vɪnˈjɛt], [bəˈloːnjə], popularly often pronounced [bəˈloːnɪ], [kæmˈpænjə], [ˈkænjən], [ˈsiːnˌjɔɹ], [ˈpɪnˌjɔn]. For **cañon** a spelling **canyon** is now commonly used. Exceptions to this rule are **poignant**, noted above, and **champagne** [ˌʃæmˈpeɪn]. The place name **Boulogne** is commonly pronounced [buˈloɪn], and for **Bourgogne** only the Anglicized forms **Burgoyne, Burgundy** are in general use. In the customary pronunciation [ˈsiːnˌjɔɹ] for **señor** the accented vowel has lost its Spanish value.

**286.** After **l**, [n] is silent in **kiln** [kɪl], though a pronunciation with [n], due to the influence of the spelling, is also heard.

**287.** For **chimney** [ˈtʃɪmnɪ], popular English often has [ˈtʃɪmlɪ], [ˈtʃɪmblɪ].

**288.** After [m], an orthographic **n** is regularly silent, except when it belongs to a succeeding syllable, as in **solemn** [ˈsɑləm], but **solemnize** [ˈsɑləmˌnaɪz]; **autumn** [ˈɔːtəm], but **autumnal** [ɔˈtʌmnəl]; **hymn** [hɪm], but **hymnal** [ˈhɪmnəl]. The influence of a head form without [n] often preserves this pronunciation even when **mn** is followed by a vowel, as in **condemn** [kənˈdɛm], **condemning** [kənˈdɛmɪŋ]; **damn** [dæm], **damning** [ˈdæmɪŋ]; **in joy and hymning** (Milton) [ɪn dʒɔɪ ænd ˈhɪmɪŋ].

In popular pronunciation [n] is often omitted in **government** [ˈgʌvəɹnˌmɛnt], pronounced [ˈgʌvəɹˌmɛnt].

For **n** [ŋ] before [k], see § 289.

[ŋ]

**289.** This sound is commonly represented in spelling by **ng**, or by **n** in the combination [ŋg], [ŋk], as in **sing, singing,** [sɪŋ], [sɪŋɪŋ], **long** [lɔŋ], **lung** [lʌŋ], **rang** [ræŋ]; **think** [θɪŋk], **minx** [mɪŋks], **Bronx** [brɔŋks], **bank** [bæŋk], **sunk** [sʌŋk], **monk** [mʌŋk], **monkey** [ˈmʌŋkɪ], **distinct** [dɪsˈtɪŋkt], **tincture** [ˈtɪŋktʃəɹ], **function** [ˈfʌŋkʃən], [fʌŋk-tʃən], **conch** [kɔŋk], etc. On the omission of [k] or [t] in the combination [ŋktʃ], see §§ 267, 339.

**290.** The prefix **in–** when stressed and followed by [k] is pronounced [ɪn–] or [ɪŋ–], as in **income** [ˈɪnˌkʌm] or [ˈɪŋˌkʌm], **incubus** [ˈɪnkjubəs] or [ˈɪŋkjubəs], **incubate** [ˈɪnkjuˌbe·t] or [ˈɪŋkjuˌbe·t]; so also with **in–** followed by **qu**, as in **inquest** [ˈɪnkwɛst] or [ˈɪŋkwɛst]. The pronunciation of **inquiry** [ɪnˈkwaɪrɪ] with stress on the first syllable, giving [ˈɪnkwɪrɪ] or [ˈɪŋkwɪrɪ], is not current in standard English.

**291.** The prefix **con–** followed by [gr] is pronounced [kɑŋ–] when it bears a stress, as in **congress** [ˈkɑŋgrɛs], **congregate** [ˈkɑŋgrɪˌge·t], **congruous** [ˈkɑŋgrʊəs]; but when not stressed it usually becomes [kən–], as in **congressional** [kənˈgrɛʃənəl], **congruity** [kənˈgruɪtɪ]. In **congregational** a pronunciation [kɑŋ–] may persist because in polysyllables of this type the first syllable bears a secondary stress.

For **Congreve, Conger, Congo,** the usual pronunciations are [ˈkɑŋˌgriv], [ˈkɑŋgəɹ], [ˈkɑŋˌgoʊ].

**292.** Followed by [k], the pronunciation of **con–** varies indifferently between [kɑn–] and [kɑŋ–], as in **concave** [ˈkɑnˌke·v] or [ˈkɑŋˌke·v], **concubine** [ˈkɑnkjubaɪn] or [ˈkɑŋkjubaɪn], **conclave** [ˈkɑnˌkle·v] or [ˈkɑŋˌkle·v], **con-**

**cord** [ˈkɑnˋkɔɹd] or [ˈkɑŋˋkɔɹd], **concourse** [ˈkɑnˋkɔɹs] **or** [ˈkɑŋˋkɔɹs], **concrete** [ˈkɑnˋkrit] or [ˈkɑŋˋkrit].

**293.** Before **qu** [kw], **gu** [gw], **n** is pronounced [ŋ] by some speakers, [n] by others, as in **banquet** [ˈbænˋkwɛt] or [ˈbæŋˋkwɛt], **Banquo** [ˈbænˋkwo] or [ˈbæŋˋkwo], **lingual** [ˈlɪngwəl] or [ˈlɪŋgwəl], **linguistic** [lɪnˈgwɪstɪk] or [lɪŋˈgwɪs-tɪk], etc., with the preference perhaps in favor of the pronunciations with [n]. In **conquer** [ˈkɑŋkəɹ], **conqueror** [ˈkɑŋkərəɹ], where **qu** is [k], the value of **n** is always [ŋ], but in **conquest** forms with [n] and [ŋ] both appear.

**294.** Before [θ], [ŋ] often becomes [n] in popular speech in **length** [lɛŋθ], **lengthen** [ˈlɛŋθən], **strength** [strɛŋθ], **strengthen** [ˈstrɛŋθən], which are pronounced [lɛnθ], [ˈlɛnθən], [strɛnθ], [ˈstrɛnθən].

**295.** A final unstressed [n] is sometimes pronounced [ŋ] in dialect speech, as in **kitchen** [ˈkɪtʃɪŋ], **chicken** [ˈtʃɪkɪŋ], **garden** [ˈgɑrdɪŋ], etc., so also facetiously in **heavens** [ˈhɛvɪŋz].

**296.** In dialect speech and sometimes also in colloquial cultivated speech, final unstressed [ŋ] becomes [n], especially in present participles, as in **singing** [ˈsɪŋɪn], **doing** [ˈduɪn], **saying** [ˈseːɪn], etc. This pronunciation is more generally heard in cultivated speech in England than in America. In both countries, however, the authority of academic opinion is strongly against it.

**297.** A final [ŋ] sometimes becomes [ŋk] in dialect speech, as **nothing** [ˈnʌθɪŋk], **singing** [ˈsɪŋɪŋk], **anything** [ˈɛnɪˋθɪŋk]. This pronunciation appears in America chiefly in the larger cities and in speakers of foreign birth or tradition. It is more common in unstressed than in stressed syllables, but pronunciations like [kɪŋk] for **king** may even be heard.

[p]

**298.** An orthographic **p** is silent in **comptroller** [kən'troːləɹ], **psalm** [sɑːm], **pseudo–** ['suːdo–], **psychology** [saɪ'kɑlədʒɪ], **pneumatic** [nju'mætɪk], **pterodactyl** [tɛro'dæktɪl], **ptomaine** ['toːˌme·n], **ptarmigan** ['tɑːɹmɪgən], **raspberry** ['ræzˌbɛrɪ], ['raːzˌbɛrɪ]. The pronunciation of **corp** is [kɔɹ], plural **corps** [kɔɹz], but in **corpse** [kɔɹps] the **p** is sounded. In **cupboard** ['kʌbəɹd] the **p** is not sounded and may be said to have been assimilated to the following **b**. The word **clapboard** shows the same change.

**299.** On the other hand, some speakers insert a [p] between **m** and a continuant consonant where no [p] is present in orthography or in standard speech, as in **warmth** [wɔɹmpθ], **lymph** [lɪmpf], **camphor** ['kæmpfəɹ], **symphony** ['sɪmpfənɪ], **samphire** ['sæmpˌfaiəɹ], **Humphrey, Humphries**, ['hʌmpfrɪ], ['hʌmpfrɪz]. The spelling **ph** in these words may partly account for the pronunciation of a [p] in them, though this spelling is of course only one of the English ways of recording [f]. A more probable explanation, however, is that a [p] is necessarily produced when the breath is allowed to issue after the formation of [m] and the tongue and lip formation for a different consonant are not immediately assumed. In the same way a [p] is sometimes present in **dreamt** [drɛmt], giving [drɛmpt]. See § 359 for **ph** pronounced [p] in the combination **phth.**

**300.** In the orthographic combination **mp** followed by a consonant, a [p] is generally pronounced, as in **unkempt** [ˌʌn'kɛmpt], **limped** [lɪmpt], **stamped** [stæmpt], **glimpse**

[glɪmps], **lamps** [læmps], **assumption** [əˈsʌmpʃən], etc., but some speakers tend to omit the [p] in these combinations, pronouncing [ˌʌnˈkɛmt], [lɪmt], [stæmt], [glɪms], [əˈsʌmʃən], etc. To most persons these seem rather careless pronunciations.

In the place names **Hampshire, Hampden, Hampton,** the **p** is usually silent.

[r], [ɹ]

**301.** On the different varieties of **r**, see §§ 39–44.

Especially in the East and South, [ɹ] is regularly omitted by many speakers before other consonants and finally, as in **party** [ˈpɑːtɪ], **large** [lɑːdʒ], **far** [fɑː], **cur** [kʌː], **war** [wɔː]. But when stressed [ɹ] is omitted finally it often leaves a trace of its existence in a weak [ə], as in **for, four** [ˈfɔːə], **there** [ˈðɛːə], **fear** [ˈfiːə], **fire** [ˈfaɪ̆ə], **fur** [ˈfʌːə], **war** [ˈwɔːə], **cur** [ˈkʌːə], **far** [ˈfɑːə].

**302.** When [ɹ] is omitted before a consonant, the preceding vowel, if not already long, is lengthened, and the difference in length may then be the only distinguishing feature between two such words as **cart** [kɑːt] and **cot** [kɑt], **hard** [hɑːd] and **hod** [hɑd], **part** [pɑːt] and **pot** [pɑt]. But between **father** and **farther** no phonetic distinction would exist, both being [ˈfɑːðə]; so also **fought** and **fort** might both be [fɔːt], **caught** and **court** might be [kɔːt], **sought** and **sort** might be [sɔːt], **laud** and **lord** might be [lɔːd], etc. In Southern speech the sound of **o** before **r** and a consonant frequently becomes a vowel between [ɔː] and [oː], which may be described as a front [ɔː]. In this pronunciation **lord** lies between **laud** and **load** and distinct from both. So also in words with **r** final, as in **tore**, the pronunciation of which suggests **taw** or **toe**, but is appreciably different to the ear.

**303.** For **burst** a popular form without [ɹ] is generally current, but is pronounced [bʌst], whereas the cultivated pronunciation is either [bəɹst] or [bʌːst]. Similar pronunciations like **nurse** [nʌs], **first** [fʌst], **curse** [kʌs], **pursy** [ˈpʌsɪ], **purslane** [ˈpʌslɪ], are to be heard only in dialect and popular speech.

**304.** For **iron** and derivatives the only current pronunciations are [ˈaɪəɹn], [ˈaɪən]. A parallel pronunciation for **apron** [ˈeːpəɹn], however, is dialectal, the standard form being [ˈeːprən]. For **irony** the pronunciation is [ˈaɪrənɪ]. For **tired** the standard pronunciation is [ˈtaɪəɹd] or [ˈtaɪəd], and so with similar words, such as **fired**, **hired**, **wired**, etc.

**305.** At the end of words after vowels, in unstressed and after [ɔː] in stressed syllables, an [ɹ] is often added which is not present in spelling or in standard use, as in **idea** [aɪˈdɪəɹ], **window** [ˈwɪndəɹ], **Hannah** [ˈhænəɹ], **Noah** [ˈnoːəɹ], etc. This is most likely to take place when the word is followed by another word beginning with a vowel, but the pronunciation is not limited to such combinations. Pronunciations like [drɔːɹ], [sɔːɹ] for **draw** [drɔː], **saw** [sɔː], occur only in illiterate or dialect speech, but one often hears [aiˈdɪəɹ], [ˈwɪndəɹ], [ˈhænəɹ], etc., especially in New England, in the speech of cultivated persons. They are localisms, however, not to be recommended for imitation. In dialect speech an **r** is often inserted before a consonant after [ɔː], as in **chalk**, pronounced [tʃɔːɹk], **dog**, pronounced [dɔːɹg], **soft**, pronounced [sɔːɹft], etc. For standard **wash** [wɔʃ], **Washington** [ˈwɔʃɪŋtən], popular speech often has [wɔːɹʃ], [ˈwɔːɹʃɪŋtən]. In such words [ɹ] probably arises from the diphthongal pronunciation of [ɔː], see § 70.

**306.** Between vowels, [r] is omitted dialectally and also by some educated speakers in a kind of feeble refined pronunciation which is not general in any locality, but is characteristic rather of individuals or small family groups, as in ['vɛːɪ] for **very**, ['kɛːɪ] for **carry**, ['ɔːəl] for **oral**, ['fʌːɪ] for **furry**, etc. This pronunciation is caused by failure to bring the tongue after the pronunciation of the preceding vowel to the position required by [r], and in most instances is probably a survival of infantile pronunciations in which the movements of the organs of speech were under imperfect command. Somewhat similar is the omission of [r] in **hundred**, pronounced ['hʌndəd], and the first [r] in **February**, pronounced ['fɛbə'wɛrɪ], for standard ['hʌndrəd], ['fɛbru'ɛrɪ]. For **February** there is also a pronunciation ['fɛbju'ɛrɪ] which is probably in part due to the analogy of **January** ['dʒænju'ɛrɪ], and is not infrequently heard in cultivated speech. The pronunciation of **library** ['laɪbrɛrɪ] as ['laɪbɛrɪ] is juvenile and dialectal.

**307.** In popular speech, [ɹ] is also omitted before consonants, especially in unstressed syllables, as in **comfortable**, **surprised**, **particular**, pronounced ['kʌmfətəbl], [sə'praizd], [pə'tɪkjuləɹ], **Saturday**, pronounced ['sætədɪ]. Also in some stressed syllables, as in **cartridge**, pronounced ['kætrɪdʒ], **partridge**, pronounced ['pætrɪdʒ].

[s]

**308.** The sound of [s] is represented in the ordinary spelling by **s**, **ss**, **c**, **sc**, **x** [ks], as in **yes** [jɛs], **best** [bɛst], **miss** [mɪs], **mistress** ['mɪstrɪs], **wasp** [wɔsp], **rice** [raɪs], **except** [ɛk'sɛpt], **accept** [æk'sɛpt], **ceiling** ['siːlɪŋ], **cincture** ['sɪŋktʃəɹ], **cinch** [sɪntʃ], **circle** ['səɹkl], **service** ['səɹvɪs],

**tax** [tæks], **buxom** [ˈbʌksəm], **scythe** [saɪð], **scene** [siːn], **scissors** [ˈsɪzəɹz]. The spelling of **scissors** is exceptional in two respects, in the spelling **sc** in a native English word for [s], and **ss** for [z]. In **schism** and derivatives, **sch** is pronounced [s], [sɪzm].

For **si, ssi, su, ssu,** pronounced [ʃ], see § 327.

**309.** The value of **c** is [s] regularly before **e, i, y,** as in **cell** [sɛl], **conceit** [kənˈsiːt], **citron** [ˈsɪtrən], **decide** [dɪˈsaɪd], **cinch** [sɪntʃ], **cycle** [ˈsaɪkl], but [k] before **a, o, u,** as in **can** [kæn], **call** [kɔːl], **coke** [koːk], **cook** [kʊk], **cup** [kʌp]. For **sacerdotal** the standard pronunciation is [ˌsæsəɹˈdoɪtəl], but sometimes a Latinized pronunciation [sækəɹ–] is heard. The Old English proper names **Cædmon, Cynewulf** are pronounced [ˈkædmən], [ˈkɪnɪˌwʊlf]. For **Celt, Celtic, Cymric** both [kɛlt], [ˈkɛltɪk], [ˈkɪmrɪk] and [sɛlt], [ˈsɛltɪk], [ˈsɪmrɪk] occur.

**310.** In the combination **stl**, the **s** is usually voiceless, as in **gristle** [ˈgrɪsl], **thistle** [ˈθɪsl], **whistle** [ˈʍɪsl], etc., but some speakers say [ˈmɪzlˌtoʊ] for **mistletoe** [ˈmɪslˌtoʊ]. For **grisly** the standard pronunciation is [ˈgrɪslɪ].

**311.** For **greasy** the common pronunciation is [ˈgriːzɪ], but some speakers carry over the consonant of the noun **grease** [griːs] to the adjective, pronouncing the adjective [ˈgriːsɪ]. A distinction is sometimes made in the meaning of [ˈgriːsɪ] and [ˈgriːzɪ], the latter being regarded as a word of unpleasant connotation. Popular usage and, in general, standard speech have only the form with [z].

**312.** For **rise** (*noun*) a pronunciation [raɪs] is sometimes heard to distinguish the noun from the verb [raɪz], but the common pronunciation is [raɪz] for both noun and verb. In some words, however, [s] is distinctive for noun, [z] for verb function, as in **advice** [æd'vaɪs], **advise** [æd'vaɪz]; **device** [dɪ'vaɪs], **devise** [dɪ'vaɪz]; **abuse** [ə'bjuːs], **abuse** (*verb*) [ə'bjuːz]; **use** [juːs], **use** (*verb*) [juːz]; **grease** [griːs], **grease** (*verb*) [griːz]. For **sacrifice** the common pronunciation is ['sækrɪˌfaɪs] for both noun and verb, but ['sækrɪˌfaɪz] is occasionally heard for the verb. For **close** as verb the pronunciation is [kloːz], as adjective, adverb and noun (as in 'cathedral close') the pronunciation is [kloːs]. In **recluse** [rɪ'kluːs] the **s** is voiceless.

**313.** The pronunciation of **Missouri** is commonly [mɪz'uːrɪ], though [mɪ'suːrɪ] is sometimes heard. The accented vowel may be [ʊ].

**314.** In **Louisville, St. Louis, Illinois** and other proper names in which a French tradition survives, pronunciations both with and without **s** are generally current. In **New Orleans** the final **s** is always pronounced, the stress being on the first syllable, as in [ˌnju 'ɔɹlənz]. The pronunciation [ˌnju ɔɹ'liːnz] is dialectal. In **Des Moines** [dɪ'mɔɪn] neither **s** is sounded. In **Illinois** when the final consonant is pronounced it is voiced. In **New Orleans** the two vowel letters of the final syllable may be given separate quality, as in [ˌnju 'ɔɹlɪənz].

**315.** In **ambergris**, though the word is of French origin, the final **s** is always sounded, and the word is treated as though it were a compound of **amber** and **grease**, being pronounced accordingly, ['æmbəɹ'griːs]. So also with **verdigris** ['vəɹdɪ'griːs], **avoirdupois** [ˌævəɹdʊ'pɔɪz]. For **bourgeois**, meaning 'middle class,' the pronunciation is ['bʊɹʒˌwɑː], but as the name of a kind of type it is [bəɹ'dʒɔɪs].

**316.** Some speakers show a marked tendency to substitute [ʃ] for [s], especially when it comes before [t], as in **worst** [wəɹst], pronounced [wəɹʃt], **distressed** [dɪs'trɛst], pronounced [dɪs'trɛʃt], **suggest** [sə'dʒɛst], pronounced [sə'dʒɛʃt], etc. The pronunciation produces a spluttery untidy effect, which most persons find very disagreeable.

**317.** For **rinse** [rɪns], [rɪnz], popular dialect speech often has [rɛntʃ]. The proper name **Rensselaer** ['rɛnsə'lɛːɹ], ['rɛnsləɹ], has a popular form ['rɛntʃləɹ]. The pronunciation of **pincers** ['pɪnsəɹz] as ['pɪntʃəɹz] is probably the result of the influence of **pinch**. It is possible that the pronunciation [rɛntʃ] for **rinse** has been affected by the analogy of **wrench** [rɛntʃ]. A half-way form, [rɛns], is also heard.

[z]

**318.** The two common spellings for [z] are **s** and **z**, as in **his** [hɪz], **phase** [feːz], **despise** [dɪ'spaɪz], **misery** ['mɪzərɪ], **accuse** [æ'kjuːz], **visor** ['vaɪzəɹ], **Townsend** ['tɑʊnzənd], **zone** [zoːn], **baize** [beːz], **lazy** ['leːzɪ], **dizzy** ['dɪzɪ], **hazard** ['hæzəɹd], **lizard** ['lɪzəɹd], etc. Hard and fast rules for **s** pronounced [z] cannot be given, because general rules are very much broken into by analogical groupings. Initial **s**, however, is never voiced, and the spellings **c**, **ss** never stand for [z], with the exception of **scissors**, see § 308, and **Missouri**, see § 313. Between vowels and in the neighborhood of voiced consonants, **s** tends to become [z] by assimilation, as in **house** [hɑʊs], **houses** ['hɑʊzɪz], but the operation of this tendency may be held in check by the influence of a head form, as in **case** [keːs], **cases** ['keːsɪz]; **gas** [gæs], **gases** ['gæsɪz]; **lease** [liːs], **leases** ['liːsɪz]; or the third singular of verbs, like **loose** [luːs], **looses** [ˈluːsɪz]. Likewise in the possessives of words ending in [s] the voiceless sound is preserved when the ending is added, as in **moose** [muːs], **moose's** [ˈmuːsɪz].

**319.** Inflectional **s** in the plurals and possessives of nouns and in the third singular present of verbs is [z], unless it is preceded by a voiceless consonant, as in **cows** [kɑʊz], **goes** [goːz], **paths** [pæðz], **wives** [waɪvz], **tubs** [tʌbz], **rides** [raɪdz]; but **cats** [kæts], **skiffs** [skɪfs], **myths** [mɪθs], **walks** [wɔːks], **steps** [stɛps], etc.

**320.** For **Mrs.** the common pronunciation is the same as for **misses**, that is, [ˈmɪsəz] or [ˈmɪsɪz], but occasionally the final consonant is voiceless, [ˈmɪsɪs]. The pronunciation with the medial consonant voiced, as in [ˈmɪzɪz], is said to be a sure test of Southern speech.[1] But the test does not work both ways. It may be true that [ˈmɪzɪz] is always Southern, but it is not true that all Southerners say [ˈmɪzɪz]. In Southern pronunciation **Mrs.** is often monosyllabic, being merely [mɪz], with perhaps the final consonant prolonged.

**321.** Words in which a stressed **s** after a vowel is followed by the ending **-ive** usually have [s], but sometimes [z], as in **abusive, conclusive, corrosive, diffusive, evasive, persuasive, incisive.** The pronunciation with **s** is to be preferred. After **n, l, r,** when **s** is under the stress it remains as [s], as in **pensive, defensive, expansive, impulsive, discursive.**

**322.** Intervocalic **s** in unstressed syllables when it is not [ʃ] or [ʒ] (see §§ 327 (*e*), 328 ff.), usually is pronounced

[1] Read, *Dialect Notes*, III, 524 (1911).

[z], as in **comparison, jettison, unison, venison,** though sometimes [s] in all these words.

The usual pronunciation of **usage** is [ˈjuːsɪdʒ], the voiceless [s] being maintained by the stress. But [ˈjuːzɪdʒ] also is heard.

**323.** In **newspaper** the less usual pronunciation is [ˈnjuːzˎpe·pəɹ], in agreement with the uncompounded form **news** [njuːz]. Generally, the voiced [z] is assimilated to the voiceless [p], giving [ˈnjusˎpe·pəɹ].

**324.** In **Chinese, Japanese, Maltese, Siamese, Soudanese,** etc., the final syllable is usually [–i·z], especially when the words stand in adjective position and are consequently lightly stressed, as in **Siamese twins** [ˈsaɪəmi·z ˈtwɪnz]. As the name of a people, for example, **the Chinese, the Japanese,** the words are more heavily stressed and are often pronounced with a voiceless consonant, [ðə tʃaɪˈniːs], [ðə dʒæpəˈniːs].

**325.** For **Kansas, Arkansas,** the pronunciation is [ˈkænzəs], [ɑɹˈkænzəs], rarely with [s] for the first consonant of the last syllable; but the pronunciation of **Arkansas** as [ˈɑɹkənˎsɔː] is the one accepted in the state and in the West generally. For **Texas** the usual pronunciation is [ˈtɛksəs], less often [ˈtɛksəz].

**326.** The pronunciation of **czar** (sometimes spelled **tzar**) and derivatives is [zɑːɹ]. In a few words, especially Greek proper names, **x** is pronounced [z], as in **Xenophon** [ˈzɛnəfən], **Xanthippe** [zænˈtɪpɪ], **Xerxes** [ˈzəɹksiz], **Xavier** [ˈzeːvɪəɹ], **Xebec** [ˈziːbɛk]. In **avoirdupois** the final consonant is always pronounced [z], see § 315.

[ʃ]

**327.** This sound is of very wide occurrence in the language and can best be treated under the heads of its various orthographic representations.

(*a*) **s**=[ʃ] in **sugar** [ˈʃʊgəɹ], **sure** [ʃʊɹ], [ʃʊəɹ], and derivatives of **sure.** The sound is not standard in any other words of this type, though occasionally heard in pronunciations like **assume** [əˈʃuːm] for [əˈsuːm], [əˈsjuːm], [ˈʃuːmæk] for **sumach** [ˈsuːmæk], especially in dialect speech.

(*b*) **sh**=[ʃ], as in **ship** [ʃɪp], **fish** [fɪʃ], **ashen** [ˈæʃən], **shackle** [ˈʃækl], **fashion** [ˈfæʃən], and a large number of other words.

(*c*) **sch**=[ʃ], but only in a few words of foreign origin, as in **schottish, schottische** [ˈʃɑtɪʃ], **schist** [ʃɪst], a term in geology, **schnapps** [ʃnæps]. For **schedule**, see § 263; for **schism**, see § 308. Ordinarily **sch**=**sk** [sk].

(*d*) **ch**=[ʃ], especially in words of French origin or words influenced by French pronunciation, as in **chef** [ʃɛf], **chalet** [ʃæˈleɪ], **chevalier** [ʃɛvəˈlɪəɹ], **cheval** [ʃɛˈvæl], **chauvinism** [ˈʃoːvɪnɪzm], **chandelier** [ˌʃændəˈlɪəɹ], **charade** [ʃəˈreːd], **chic** [ʃik], **chassis** [ʃæˈsiː], **champagne** [ʃæmˈpeːn], **chiffonier** [ʃɪfəˈnɪəɹ] (very commonly also [ʃɛf–]), **chauffeur** [ˈʃoːfəɹ] or [ʃoˈfəɹ], **chivalry** [ˈʃɪvəlrɪ], **chagrin** [ʃəˈgrɪn], **cheroot** [ʃəˈruːt], **chaise** [ʃeːz], **chamois** [ˈʃæmwɑ] (as the name of the animal), [ˈʃæmɪ] (as the name of the skin of commerce), **chiffon** [ˈʃɪfɔn], **chemise** [ʃɛˈmiːz], **chicanery** [ʃɪˈkeːnɪrɪ], **mustache** [məsˈtæʃ]; also in proper names, as in **Charlotte** [ˈʃɑːɹlət], **Champlain** [ʃæmˈpleːn], **Charlevoix** [ˈʃɑːɹləvɔɪ], **Cheyenne** [ˈʃaɪˈɛn], **Chenango** [ʃəˈnæŋgo], **Chicago** [ʃɪˈkɑːgo] or [ʃɪˈkɔːgo], **Michigan** [ˈmɪʃɪgən], **Cheboygan** [ʃɪˈbɔɪgən], **Chatauqua** [ʃəˈtɔːkwə]. But [ʃ] for **ch** is not universal in native American place names, some having [tʃ], as in **Chippewa** [ˈtʃɪpɪˌwɔː], **Chillicothe** [tʃilɪˈkɔːθɪ], **Chicopee** [ˈtʃɪkoˌpiː], **Cherokee** [ˈtʃɛroˌkiː], **Chattanooga** [tʃætəˈnuːgə].

For **chivalry** [ˈʃɪvəlrɪ] and derivatives a pronunciation [ˈtʃɪvəlrɪ] also obtains in England, but is never heard in America except as a Briticism.

An occasional pronunciation [pəˈroːʃəl] is heard for the standard **parochial** [pəˈroːkɪəl].

(*e*) Under this and the following heads are grouped instances in which an original [s] or [t], followed by an unstressed mid or high front sound, [e], [ɪ] or [ju], combined with the vowel to form [ʃ].

**ce**=[ʃ], as in **ocean** [ˈoːʃən], and in the ending **-aceous**, as in **herbaceous** [həɹˈbeːʃəs], **crustaceous** [krʌsˈteːʃəs], etc. For **oceanic** both [oʃɪˈænɪk] and [osɪˈænɪk] occur.

(*f*) **ci**=[ʃ], as in **musician** [mjuˈzɪʃən], **social** [ˈsoːʃəl], **gracious** [ˈgreːʃəs], **sufficient** [səˈfɪʃənt], **ancient** [ˈeːnʃənt], also [ˈeːntʃənt], **pacient** [ˈpeːʃənt], **racial** [ˈreːʃəl], **precious** [ˈprɛʃəs], **preciosity** [prɛʃɪˈɔsɪtɪ].

In the endings **-ciate**, **-ciation**, considerable difference of usage occurs, the general tendency of popular speech being to pronounce **ci** as [ʃ], but in cultivated speech this tendency is sometimes interrupted, especially in formal discourse, in which the pronunciation [sɪ] is often preferred as being nearer to the spelling, as in **enunciate** [ɪˈnʌnʃɪˌe·t] or [ɪˈnʌnsɪˌe·t], **associate** and derivatives [əˈsoːʃɪˌe·t] or [əˈsoːsɪˌe·t], **pronunciation** [proˌnʌnʃɪˈeːʃən] (but perhaps more commonly [proˌnʌnsɪˈeːʃən], either from a desire to distinguish **ci** and **ti** in the word, or it may be because one is likely to be self-conscious in pronouncing this word), **officiate** [ɔˈfɪʃɪˌe·t] or [ɔˈfɪsɪˌe·t], **emaciated** [ɪˈmeːʃɪˌetəd] or [ɪˈmeːsɪˌe·təd], **appreciate** [æˈpriːʃɪe·t], **appreciation** [æpriʃɪˈeːʃən] or [æprisɪˈeːʃən]. In words like

**appreciation, enunciation, association,** etc., the **ci** is likely to be pronounced [sɪ] to avoid bringing two [ʃ]-sounds close together.

(*g*) **sci**=[ʃ], as in **conscious** [ˈkɑnʃəs], **conscience** [ˈkɑnʃəns], **omniscient** [ɔmˈnɪʃənt], **luscious** [ˈlʌʃəs].

In formal speech instead of [ʃ], sometimes [sɪ] is heard for **sci**, especially in learned words, like **omniscient** [ɔmˈnɪsɪənt], **prescience** [ˈprɛsɪəns].

(*h*) **si**=[ʃ], as in **mansion** [ˈmænʃən], **dimension** [dɪˈmɛnʃən], **transient** [ˈtrænʃənt], in formal speech often [ˈtrænsɪənt], **Asia** [ˈeːʃə], but also [ˈeːʒə], **fuchsia** [ˈfjuːʃə]. In **transient** the consonant is sometimes voiced, giving [ˈtrænʒənt]. In **Persia** [ˈpəɹʒə] it is always voiced. See § 333 (*a*).

The variant spelling **x** for [ks] appears in **noxious** [ˈnɑkʃəs], **anxious** [ˈæŋkʃəs]. For **axiom** the standard pronunciation is [ˈæksɪəm], the general tendency, which would produce [ˈækʃəm], being held in check by the learned character of the word.

(*i*) **se**=[ʃ], as in **nausea** [ˈnɔːʃə] and derivatives, but also pronounced [ˈnɔːʃɪə], [ˈnɔːsɪə], [ˈnɔːʒə], [ˈnɔːʒɪə], [ˈnɔːzɪə].

(*j*) **su**=[ʃ], the vowel also persisting, as in **insular** [ˈɪnʃuləɹ], **peninsula** [pɛnˈɪnʃulə], **sensual** [ˈsɛnʃuəl], **sexual** [ˈsɛkʃuəl], **consular** [ˈkɑnʃuləɹ], **luxury** [ˈlʌkʃərɪ], less frequently [ˈlʌgʒərɪ].

In all these words, which differ from those under (*a*) in that **s** is followed by **u** in an unstressed syllable, pronunciations with [sj] also occur, as in [ˈɪnsjuləɹ], [ˈsɛnsjuəl], etc., especially in formal and conscious speech. It is the [j] element in [ju] that causes the [s]-sound to become [ʃ].

(*k*) **ssi**=[ʃ], as in **mission** [ˈmɪʃən], **passion** [ˈpæʃən], **discussion** [dɪsˈkʌʃən], **confession** [kənˈfɛʃən], **Ossian**

[ˈɔʃən] or in careful pronunciation [ˈɔʃɪən], **Russia** [ˈrʌʃə], **Prussia** [ˈprʌʃə].

(*l*) **ssu**=[ʃ], the vowel also persisting, as in **issue** [ˈɪʃu], **tissue** [ˈtɪʃu], **fissure** [ˈfɪʃʊɹ] or [ˈfɪʃəɹ], **pressure** [ˈprɛʃʊɹ] or [ˈprɛʃəɹ], **commissure** [ˈkɑmɪˌʃʊɹ], a term in biology.

A careful pronunciation, as in [ˈɪsju] or [ˈɪʃju], is sometimes cultivated in these words, see also under (*j*). On the other hand, a slighter colloquial form is also to be observed, as in [ˈtɪʃə] for **tissue**, especially as adjective in the phrase **tissue paper.**

(*m*) **te**=[tʃ], as in **righteous** [ˈraɪtʃəs], sometimes also **courteous** [ˈkəɹtʃəs], though more commonly [ˈkəɹtɪəs]. Other words in –**eous**, as **duteous**, **piteous**, **plenteous**, **bounteous**, **beauteous**, have only the pronunciation [ˈdjutɪəs], etc., in agreement with their head forms **duty**, **pity**, **plenty**, **bounty**, **beauty.**

In **amateur** the stress falls in cultivated speech on the last syllable, [æməˈtəɹ], but quite generally in familiar speech, especially in such phrases as "amateur theatricals," "amateur standing," etc., the stress is on the first syllable, giving [ˈæmətʃəɹ].

(*n*) **ti**=[ʃ], as in **position** [pəˈzɪʃən], **nation** [ˈneːʃən], **essential** [ɪˈsɛnʃəl], **Titian** [ˈtɪʃən], **rational** [ˈræʃənəl], **ratio** [ˈreːʃo], **sentient** [ˈsɛnʃənt], though also [ˈsɛntɪənt] as a learned word.

For **otiose**, **otium**, the recognized dictionary pronunciations are [oʃɪˈoːs], [ˈoːʃɪəm], but the words are not current in colloquial use, and for that reason most speakers when compelled to pronounce them would follow the spelling.

For **ratiocination** both [ˌrætɪosɪˈneːʃən] and [ˌræʃɪosɪˈneːʃən] are in good use.

In words like **differentiation**, **negotiation**, **substantia-**

**tion**, the first **ti** is often pronounced [sɪ] and the second [ʃ], perhaps from a disinclination to have two [ʃ]-sounds close together, see above, under (*f*). In **differentiation** the influence of **difference** may also be of some weight. In **differentiate**, **negotiate**, **substantiate**, the value of **ti** is commonly [ʃɪ], and it remains so with probably the majority of speakers in **differentiation**, etc.

When **ti** is preceded by [s], the [t] assibilates to [ʃ], but at the same time remains as [t] to avoid the juxtaposition of [s] and [ʃ], as in **question** [ˈkwɛstʃən], **suggestion** [səˈdʒɛstʃən], **Christian** [ˈkrɪstʃən], etc. The pronunciation [ˈkrɪstɪən] is very formal. See § 339.

When **ti** is preceded by [n], ordinarily the **ti** is pronounced [ʃ], as in **mention** [ˈmɛnʃən], **attention** [əˈtɛnʃən], **convention** [kənˈvɛnʃən], etc.; but when a word is strongly stressed, the sound may become [tʃ], as in **Don't even mention it** [doːnt iːvn ˈmɛntʃən ɪt], or in **attention** as a military command, which is reduced merely to the final syllable [tʃʌn], with of course heavy stress. In such words the organic position for [t] is already assumed for the pronunciation of [n], and the special emphasis merely carries over the continuant [n] to a stop [t].

The history of these words in **ti** runs parallel in everything except orthography to words in **si**. Words of this type were first introduced into the language from French in the early Middle English period, and at the time of their appearance in the language they had already acquired in French a pronunciation [sɪ]. This pronunciation Modern French still retains in words like **nation**, **intention**, etc. Sometimes in the earlier periods one finds **t** replaced by **c** in spelling, as in **nacion** for **nation** [ˈnæsɪən]. The influence of Latin orthography, however, was strong enough to prevent the carrying through of this rationalizing process in spelling, which would have resulted in a consistent spelling with **c** or **s** for **t** in words of this type. Instead a certain amount of inconsistency now appears in English spelling, as in **(in)tention** and **(ex)tension, vicious** and **vitiate**, both of these being pairs of etymologically the same word, or **mention** and **(di)mension**, etymologically different, but phonetically the same. Occasionally words with **cti** are written with **x**, as in **connection, connexion** [kə'nɛkʃən], **inflection, inflexion** [ɪn'flɛkʃən], etc.

(*o*) **tu**=[tʃ], as in **nature** ['neːtʃəɹ], **feature** ['fiːtʃəɹ], **creature** ['kriːtʃəɹ], **moisture** ['mɔɪstʃəɹ], **fortune** ['fɔɹtʃən], **actual** ['æktʃuəl], **virtuous** ['vəɹtʃuəs], **furniture** ['fəɹnɪtʃəɹ], etc. Formal pronunciations, e.g., ['neːtʃʊɹ], ['fiːtʃʊɹ], etc., may occur.

For **literature** and other words of three or four syllables which may have a secondary stress on the final syllable, two pronunciations occur, ['lɪtərətʃəɹ] or ['lɪtərəˌtjʊɹ], the latter being the more formal and careful style.

The influence of **manufacture** [mænju'fæktʃəɹ] often produces a popular pronunciation [mænju'fæktʃərɪ] for **manufactory**, which in standard pronunciation is always [mænju'fæktərɪ].

The change of **tu** to [tʃ] implies a pronunciation of **u** as [ɪu] or [ju], that is, ['neːtjuɹ], ['fiːtjuɹ], etc. This pronunciation is historically recorded, and it was not until towards the close of the eighteenth century that the combination [tju] became [tʃu] in generally accepted English. In fact, [tju] may still be heard occasionally in formal pronunciation. It was perhaps natural for the [t] to be retained, since it was pronounced, even when with the following sound it produced a [ʃ], giving for older **nature** ['neːtjuɹ] the pronunciation ['neːtʃuɹ]. In a word like **nation**, however, it was pointed out above that the **t** was never sounded as [t] in English, but only as [s], and the combination therefore developed as **si** into [ʃ]. If **nation** and similar words had come into the language with **t** sounded, for example [ˈneːtɪɔn], no doubt a pronunciation [ˈneːtʃən] would have resulted instead of [ˈneːʃən]; and so also with [tʃ] for other words of this type. In short, the development of **tu** into [tʃ] is a relatively late and exclusively English process, whereas the development of **ti** into [ʃ] is not what it seems to be, but merely the development of a French [sɪ] into [ʃ].

The pronunciation of **u** in the combination **tu** as [u], not [ju], resulted merely in a weakening of the vowel without any change in the character of the preceding consonant. Thus arose dialect pronunciations like *critter* for **creature,** *nater*, *nateral* for **nature, natural,** etc.

When the combination **tu** is under the stress, it remains [tju], as in **mature** [məˈtjuɹ] or [məˈtjʊɹ], **institute** (*noun*) [ˈɪnstɪˌtjut], **institution** [ɪnstɪˈtjuʃən], **astute** [æsˈtjuːt], and in initial stressed syllables, as in **tuber, Tudor, tunic, tutor,** and the monosyllables **tube** and **tune.** Even in these stressed syllables the combination **tu** was formerly pronounced [tʃu], but this is heard now only as a humorous pronunciation.

[ʒ]

**328.** This is the voiced equivalent of [ʃ] and is orthographically represented by **j**, **g**=[dʒ], or by **s** or **z** before unstressed **i** or **u**, often also by **d** before unstressed **i** or **u.**

**329.** As the second element of the compound sound [dʒ], this consonant appears in **join** [dʒɔɪn], **judge** [dʒʌdʒ], **gem** [dʒɛm], **gage** [geːdʒ], **suggest** [səˈdʒɛst], **allege** [əˈlɛdʒ], **ledge** [lɛdʒ], **bridge** [brɪdʒ], **magic** [ˈmædʒɪk].

**330.** For **malinger** the standard pronunciation is [məˈlɪndʒəɹ], though occasionally speakers are led to pronounce the word as though it were a variant form of **linger** [ˈlɪŋgəɹ].

**331.** For **margarine**, or the compound **oleomargarine**, the common pronunciation is [ˈmaːɹdʒərɪn] or [ˈmaːɹdʒəˌriːn], the historically correct pronunciation [ˈmaːɹgərɪn] being now rarely heard.

**332.** For **longevity**, **longitude**, the pronunciation is always [lɔnˈdʒɛvɪtɪ], [ˈlɔndʒɪˌtjuːd]. For **gibber**, **gibbering**, it may be [ˈdʒɪbəɹ], [ˈdʒɪbərɪŋ] or [ˈgɪbəɹ], [ˈgɪbərɪŋ], but for **gibberish** it is always [ˈgɪbərɪʃ]. In **gibbet**, **gibe**, **giblets**, **gill** (*quarter pint*), **gin** (shortened form of **engine** and also shortened form of **Geneva**), **ginseng**, **gist**, the initial consonant is always [dʒ]. A dictionary should be consulted for a list of the words containing **g** before front vowels.

**333.** Other occurrences of [ʒ] are:

(*a*) **si**=[ʒ], as in **derision** [dɪˈrɪʒən], **vision** [ˈvɪʒən], **fusion** [ˈfjuːʒən], **abrasion** [əˈbreːʒən], **occasion** [əˈkeːʒən], **erosion** [ɪˈroːʒən], **osier** [ˈoːʒəɹ], **Frasier** [ˈfreːʒəɹ] or [ˈfreːʒjəɹ], **hosier** [ˈhoːʒəɹ] or [ˈhoːʒjəɹ], **gymnasium** [dʒɪmˈneːʒəm], **symposium** [sɪmˈpoːʒəm], though for these last two words a learned pronunciation [–zɪəm] is also heard.

(*b*) **zi**=[ʒ], as in **glazier** [ˈgleːʒəɹ] or [ˈgleːʒjəɹ], also written **glasier**, **Frazier** [ˈfreːʒəɹ] or [ˈfreːʒjəɹ].

(*c*) **su**=[ʒ], with the vowel also persisting, as in **treasure** [ˈtrɛʒəɹ], **pleasure** [ˈplɛʒəɹ], **leisure** [ˈlɛʒəɹ] or [ˈliːʒəɹ], **closure** [ˈkloːʒəɹ], **erasure** [ɪˈreːʒəɹ]; **usual** [ˈjuːʒuəl] or [ˈjuːʒjuəl], **visual** [ˈvɪʒuəl] or [ˈvɪʒjuəl], **casual** [ˈkæʒjuəl] or [ˈkæzjuəl].

The standard pronunciation of **Jesuit** is [ˈdʒɛzjuɪt], less commonly [ˈdʒɛʒjuɪt].

In **luxurious** the standard pronunciation is [lʌgˈʒʊrɪəs].

(*d*) **zu** = [ʒ], in **azure** [ˈeːʒəɹ] or [ˈæʒəɹ].

(*e*) **di** = [dʒ], in **cordial** [ˈkɔɹdʒəl], **soldier** [ˈsoːldʒəɹ], and sometimes in other words in **–ial**, **–ient**, **–ious**, **–ium**, as in **medial, obedient, expedient, tedious, medium, radium, tedium**, but usually in these words the endings have the value [–ɪəl], [–ɪənt], [–ɪəs], [–ɪəm].

In **grandeur**, **de** = [ʒ], [ˈgrændʒəɹ].

(*f*) **du** = [dʒu], in **modulate** [ˈmɑdʒuˌle·t], **nodule** [ˈnɑdʒul], **schedule** [ˈskɛdʒul], **pendulum** [ˈpɛndʒuləm], **individual** [ɪndɪˈvɪdʒuəl], etc. Instead of [dʒu] in these words, careful and formal speech often has [dju], but the normal tendency is to pronounce [dʒu].

(*g*) **ti** = [ʒ], in **equation** [ɪˈkweːʒən], but also, in accordance with the usual value of **ti** as [ʃ], [ɪˈkweːʃən]. The pronunciation with [ʒ] seems to have arisen by analogy to such words as **invasion, abrasion**, etc.

**334.** In some words of French origin, **g** is pronounced [ʒ], as in **rouge** [ruːʒ], **menage** [mɛˈnɑːʒ], **cortege** [kɔɹˈteːʒ], **mirage** [mɪˈrɑːʒ], **camouflage** [ˌkæmuˈflɑːʒ], **persiflage** [ˌpəɹsɪˈflɑːʒ].

**335.** The proper name **Mosher** is usually [ˈmoːʒəɹ]. It is also spelled **Mosier, Mozier.**

### [t]

**336.** This sound is commonly represented by **t, tt**, but also by **d** in the preterites of many verbs when the ending **–(e)d** is assimilated to a preceding voiceless consonant. Examples of [t] are **talk** [tɔːk], **lettuce** [ˈlɛtɪs], **missed**

[mɪst], **slipped** [slɪpt], **coughed** [ˈkɔːft], **wished** [wɪʃt], and hosts of other words.

**337.** An orthographic **t** is silent in **argot** [ˈɑːɹgo], **depot** [ˈdiːpo], **ballet** [bæˈleɪ] or [ˈbælɪ], **buffet** [bʊˈfeɪ], **chalet** [ʃæˈleɪ], **valet** [væˈleɪ] or [ˈvælɪ], but more fashionably now [ˈvælɪt], **parquet** [pɑɹˈkeɪ] as the name of a part of a theater, but [pɑɹˈkɛt] as the name of a kind of flooring. All these words are of comparatively recent French origin. In **trait**, final **t** is not pronounced in British usage, but in America it is always pronounced.

**338.** In the orthographic combination **–ction**, the **t** is silent, as in **perfection** [pəɹˈfɛkʃən], **suction** [ˈsʌkʃən], **function** [ˈfʌŋkʃən], **diction** [ˈdɪkʃən], **action** [ˈækʃən], etc. In the combination **–ctu–**, usage varies between [ktʃ] and [kʃ], as in **actual** [ˈæktʃuəl] or [ˈækʃuəl], **juncture** [ˈdʒʌŋk-tʃəɹ] or [ˈdʒʌŋkʃəɹ], **puncture** [ˈpʌŋktʃəɹ] or [ˈpʌŋkʃəɹ], **lecture** [lɛktʃəɹ] or [ˈlɛkʃəɹ], **manufacture** [manjuˈfæktʃəɹ] or [mænjuˈfækʃəɹ], etc., though in formal and careful speech the pronunciation with [t] is preferred.

**339.** In the combinations **–sti–**, **–stu–**, a [t] is always pronounced in cultivated speech, pronunciations like [ɛgzˈɔːsʃən], [ˈkwɛsʃən], [ˈfɪksʃəɹ], [ˈmɪksʃəɹ] for **exhaustion** [ɛgzˈɔːstʃən], **question** [ˈkwɛstʃən], **fixture** [ˈfɪkstʃəɹ], **mix-ture** [ˈmɪkstʃəɹ] being slovenly English.

**340.** In the combinations **stl**, **stn**, **ftn**, no [t] is pro-nounced, as in **epistle** [ɪˈpɪsl], **thistle** [ˈθɪsl], **nestle** [ˈnɛsl], **jostle** [ˈdʒɔsl], **hustle** [ˈhʌsl], **soften** [ˈsɔfn], **often** [ˈɔfn], **listen** [ˈlɪsn], **fasten** [ˈfæsn], **chasten** [ˈtʃeːsn], **moisten** [ˈmɔɪsn], **chestnut** [ˈtʃɛsˌnʌt]. In connected discourse, the combination **stn** appears in **must not**, which is commonly pronounced [ˈmʌsnt], except in precise speech where the words are consciously held apart. In **often** there is some tendency to restore the **t** in pronunciation, through the influence of spelling. But [ˈɔfn] is still the prevailing form. In rapid colloquial speech the combination **let us** frequently becomes [lɛs], e.g., **Let us go and see** [lɛs goː n siː].

**341.** For the orthographic combinations **nch**, **lch**, a pronunciation [ntʃ], [ltʃ] is generally current, though less frequently one also hears [nʃ], [lʃ], as in **pinch** [pɪntʃ] or [pɪnʃ], **bench** [bɛntʃ] or [bɛnʃ], **launch** [lɔːntʃ] or [lɔːnʃ], **filch** [fɪltʃ] or [fɪlʃ], **belch** [bɛltʃ] or [bɛlʃ], **gulch** [gʌltʃ] or [gʌlʃ]. For **Welsh** the spelling usually preserves a pronunciation [wɛlʃ], but in the verb and noun probably derived from this word, meaning to slide from under one's obligations, both spellings occur, **welch**, **welcher** and **welsh**, **welsher**, and a corresponding variation in pronunciation. In American usage the pronunciation of all these words with [ntʃ], [ltʃ] is to be preferred. See § 246. For the combination **ns**, the pronunciation in America is usually [nts], as in **dense** [dɛnts], not distinguishable from **dents**, **mince** [mɪnts], not distinguishable from **mints**, etc. But some speakers say [dɛns], [mɪns] for **dense**, **mince**, etc.

**342.** A [t] is often omitted in the popular dialects after [p], as in [slɛp], [kɛp], [krɛp] for **slept** [slɛpt], **kept** [kɛpt], **crept** [krɛpt].

**343.** A [t] is sometimes added in popular speech after [s] in words where it does not appear in standard speech, as in [wʌnst], [twaɪst] for **once**, **twice**, [wɪʃt] for **wish**, [əˈkrɔst] for **across**, [kloːst] for **close**. So also [əˈtækt] for **attack** [əˈtæk]. On the other hand, [t] is frequently omitted after [s] in popular speech, as in [dʒʌs], [rɪs], [hoːs], [nɛks] for **just** [dʒʌst], **wrist** [rɪst], **host** [hoːst], **next** [nɛkst], etc. In **waistcoat, Westcott**, the final consonant of the first syllable is usually silent, both words being pronounced [ˈwɛskət]. But **waistcoat** is rarely used in America, the common word being **vest.** In **locust** few cultivated speakers would acknowledge omitting the final consonant, yet in current speech it is doubtful if one ever hears it.

**344.** In the combination [kt], [t] is sometimes omitted in the popular dialects, **insect** [ˈɪnsɛkt], **contact** [ˈkɑntækt], **perfect** [ˈpəɹfɪkt], **aqueduct** [ˈækwɪˌdʌkt], becoming [ˈɪnsɛk], [ˈkɑntæk], [ˈpəɹfɪk], [ˈækwɪˌdʌk], etc.

**345.** For **partner** [ˈpɑːɹtnəɹ], popular speech often has [ˈpɑːɹdnəɹ].

**346.** In **asked** [aːskt], [æskt], many speakers pronounce no [t], saying [æsk], especially when the next word begins with a consonant; or some speakers omit [k], lengthening the preceding consonant, as in [æsːt]. In no case, not even in the most formal or careful speech, are both a fully articulated [k] and [t] pronounced. What happens in cultivated speech is that after [s] the tongue position for [k] is assumed, but is held without explosion until the position for [t] has been reached. There is thus only one genuine stop consonant in **asked**. Other words of this type, like **basked, masked**, etc., are not in familiar use and are consequently likely to be pronounced with emphasis on the orthographic elements of the words. See § 15.

In a combination like **next time**, usually only one **t** is pronounced, as in [nɛks taɪm]; in **next station** both **s** and **t** of **next** are usually silent in cultivated colloquial speech, as in [nɛk 'steːʃən]. And as a matter of fact, even the [k] is often not fully articulated; the stoppage for [k] is assumed, but the explosion is not completed.

In the spelling **eighth**, the **th** stands for **tth**, though the explosion for the **t** is not completely made. The **gh** being silent, the phonetic form of the word is approximately [eːtθ].

[θ]

**347.** The spelling for this sound is always **th**, but this spelling stands for both [θ] and [ð], see §§ 30, 31.

Examples of [θ] are **path** [paːθ], [pæθ], **thin** [θɪn], **faith** [feːθ], **both** [boːθ], **month** [mʌnθ], **froth** [frɔθ], **frothy** ['frɔθɪ], **myth** [mɪθ], **mythology** [mɪ'θɑlədʒɪ].

**348.** A **th** of the spelling is pronounced [t] in **thyme** [taɪm], **Thomas** ['tɑməs], ['tɔməs], **Thompson** ['tɑmpsən], ['tɔmpsən]. For **isthmus** only ['ɪsθməs] is current in America, but in England both ['ɪsθməs] and ['ɪstməs]. In rapid speech the word may become ['ɪsməs]. For **Esther** the common pronunciation is ['ɛstəɹ], but occasionally also ['ɛsθəɹ]. The **Thames**, a river in England and in Connecticut, is always [tɛmz]. The proper name **Anthony** is usually ['ænθənɪ], sometimes ['æntənɪ], though when pronounced in the latter way, it is usually made to conform in spelling.

**349.** In the combination [fθ], [sθ], popular speech often has [t] for [θ], as in [fɪft] for **fifth** [fɪfθ] or [fɪftθ], [sɪkst] for **sixth** [sɪksθ] or [sɪkstθ]. In **months** popular speech often omits [θ], pronouncing the word [mʌns].

**350.** For standard **height** [haɪt], popular usage also has [haɪtθ], parallel to **width, breadth, length.**

[ð]

**351.** This sound is the voiced equivalent of [θ] and is spelled **th.** In the earlier stages of the language [ð] occurred only between vowels or between a voiced consonant and a vowel. In relatively unstressed position, however, voiceless continuants tend to become voiced, [θ] becoming [ð], and many words like **this** [ðɪs], **that** [ðæt], **they** [ðeɪ], **thou** [ðaʊ], **then** [ðɛn], **than** [ðæn], **though** [ðoʊ], **with** [wɪð], which are only slightly stressed in the word groups in which they occur, have now [ð] instead of earlier [θ]. Analogy and the loss of vowels in unstressed syllables also obscure the old rule, so that now [ð] appears not only between vowels, but also finally in words like **bathe** [beːð], **breathe** [briːð], **lathe** [leːð], **clothe** [kloːð], **sheathe** [ʃiːð], **wreathe** [riːð], and many others.

**352.** Singular nouns with final [θ] may change to [ð] in the plural, as in **path** [pæθ], **paths** [pæðz], **bath** [bæθ], **baths** [bæðz], **moth** [mɔθ], **moths** [mɔðz]; but the analogy of the singular may maintain [θ] in the plural, as in **Goth** [gɔθ], **Goths** [gɔθs], **breath** [brɛθ], **breaths** [brɛθs], **death** [dɛθ], **deaths** [dɛθs]. A plural **moths** [mɔθs] is recorded in the dictionaries, but the only form the writer has ever heard is [mɔðz].

**353.** For **rhythm** both [rɪðm] and [rɪθm] occur, the former being much the more common. The same diversity of use appears in derivatives, as in **rhythmic, rhythmical**, but some speakers who pronounce [rɪðm] in the simple word, say [ˈrɪθmɪk], [ˈrɪθmɪkl] in the derivatives, the reason being that in the derivatives the consonant stands at the end of a syllable, not between two voiced sounds, as in [rɪðm].

**354.** For **asthma** the current formal pronunciation is [ˈæzðmə], though often also [ˈæzmə]. The British pronunciation is [ˈæsθmə], [ˈæsmə] or [ˈæstmə].

**355.** Before [z], in popular speech [ð] is often omitted, as in **clothes** [kloːðz] pronounced [kloːz], **oaths** [oːðz] pronounced [oːz], etc.

**356.** In the popular dialects [θ], [ð] sometimes completely disappear, being replaced by [t] and [d], as in **think** pronounced [tɪŋk], **that** pronounced [dæt], **with** pronounced [wɪt] or [wɪd].

[f]

**357.** The representation of [f] in the ordinary spelling is **f**, **ff**, **gh** or **ph**, as in **find** [faɪnd], **stiff** [stɪf], **sniffed** [snɪft], **rough** [rʌf], **cough** [kɔːf], **Brough** [brʌf], **laugh** [laːf], [læf], **nephew** [ˈnɛfju], **philosophy** [fɪlˈɔsəfɪ], **sylph** [sɪlf]. For **lieutenant** [luˈtɛnənt] the pronunciation [lɛfˈtɛnənt], [lɪf–], is sometimes heard, but it is not general with any group of American speakers. It is common in England. For **nephew** both [ˈnɛfju] and [ˈnɛvju] occur, though the former is the more general pronunciation. For **hiccough** the only pronunciation is [ˈhɪkəp]. For the history of this word, see the New English Dictionary.

**358.** In the connected discourse of colloquial usage, a final [v] is sometimes assimilated to a succeeding voiceless consonant, becoming [f], as in **I have to go** [ə ˈhæf tə ˈgoʊ]. But what might be permissible in this phrase, is not permissible generally, e.g., one cannot say **I'd love to go** [aɪd ˈlʌf tə ˈgoʊ].

**359.** In the combination **phth** the pronunciation [f] for **ph** is sometimes replaced by [p], as in **diphthong** [ˈdɪfθɔŋ] or [ˈdɪpθɔŋ], **diphtheria** [dɪfˈθɪrɪə] or [dɪpˈθɪrɪə], **naphtha** [ˈnæfθə] or [ˈnæpθə]. The pronunciation with [f] is perhaps to be preferred, though usage is far from being uniform. See § 299. For **phthisic** the accepted pronunciation is [ˈtɪzɪk], but **phthisis** is said to be pronounced [ˈθaɪsɪs]. Neither word is in common use.

### [v]

**360.** This sound is the voiced equivalent of [f], and is commonly represented by **v**, as in **live** [lɪv] (*verb*), [laɪv] (*adj.*), **vivid** [ˈvɪvɪd], **shoved** [ʃʌvd], **dived** [daɪvd]. In **nephew** [ˈnɛvju] and **Stephen** [ˈstiːvən] it is spelled **ph.**

**361.** When [f] of a main form becomes voiced in an inflectional form, the spelling always changes to **v**, as in **wife** [wɑɪf], **wives** [waɪvz], **loaf** [loːf], **loaves** [loːvz], etc., but **wife's** [waɪfs], **griefs** [griːfs], **laughs** [laːfs], [læfs], third singular present of the verb, or plural of the noun, where the consonant remains unchanged.

Some plurals have both a form with [f] and one with [v], as in **hoof** [huːf], **hoofs** [huːfs] or **hooves** [huːvz]; **scarf** [skɑːɹf], **scarfs** [skɑːɹfs] or **scarves** [skɑːɹvz]. The plural of **staff** is **staffs**, except as a technical term in music, where it is **staves** [steːvz].

**362.** In archaic and poetic style an intervocalic [v] is sometimes omitted, the omission being indicated by the apostrophe, as in **e'er** [ɛːəɹ] for **ever, o'er** [ɔːəɹ] for **over,** etc.

**363.** The preposition **of** usually stands in unstressed position and is pronounced [əv], or in rapid speech [ə], as in **five o'clock** [faɪv ə klɑk], **time of day** [taɪm ə deɪ], **man of war** [mæn ə wɔːɹ].

**364.** Final [v] in **give** is sometimes omitted before [m] in colloquial speech, **give me** [ˈgɪv mɪ] becoming [ˈgɪ mɪ]. This is spelled in dialect orthography as *gimme*, and though by no means limited to illiterate or dialect use, under the influence of the printed and written language it is coming to be more and more discredited. Cf. **let me** pronounced [ˈlɛmɪ], and see above, § 100.

[w]

**365.** The spelling of this sound is commonly **w**, as in **win** [wɪn], **swing** [swɪŋ], **twig** [twɪg], **between** [bɪˈtwiːn], or **u**, as in **languid** [ˈlæŋgwɪd], **language** [læŋˈgwɪdʒ], **persuade** [pəɹˈsweːd], and **u** after **q**, as in **quire** [ˈkwaɪəɹ], **question** [ˈkwɛstʃən], **quack** [kwæk], **conquest** [ˈkɑnkwɛst] or [ˈkɑŋkwɛst].

**366.** The spelling **gu** represents usually [g], as in **guard** [gɑːɹd], **guest** [gɛst], **guide** [gaɪd], **guess** [gɛs], **guile** [gaɪl], etc., but in a few words of foreign origin, as in **guano** [ˈgwɑːno], **guava** [ˈgwɑːvə], and in **Guelph** [gwɛlf], the **u** is pronounced.

**367.** The sound [w] appears in **one** [wʌn], **once** [wʌns], in pronunciaton but not in spelling. The verb **won** and **one** are exact homonyms. A **w** appears in the spelling of **two** [tuː], **sword** [sɔːɹd], but not in pronunciation. Before **r** a silent **w** is frequently written, as in **wring** [rɪŋ], **write** [wraɪt], **wrap** [ræp], **wrist** [rɪst], etc. For **choir** the pronunciation is the same as for **quire**, that is [ˈkwaɪəɹ].

**368.** In a few words of French origin the ending **–oir** is pronounced [–wɑɹ] or [–wɔɹ], as in **memoir** [ˈmɛmwɑɹ], [ˈmɛmwɔɹ], **reservoir** [ˈrɛzəɹˌvwɑɹ], [ˈrɛzəɹˌvwɔɹ]; but **reservoir** is also often pronounced without [w], as [ˈrɛzəɹˌvɔɪəɹ].

**369.** An initial **w** of an unstressed syllable following a stressed one sometimes weakens and disappears, as regularly in **answer** [ˈænsəɹ], and in the combination **qu** in **chequer** [ˈtʃɛkəɹ], **conquer** [ˈkɑŋkəɹ], **liquor** [ˈlɪkəɹ]. In compositional syllables, like -**ward**, -**worth**, -**wich**, -**wick**, which have a secondary stress in American speech, **w** is generally pronounced when written; but in **toward**, **towards** [tɔːɹd], [tɔːɹdz] the words are monosyllables without [w]. Thus in proper names, as in **Woodward**, **Woolworth**, **Woolwich** (Maine), **Norwich**, **Greenwich**, etc., [w] is pronounced, except that one may occasionally hear [ˈgriːnɪtʃ], [ˈgrɪnɪtʃ], as a literary or acquired pronunciation. In the town in Connecticut of that name, the local pronunciation is [ˈgriːnˌwɪtʃ].

**370.** A **w** frequently appears in spelling, at the ends of words, which has no consonantal value but is merely an orthographic survival from an earlier [w] which became vocalic and which would thus be more accurately represented by **u**. Conventional spelling, however, rarely permits **u** to stand at the end of a word, exceptions being **thou** [ðɑʊ], and a few foreign words like **gnu** [nuː], **zebu** [ˈziːˌbu·]. A vocalized **w** stands in the spelling of **draw** [drɔː], **know** [noʊ], **sow** [soʊ], [sɑʊ], **few** [fjuː], **grew** [gruː], **now** [nɑʊ], etc. The spelling with **w** persists in derivative forms, but is silent there also, as in **drawing** [ˈdrɔːɪŋ], **sower** [ˈsoːəɹ], **fewer** [ˈfjuːəɹ].

**371.** A **w** with no consonantal value appears occasionally in spelling before consonants, as in **bawl** [bɔːl], **yawl** [jɔːl], **hawk** [hɔːk], **bowl** [boːl], **howl** [hɑʊl], **brown** [brɑʊn], **drowse** [drɑʊz], **newt** [njuːt], **mewl** [mjuːl], or before a weak syllable with [ɹ], [l], [n], as in **power** [ˈpɑʊəɹ], **towel** [ˈtɑʊəl], **Owen** [ˈoːən], **Cowan** [ˈkɑʊən], etc.

[ʍ]

**372.** This sound is the voiceless equivalent of [w], and in America it is generally pronounced wherever written **wh**, as in **what** [ʍɑt], **which** [ʍɪtʃ], **wheat** [ʍiːt], **whit** [ʍɪt], **white** [ʍaɪt], **whisper** [ˈʍɪspəɹ], etc. Some speakers, however, pronounce all these voiceless sounds voiced, as in **whit** [wɪt] not distinguished from **wit**, **white** [waɪt] not distinguished from **wight**. Though not vulgarisms, such pronunciations are usually discountenanced by careful speakers and in formal instruction. In standard British speech of the Southern type **w** and **wh** are generally both pronounced as [w].

**373.** In **who** and derived forms of **who**, **whole**, the initial consonant is neither [w] nor [ʍ], but [h], as in [huː], [hoːl]. So also **whoop**, **whooping-cough**, which may be spelled **hoop**, **hooping-cough**, are pronounced [huːp], [ˈhuːpɪŋ-] or [ˈhʊpɪŋˌkɔːf].

## EXERCISES

(1) Make a collection of sounds not used in articulate speech (e.g., the sigh, cough, cluck, click, sniff, 'humph,' 'huh,' 'eh,' 'hm,' the sound for calling a cat, for starting horses, etc.), and analyze them phonetically. Record them in phonetic script, inventing symbols when necessary. See §§ 3, 4.

(2) Take a page of any ordinary English prose and make a list in phonetic script of all the words containing (*a*) voiced stops, (*b*) voiceless stops, (*c*) voiced continuants, (*d*) voiceless continuants.

(3) In these words, note what sounds have been affected, and in what way, by their proximity to other sounds. See § 6.

(4) Make a list from the same passage of all words containing fricative continuants, lateral continuants and nasal continuants.

(5) Make lists in phonetic script of all the words on this same page which contain the same vowel sound.

(6) Go through this page and note the instances in which the ordinary spelling is the same or approximately the same as the phonetic transcriptions.

(7) In the same passage, observe where the breaks or pauses come in natural easy reading. Transcribe the passage into these 'breath groups' instead of the usual division into words. See § 100.

A minute study of a single passage, such as is suggested in Exercises 2–7, is better preliminary discipline than the study of scattering texts.

(8) Practice the vowel sounds in sequence, starting with the lowest unround vowel and proceeding to the highest, then the lowest rounded vowel, proceeding to the highest; reverse the process, starting with the high vowels.

(9) Practice such pairs of sounds as [e] and [ɛ], [i] and [ɪ], [u] and [ʊ], [o] and [ɔ], [ʌ] and [ʌː], [ɔ] and [ɔː], until the distinction between tense and slack sounds is quite clear.

(10) Pronounce the sentences **It was covered with furs, It was covered with firs, It was covered with furze, It was covered with fuzz**, to a hearer, and see if he can tell when you mean **furs, firs, furze, fuzz.** If you do not pronounce these words alike, analyze the organic differences.

As a similar exercise pronounce the sentence **The container was well caulked** and **The container was well corked**, and see if a hearer can tell which word you have in mind. If so, extend the experiment to other persons to see if the words are always audibly distinct.

(11) Make a collection of difficult phrases, like **Peter Piper pickt a peck of pickled peppers, She sells sea-shells**, etc., and analyze their phonetic character. Make a collection of phrases which are memorable not for their difficulty but for their phonetic 'haunting' quality, agreeable or disagreeable, e.g., **a pink trip slip for a five cent fare; the exhaustless grace of Niagara's emerald curve; the multitudinous seas incarnadine**, etc. Each person's list will naturally be different from any other. Make a list of alliterative phrases, like **bag and baggage, stock and stone, head and heels, time and tide.** Make a list of striking alliterative phrases, such as are often met with in newspaper headlines. An interesting study of consonant sounds can be made on the basis of Lyly's

*Euphues*, or still better, George Pettie's *Petite Pallace of Pleasure* (1576), in which the resources of the language in sounds are utilized with the utmost ingenuity for the purpose of stylistic ornamentation.

(12) Take a word containing an initial voiceless stop, e.g., **pay**, and practice this stop with and without audible aspiration until the difference becomes clear. See § 13. Then pronounce words containing a voiceless stop between voiced sounds, as in **witty**, **putty**, **potato**, **dainty**, **bottle**, **pippin**, **winter**, **better**, **water**, **stopper**, etc., with weak and with audible aspiration, and note which is the better pronunciation. See § 14.

(13) Analyze fully the phonetic elements of a number of words like **stripped**, **booked**, **robbed**, **drugged**. See § 15.

(14) Repeat pairs of words like **sit** and **sin**, **pit** and **pin**, **bid** and **bin**, **did** and **din**, and then segregate the final consonants in order to study the difference between stop consonants and nasal continuants.

(15) Repeat pairs of words like **sin** and **sing**, **win** and **wing**, to make clear the difference between [n] and [ŋ].

(16) Repeat groups of words like **sin**, **sing**, **sink**; **win**, **wing**, **wink**; **thin**, **thing**, **think**, and then analyze their phonetic elements.

(17) Note the sound of [n] in **fount**, **found**; **shunt**, **shunned**; **sun**, **sunset**, **Sunday**, **sunbeam**. Is it equally long in all these words? Study in general the length of the continuant consonants in different combinations.

(18) Note the length of the vowel in **led**, **let**; **bed**, **bet**; **said**, **set**; **sad**, **sat**; **hod**, **hot**, etc. Though these are all short vowels, are they all equally short? Cf. § 80.

(19) Examine all the occurrences of [z] on a page of ordinary prose, and note in what instances the sound ends in a voiceless vanish. See § 36.

(20) Study the difference in the sound of [ŋ] in **sing** and **song**, and collect other words illustrating the same difference.

(21) Study the sound of [k] in **keel** and **call**, of [g] in **geese** and **gall**, of [h] in **heel** and **haul**, and add other illustrations of the same variation in the quality of the consonant.

(22) Imitate the speech of one who has a cold in the head, and indicate its phonetic character in transcription.

(23) Take a passage of ordinary colloquial prose and pronounce the vowels as nasally as you can, that is, caricature it. Then pronounce the vowels with as little nasalization as possible. Does your own speech fall between these two extremes?

(24) Observe in the speech of those with whom you come in contact, any manner of speech which might be characterized as 'drawling,' and describe its phonetic character.

(25) Some of the vague descriptive adjectives which are occasionally applied to speech or to special sounds are 'broad,' 'rough,' 'flat,' 'liquid,' 'thin,' 'mushy,' 'muddy,' 'crisp,' 'sharp.' Add others to this list, and endeavor to determine what is meant by them in terms of the organic analysis of speech.

(26) Make a collection of those speech characteristics which in your estimation are evidences (*a*) of special refinement or distinction in speech, (*b*) of 'common' or unrefined speech. Try to determine how generally your judgments would be acceptable to others.

(27) Examine the pronunciation of **r** in the speech of as many different persons as possible, and note how many types of **r**-sound are distinguishable within the range of your observation.

(28) Start a list of words which may be stressed in two or more different ways.

(29) Transcribe in phonetic notation (*a*) first your own speech in detached phrases as you can hear yourself pronounce them, (*b*) your own speech in connected conversation, (*c*) your own speech as you hear it in reading aloud.

(30) Transcribe in phonetic notation the speech of some other person or persons than yourself. For this purpose, choose one or two individuals whose speech you have the best opportunity of studying, and preferably whose speech impresses you as being ordinarily somewhat different from your own. Proceed very slowly at first, transcribing only phrases which you are sure you have heard correctly.

(31) Take a passage of English prose and transcribe it first into very formal literary style, then into ordinary reading style, and then into very familiar colloquial style.

(32) If your own speech is of the Eastern American type, transcribe a passage illustrating it into Western American speech, etc.

(33) Transcribe the passages of dialect speech given in this volume into informal standard speech.

(34) Make a transcription of some dialect speech with which you are orally familiar. Indicate the elements in this pronunciation which are really dialectal and those which are merely standard colloquial.

(35) Transcribe the passages of British pronunciation given in this volume into standard American pronunciation.

These exercises are not systematically arranged, and are not intended to be exhaustive either of the topics discussed in this book or of the points of interest which may engage the attention of the student of phonetics. They are merely suggestive, and the number of them will readily be increased in the practical work of the class-room.

# BIBLIOGRAPHICAL NOTE

Of the numerous works on general phonetics, perhaps the most useful brief books in English are *Elements of Phonetics* by Walter Rippmann (on the basis of Viëtor's *Kleine Phonetik*), published by J. M. Dent and Sons; *Introduction to Phonetics* by Laura Soames (The Macmillan Co.); *General Phonetics* by G. Noël-Armfield (W. Heffer and Sons, Cambridge, Eng., 1915). For special studies of English pronunciation, reference may be made to *The Pronunciation of English* by Daniel Jones (Cambridge University Press), and to various other publications by Jones, including *A Phonetic Dictionary of the English Language* by Hermann Michaelis and Daniel Jones (Carl Meyer, Hannover and Berlin); *The Pronunciation of English in Scotland* by William Grant (Cambridge University Press); *Northern English* by R. J. Lloyd (Teubner, Leipzig and Berlin, 1908), particularly valuable for the comparison of British and American English; *The Sounds of Spoken English* by Walter Rippmann (J. M. Dent and Sons). Little has been done in the way of special study of American speech, but reference should be made to Professor Grandgent's article, *English in America*, in *Die Neueren Sprachen*, II, 443–467 (1894), where a further bibliography of publications by Professor Grandgent will be found; also in the same journal, II, 520–528, a group of phonetic transcriptions. *From Franklin to Lowell, A Century of New England Pronunciation*, by Professor Grandgent, in the Publications of the Modern Language Association, XIV, 207–239, gives a valuable historical survey of New England speech. The various numbers of *Dialect Notes*, the publication of the American Dialect Society, should also be consulted. On the general question of standard, the student may consult the two books by Professor Lounsbury, *The Standard of Usage in English* and *The Standard of Pronunciation in English* (Harpers, New York). For the general history of English sounds, see Jespersen, *A Modern English Grammar*, Part I, Sounds and Spellings (Winter, Heidelberg, 1909). As a number of the books mentioned in this note are appearing from time to time in new editions, it is advisable in ordering always to ask for the latest edition.

# TRANSCRIPTIONS

## I

### **ʹdeɪ-ˋdriːmz**

æz aɪ wəz stɛpɪŋ əʹʃɔːɹ, aɪ wəz ʹgriːtɪd baɪ ʹmɪstəɹ bəɹn, hu ʹpæsɪz ðə ʹsʌməɹ ɔn ðɪ ʹaɪlənd, nd hu ʹhɑspɪtəblɪ æskt ɪf aɪ wəɹ ʹgoːɪŋ hɪz weɪ. hɪz weɪ wəz tɔːɹd ðə ʹsʌðəɹn ɛnd əv ðɪ ʹaɪlənd, nd aɪ sɛd jɛs. hɪz ʹpɑkɪts wəɹ fʊl əv ʹpeːpəɹz nd hɪz brɑʊ əv ʹrɪŋklz; so ʍɛn wɪ riːtʃt ðə pɔɪnt ʍɛɹ hiː ʃʊd təɹn ɔːf, aɪ æskt ɪm tə lɛt mɪ əʹlaɪt, ɔlʹðoː hi wəz ʹvɛrɪ ʹæŋkʃəs tə ʹkærɪ mi ʍɛrʹɛvəɹ aɪ wəz ʹgoːɪŋ.

"aɪm ʹoːnlɪ ʹstroːlɪŋ əʹbɑʊt," aɪ ʹænsəɹd, æz aɪ ʹklæmbəɹd ʹkɛːɹfəlɪ ɑʊt əv ðə ʹwægn.

"ʹstroːlɪŋ əʹbɑʊt?" æskt hiː, ɪn ə bɪʹwɪldəɹd ʹmænəɹ; "du ʹpiːpl stroːl əʹbɑʊt, ʹnɑʊ-ə-ˋdeɪz?"

"səmʹtaɪmz," aɪ ʹænsəɹd, ʹsmaɪlɪŋ, æz aɪ pʊld maɪ ʹtrɑʊzəɹz dɑʊn ʹovəɹ maɪ buːts, fɔɹ ðe· hæd drægd ʌp, æz aɪ stɛpt ɑʊt əv ðə ʹwægn, "nd bɪʹsaɪd, ʍɑt kn n oːld ʹbʊˋkːiːpəɹ du ʹbɛtəɹ ɪn ðə dʌl ʹsiːzn ðən stroːl əʹbɑʊt ðɪs ʹplɛznt ʹaɪlənd, n wɔtʃ ðə ʃɪps æt siː?"

bəɹn lʊkt æt mi ẇɪð hɪz ʹwɪərɪ aɪz. "aɪd gɪv faɪv ʹðɑʊzənd ʹdɑləɹz ə ʹjɪəɹ fɔɹ ə dʌl ʹsiːzən," sɛd hiː, "bət æz fəɹ ʹstroːlɪŋ, aɪv fəɹʹgɑtn hɑʊ."

æz hi spoːk, hɪz aɪz ʹwɔndəɹd ʹdriːmɪlɪ əʹkrɔs ðə fiːldz nd wʊdz, nd wəɹ ʹfæsnd əʹpɔn ðə ʹdɪstənt seɪlz.

“ɪt ɪz ˈplɛznt,” hi sɛd ˈmjuzɪŋlɪ, ænd fɛl ˈɪntʊ ˈsaɪ-
25 ləns. bət aɪ həd no taɪm tə spɛːɹ, so aɪ wɪʃt ɪm ˌgʊd-
ˈæftəɹˌnuːn.

“aɪ hoːp jəɹ waɪf s wɛl,” sɛd bəɹn tə mɪ, æz aɪ
təɹnd əˈweɪ. ˈpʊəɹ bəɹn! hi droːv ɔn əˈloːn ɪn hɪz
ˈwægn.

30 bət aɪ me·d heːst tə ðə moːst ˈsɑlɪˌtɛrɪ pɔɪnt əpɔn
ðə ˈsʌðəɹn ʃɔːɹ, ænd ðɛːɹ sæt, glæd tə bi so ˈnɪəɹ ðə
siː. ðɛɹ wəz ðæt wɔːɹm, ˌsɪmpəˈθɛtɪk ˈsaɪləns ɪn ðɪ
ɛːɹ, ðət gɪvz tə ˈɪndɪn-ˈsʌməɹ deɪz ˈɔlˌmo·st ə ˈhjumən ˈtɛndəɹnəs əv ˈfiːlɪŋ. ə ˈdɛlɪkɪt heɪz, ðət siːmd
35 ˈoːnlɪ ðə ˈkaɪndlɪ ɛːɹ me·d ˈvɪzɪbl, hʌŋ ovəɹ ðə siː.
ðə ˈwɔtəɹ læpt ˈlæŋgwɪdlɪ əˈmʌŋ ðə rɑks, ænd ðə
ˈvɔɪsəz əv ˈtʃɪldrən ɪn ə boːt bɪˈjɔnd, ræŋ ˈmjuzɪkəlɪ,
ænd ˈgrædʒuəlɪ rɪˈsiːdɪd, ənˈtɪl ðe· wəɹ lɔst ɪn ðə
ˈdɪstəns.

40 ɪt wəz sʌm taɪm bɪˈfɔːɹ aɪ wəz əˈwɛːɹ əv ðɪ ˈɑʊt-
ˌlaɪn əv ə lɑːɹdʒ ʃɪp, drɔːn ˈveːglɪ əˈpɔn ðə mɪst, ʍɪtʃ
aɪ səˈpoːzd, æt fəɹst, tə bi ˈoːnlɪ ə kaɪnd əv mɪˈrɑːʒ.
bət ðə mɔːɹ ˈstɛdˌfæstlɪ aɪ geɪzd, ðə mɔːr dɪsˈtɪŋkt ɪt
bɪˈkeːm, ænd aɪ kʊd no ˈlɔŋgəɹ dɑʊt ðæt aɪ sɔː ə
45 ˈsteːtlɪ ʃɪp ˈlaɪɪŋ æt ˈæŋkəɹ, nɑt mɔːɹ ðən hæf ə maɪl
frəm ðə lænd.

“ɪts n ɪkˈstrɔːɹdɪˌnɛrɪ pleːs tə ˈæŋkəɹ,” aɪ sɛd tə
ˌmaɪˈsɛlf, “ɔɹ kæn ʃi bi əˈʃɔːɹ?”

ðɛɹ wəɹ no saɪnz əv dɪsˈtrɛs; ðə seɪlz wəɹ ˈkɛːɹfəlɪ
50 kluːd ʌp, ænd ðɛɹ wəɹ no ˈseːləɹz ɪn ðə tɑps, nɔɹ
əˈpɔn ðə ʃrɑʊdz. ə flæg, əv ʍɪtʃ aɪ kʊd nɑt siː ðə
dɪˈvaɪs ɔɹ ˈneːʃən, hʌŋ ˈhɛvɪlɪ æt ðə stəɹn, ænd lʊkt
æz ɪf ɪt hæd ˈfɔːln əˈsliːp. maɪ ˈkjʊrɪˈɑsɪtɪ bɪˈgæn tə
bi ˈsɪŋgjuləɹlɪ ɪkˈsaɪtɪd. ðə fɔːɹm əv ðə ˈvɛsl siːmd
55 nɑt tə bi ˈpəɹmənənt; bət wɪðˈɪn ə ˈkwɔɹtəɹ əv ən
ˈɑʊəɹ, aɪ wəz ˈʃʊəɹ ðæt aɪ hæd siːn hæf ə ˈdʌzn ˈdɪf-

rənt ʃɪps. æz aɪ geɪzd, aɪ sɔː no mɔːɹ seɪlz nɔɹ mæsts,
bət ə lɔŋ reɪndʒ əv ˈɔːɹəɹz, ˈflæʃɪŋ laɪk ə ˈgoːldn frɪndʒ,
ɔɹ streːt nd stɪf, laɪk ðə lɛgz əv ə ˈsiː-ˌmɔnstəɹ.
60 "ɪts sʌm ˈbloːtɪd kræb, əɹ ˈlɑbstəɹ, ˈmægnɪˌfaɪd baɪ
ðə mɪst," aɪ sɛd tə maɪˈsɛlf, kəmˈple·səntlɪ.
bʌt, æt ðə seːm ˈmoːmənt, ðɛɹ wəz ə ˈkɑnsɛnˌtre·tɪd
ˈflæʃɪŋ nd ˈbleːzɪŋ ɪn wʌn spɑt əˈmʌŋ ðə ˈrɪgɪŋ, ænd
ɪt wɑz æz ɪf aɪ sɔː ə bɪˈætɪfaɪd ræm, ɔɹ, mɔːɹ ˈtruːlɪ, ə
65 ˈʃiːp-ˌskɪn, ˈsplɛndɪd æz ðə hɛːɹ əv ˌbɛrəˈnaɪsɪ.
"ɪz ðæt ðə ˈgoːldn fliːs?" aɪ *θ*ɔːt. "bət ˈʃʊəɹlɪ, ˈdʒeː-
sən nd ðɪ ˈɑːɹgəˌnɔːts hæv gɔːn hoːm lɔŋ sɪns. du
ˈpiːpl goː ɔn ˈgoːld-ˌfliːsɪŋ ɛkspɪˈdɪʃənz nɑʊ?" aɪ æskt
maɪˈsɛlf, ɪn pəɹˈplɛksɪtɪ. "kæn ðɪs bi ə kælɪˈfɔɹnjə
70 ˈstiːməɹ?"
hɑʊ kʊd aɪ hæv *θ*ɔːt ɪt ə ˈstiːməɹ? dɪd aɪ nɑt siː
ðoːz seɪlz, "*θ*ɪn ənd ˈsɪəɹ"? dɪd aɪ nɑt fiːl ðə ˈmɛlən-
ˌkɑlɪ əv ðæt ˈsɑlɪˌtɛrɪ bɑːɹk? ɪt hæd ə ˈmɪstɪk ˈɔːrə;
ə ˈbɔrɪəl ˈbrɪljənsɪ ˈʃɪməɹd ɪn ɪts weːk, fɔɹ ɪt wəz
75 ˈdrɪftɪŋ ˈsiːwəɹd. ə streɪndʒ ˈfɪəɹ ˈkəɹdld əˈlɔŋ maɪ
veɪnz. ðæt ˈsʌməɹ sʌn ʃoːn kuːl. ðə ˈwɪərɪ ˈbætəɹd
ʃɪp wəz gæʃt, æz ɪf nɔːd baɪ aɪs. ðɛɹ wəz ˈtɛrəɹ ɪn
ðə ɛːɹ, æz ə "ˈskɪnɪ hænd so brɑʊn" weɪvd tʊ mi
frəm ðə dɛk. aɪ leɪ æz wʌn bɪˈwɪtʃt. ðə hænd əv ðɪ
80 ˈeːntʃənt ˈmærɪnəɹ siːmd tə bi ˈriːtʃɪŋ fɔɹ mi, laɪk ðə
hænd əv dɛ*θ*.
dɛ*θ*? ʍaɪ, æz aɪ wəz ˈɪnlɪ ˈpreːɪŋ pruːz fəɹˈgɪvnəs
fɔɹ maɪ ˈsɑlɪˌtɛrɪ ˈræmbl nd ˈkɑnsɪˌkwɛnt dɪˈmaɪz, ə
glæns laɪk ðə ˈfʊlnəs əv ˈsʌməɹ ˈsplɛndəɹ gʌʃt ovəɹ
85 mi; ðɪ ˈoːdəɹ əv ˈflɑʊəɹz ənd əv ˈiːstəɹn gʌmz me·d
ɔːl ðɪ ˈætməsˌfɪəɹ. aɪ briːðd ðɪ ˈɔrɪˌɛnt, ənd leɪ
drʌŋk wɪð bɑːm, ʍaɪl ðæt streɪndʒ ʃɪp, ə ˈgoːldn
ˈgælɪ nɑʊ, wɪð ˈglɪtərɪŋ ˈdreːpɛˌriz fɛsˈtuːnd wɪð
ˈflɑʊəɹz, peːst tʊ ðə ˈmɛʒəɹd biːt əv ˈɔːəɹz əˈlɔŋ ðə

90 kaːm, ənd ˈkliəˈpeːtrə smaɪld əˈluːrɪŋlɪ fram ðə greˑt ˈpædʒənts haːɹt.

waz ðɪs ə baːɹdʒ fɔɹ ˈsʌməɹ ˈwɔtəɹz, ðɪs pɪˈkjuljəɹ ʃɪp aɪ sɔː? ɪt hæd ə ˈruɪnd ˈdɪgnɪtɪ, ə ˈkʌmbrəs ˈgrændʒəɹ, ɔlˈðoː ɪts mæsts wəɹ ˈʃætəɹd, nd ɪts seɪlz 95 rɛnt. ɪt hʌŋ ˈpritəɹˈnætʃɛrɪlɪ stɪl əˈpɔn ðə siː, æz ɪf tɔɹˈmɛntɪd nd ɪgˈzɔːstɪd baɪ lɔŋ ˈdraɪvɪŋ nd ˈdrɪftɪŋ. aɪ sɔː no ˈseːləɹz, bət ə greˑt ˈspænɪʃ ˈɛnsaɪn ˈfloːtɪd ˈovəɹ, ænd weɪvd, ə fjuˈnɪrɪəl pluːm. aɪ njuː ɪt ðɛn. ðɪ aɹˈmaːdə wəz lɔŋ sɪns ˈskætəɹd; bət ˈfloːtɪŋ faːɹ

100 ɔn ˈdɛsoˈleˑt ˈreːmɪ siːz,

lɔst fɔr ˈsɛntʃʊˈriz, ənd əˈgɛn rɪˈstɔɹd tʊ saɪt, ˈhɪəɹ leɪ wʌn əv ðə ˈfeːtɪd ʃɪps əv speɪn. ðə hjudʒ ˈgælɪjən siːmd tə fɪl ɔːl ðɪ ɛːɹ, bɪlt ʌp əˈgɛnst ðə skaɪ, laɪk ðə ˈgɪldɪd ʃɪps əv klɔːd lɔˈreɪn əˈgɛnst ðə ˈsʌnˈsɛt.

105 bət ɪt flɛd, fɔɹ naʊ ə blæk flæg ˈflʌtəɹd æt ðə ˈmæstˈhɛd — ə lɔŋ loʊ ˈvɛsl ˈdaːɹtɪd ˈswɪftlɪ ʍɛːɹ ðə væst ʃɪp leɪ; ðɛɹ keˑm ə ʃrɪl ˈpaɪpɪŋ ˈʍɪsl, ðə klæʃ əv ˈkʌtlɪsəz, fɪəɹs ˈrɪŋɪŋ oʊðz, ʃaɹp ˈpɪstəl kræks, ðə ˈθʌndəɹ əv kəˈmænd, ənd ˈovəɹ ɔːl ðə ˈgʌstɪ jɛl əv ə 110 dɪˈmoˑnɪæk ˈkɔrəs,

maɪ neɪm wəz rabəɹt kɪd, ʍɛn aɪ seɪld.

— ðɛɹ wəɹ no klaʊdz ˈlɔŋgəɹ, bət ˈʌndəɹ ə sɪˈriːn skaɪ aɪ sɔː ə baːɹk ˈmʌvɪŋ wɪð ˈfɛstəl pɔmp, θrɔŋd wɪð greɪv ˈsɛnəˈtɔɹz ɪn ˈfloːɪŋ roːbz, ənd wʌn wɪð ˈdjukəl 115 ˈbanɪt ɪn ðə mɪdst, ˈhoːldɪŋ ə rɪŋ. ðə smuːð baːɹk swæm əˈpɔn ə siː laɪk ðæt əv ˈsʌðəɹn ˈlætɪˈtjudz. aɪ sɔː ðə ˈbutʃɛnˈtɔro ənd ðə ˈnʌptʃəlz əv ˈvɛnɪs ənd ðɪ ˈeˑdrɪˈætɪk.

huː wəɹ ðoːz ˈkʌmɪŋ ˈovəɹ ðə saɪd? huː ˈkraʊdɪd 120 ðə boːts, ənd spræŋ ˈɪntʊ ðə ˈwɔtəɹ, mɛn ɪn oːld ˈspænɪʃ ˈaːɹməɹ, wɪð pluːmz nd sɔːɹdz, ənd ˈbɛːrɪŋ ə

glɪtərɪŋ krɔs? huː wəz hiː ′stændɪŋ ə′pɔn ðə dɛk
wɪð ′foːldɪd ɑːɹmz ænd ′geɪzɪŋ tɔːɹdz ðə ʃɔːɹ, æz ′lʌvəɹz
ɔn ðɛɹ ′mɪstrɪsəz ænd ′mɑːɹtɪɹz ə′pɔn ′hɛvn? ′ovəɹ
125 ʍɑt ′dɪstænt ænd tu′mʌltʃuəs siːz hæd ðɪs smɔːl
kræft ɪ′ske·pt frɑm ′ʌðəɹ ′sɛntʃuriz ænd ′dɪstænt
ʃɔːɹz? ʍɑt sɑʊndz əv ′fɔrɪn hɪmz, fəɹ′gɑtn nɑʊ, wəɹ
ðiːz, ænd ʍɑt so′lɛmnɪtɪ əv ′di·bɑɹ′keːʃən? wɑz ðɪs
greɪv fɔːɹm ko′lʌmbəs?

## Day-dreams

As I was stepping ashore, I was greeted by Mr. Bourne, who passes the summer on the island, and who hospitably asked if I were going his way. His way was toward the southern end of the island, and I said yes. His pockets were full of papers and his brow of wrinkles; so when we reached the point where he should turn off, I asked him to let me alight, although he was very anxious to carry me wherever I was going.

"I am only strolling about," I answered, as I clambered carefully out of the wagon.

"Strolling about?" asked he, in a bewildered manner; "do people stroll about, now-a-days?"

"Sometimes," I answered, smiling, as I pulled my trousers down over my boots, for they had dragged up, as I stepped out of the wagon, "and beside, what can an old bookkeeper do better in the dull season than stroll about this pleasant island, and watch the ships at sea?"

Bourne looked at me with his weary eyes.

"I'd give five thousand dollars a year for a dull season," said he, "but as for strolling, I've forgotten how."

As he spoke, his eyes wandered dreamily across the fields and woods, and were fastened upon the distant sails.

"It is pleasant," he said musingly, and fell into silence. But I had no time to spare, so I wished him good-afternoon.

"I hope your wife is well," said Bourne to me, as I turned away. Poor Bourne! He drove on alone in his wagon.

But I made haste to the most solitary point upon the southern shore, and there sat, glad to be so near the sea. There was that warm, sympathetic silence in the air, that gives to Indian-summer days almost a human tenderness of feeling. A delicate haze, that seemed only the kindly air made visible, hung over the sea. The water lapped languidly among the rocks, and the voices of children in a boat beyond, rang musically, and gradually receded, until they were lost in the distance.

It was some time before I was aware of the outline of a large ship, drawn vaguely upon the mist, which I supposed, at first, to be only a kind of mirage. But the more steadfastly I gazed, the more distinct it became, and I could no longer doubt that I saw a stately ship lying at anchor, not more than half a mile from the land.

"It is an extraordinary place to anchor," I said to myself, "or can she be ashore?"

There were no signs of distress; the sails were carefully clewed up, and there were no sailors in the tops, nor upon the shrouds. A flag, of which I could not see the device or the nation, hung heavily at the stern, and looked as if it had fallen asleep. My curiosity began to be singularly excited. The form of the vessel seemed not to be permanent; but within a quarter of an hour, I was sure that I had seen half a dozen different ships. As I gazed, I saw no more sails nor masts, but a long range of oars, flashing like a golden fringe, or straight and stiff, like the legs of a sea-monster.

"It is some bloated crab, or lobster, magnified by the mist," I said to myself, complacently.

But, at the same moment, there was a concentrated flashing and blazing in one spot among the rigging, and it was as if I saw a beatified ram, or, more truly, a sheep-skin, splendid as the hair of Berenice.

"Is that the golden fleece?" I thought. "But, surely, Jason and the Argonauts have gone home long since. Do people go on gold-fleecing expeditions now?" I asked myself, in perplexity. "Can this be a California steamer?"

How could I have thought it a steamer? Did I not see those sails, "thin and sere"? Did I not feel the melancholy of that solitary bark? It had a mystic aura; a boreal brilliancy shimmered in its wake, for it was drifting seaward. A strange fear curdled along my veins. That summer sun shone cool. The weary, battered ship was gashed, as if gnawed by ice. There was terror in the air, as a "skinny hand so brown" waved to me from the deck. I lay as one bewitched. The hand of the ancient mariner seemed to be reaching for me, like the hand of death.

Death? Why, as I was inly praying Prue's forgiveness for my solitary ramble and consequent demise, a glance like the fulness of summer splendor gushed over me; the odor of flowers and of eastern gums made all the atmosphere. I breathed the orient, and lay drunk with balm, while that strange ship, a golden galley now, with glittering draperies festooned with flowers, paced to the measured beat of oars along the calm, and Cleopatra smiled alluringly from the great pageant's heart.

Was this a barge for summer waters, this peculiar ship I saw? It had a ruined dignity, a cumbrous grandeur, although its masts were shattered, and its sails rent. It hung preternaturally still upon the sea, as if tormented and exhausted by long driving and drifting. I saw no sailors, but a great Spanish ensign floated over, and waved, a funereal plume. I knew it then. The armada was long since scattered; but, floating far

on desolate rainy seas,

lost for centuries, and again restored to sight, here lay one of the fated ships of Spain. The huge galleon seemed to fill all the air, built up against the sky, like the gilded ships of Claude Lorraine against the sunset.

But it fled, for now a black flag fluttered at the mast-head — a long low vessel darted swiftly where the vast ship lay; there came a shrill piping whistle, the clash of cutlasses, fierce ringing oaths, sharp pistol cracks, the thunder of command, and over all the gusty yell of a demoniac chorus,

My name was Robert Kidd, when I sailed.

— There were no clouds longer, but under a serene sky I saw a bark moving with festal pomp, thronged with grave senators in flowing robes, and one with ducal bonnet in the midst, holding a ring. The smooth bark swam upon a sea like that of southern latitudes. I saw the *Bucentoro* and the nuptials of Venice and the Adriatic.

Who were those coming over the side? Who crowded the boats, and sprang into the water, men in old Spanish armor, with plumes and swords, and bearing a glittering cross? Who was he standing upon the deck with folded arms and gazing towards the shore, as lovers on their mistresses and martyrs upon heaven? Over what distant and tumultuous seas had this small craft escaped from other centuries and distant shores? What sounds of foreign hymns, forgotten now, were these, and what solemnity of debarkation? Was this grave form Columbus?

## REMARKS

This passage from *Prue and I*, by George William Curtis, was chosen for transcription because it calls for a considerable range of styles, from familiar colloquial to a formal poetic and rhetorical style. It is transcribed into what seem to the author the least questionable forms of standard speech, that is, the forms least limited by geographical or other considerations. It is not to be taken therefore as a record of the author's individual pronunciation, but of what in his judgment is as satisfactory a representation as can be made of an accepted general standard in American speech. The author's native speech is that of Southern Ohio, though for the past twenty years he has been a resident of New York City, and it is of course quite likely that his observations have been, in some degree, colored by his early habits of speech.

[deɪ-driːmz]. The diphthongal quality in [deɪ-] is not strongly marked, but sufficiently so to justify recording it, and so generally in final position and also before voiced consonants, e.g., [deɪz], l. 12, [seɪlz], l. 23, etc.

l. 2. [bəɹn]. The name might also be pronounced [ˈbuːɹn], [ˈbuːəɹn].

[ˈpæsɪz]. Some speakers might say [ˈpæsəz], and so generally with final unstressed syllables in –**es**, –**ed**.

[ˈhɑspɪtəblɪ]. Or [ˈhɔspɪtəblɪ], but not with the stress on the second syllable. This variation between [ɑ] and [ɔ] occurs in a number of other words.

l. 3. [æskt]. Or [ɑːskt], [aːskt].

l. 5. [ˈpɑkɪts]. Or [ˈpɔkɪts]. Is [ˈpɑkəts] permissible?

l. 6. [ʍɛːɹ]. The vowel in **where**, **there**, when these are slightly stressed words, should be transcribed as short, [ʍɛɹ], [ðɛɹ].

l. 7. [ɪm]. More formally, [hɪm].

[ˈæŋkʃəs]. Better than [ˈæŋʃəs].

l. 13. [səmˈtaɪmz]. The word might also be pronounced [ˈsʌm-ˌtaɪmz].

l. 15. [nd bɪˈsaɪd], etc. Informal conversational style.

l. 19. [ˈwɪərɪ]. Or [ˈwiːrɪ], though less commonly.

l. 22. [ˈwɔndəɹd]. Or [ˈwɑndəɹd].

l. 23. [fiːldz]. Less correctly, [fiːlz].

l. 24. [ænd fɛl], etc. This clause is transcribed in slow and formal style. The sentence immediately following is again brisker and more informal.

l. 30. [meˑd]. The vowel is half-long or short here, because so slightly stressed.

l. 54. [ˈvɛsl]. Sometimes pronounced [ˈvɛsəl] or [ˈvɛsɛl], but not in standard speech.

l. 62. [bʌt]. Usually unemphatic, [bət], but stressed here.

l. 64. [wɑz]. Somewhat emphatic here.

l. 72. [ˈsɪəɹ]. Perhaps also [ˈsiəɹ].

[ˈmɛlənˌkɑlɪ]. Or [ˈmɛlənˌkɔlɪ]; so also **solitary**, l. 73, [ˈsɑlɪˌtɛrɪ] or [ˈsɔlɪˌtɛrɪ].

l. 86. [ˈɔrɪˌɛnt]. Or [ˈorɪˌɛnt]. Less formally, [ˈɔrɪənt].

l. 92. [wɑz]. Unstressed, but formal because of its important position in the sentence.

l. 98. [njuː]. Often pronounced [nuː].

l. 113. [pɔmp]. Or [pɑmp], but in this word [ɔ] is more general than [ɑ].

l. 114. [ˈsɛnəˌtɔɹz]. Formal pronunciation.

l. 124. [ˈmɑːɹtɪɹz]. Less formally, [ˈmɑːɹtəɹz]; so also [ˈdɪstənt], l. 125, [ˈsɛntʃərɪz], l. 126, [səˈlɛmnɪtɪ], l. 128, [kəˈlʌmbəs], l. 129.

## II

### ðə ˈlɔŋɪŋ əv ə mæn əv ˈsaɪəns

maɪ fəɹst stɛp, əv kɔɹs, wɑz tə faɪnd ˈsjutəbl
əˈpɑːɹtmənts. ðiːz aɪ əbˈteːnd, ˈæftəɹ ə ˈkʌpl əv deːz
səɹtʃ, ɪn fɔːɹθ ˈævənju; ə ˈvɛrɪ ˈprɪtɪ ˈsɛkənd-ˎflɔːɹ un-
ˈfəɹnɪʃt, kənˈteːnɪŋ ˈsɪtɪŋ-ˎruːm, ˈbɛd-ˎruːm, ænd ə
5 ˈsmɔːləɹ əˈpɑːɹtmənt ʍɪtʃ aɪ ɪnˈtɛndɪd tə fɪt ʌp æz ə
ˈlæbərəˎtɔrɪ. aɪ ˈfəɹnɪʃt maɪ ˈlɑdʒɪŋz ˈsɪmplɪ, bət
ˈræðəɹ ˈɛləgəntlɪ, ænd ðɛn dɪˈvoːtɪd ɔːl maɪ ˈɛnəɹdʒiz
tʊ ðɪ əˈdɔɹnmənt əv ðə tɛmpl əv maɪ ˈwəɹʃɪp. aɪ
ˈvɪzɪtɪd paɪk, ðə ˈsɛləˎbre·tɪd ɑpˈtɪʃən, ænd pæst ɪn
10 rɪˈvjuː hɪz ˈsplɛndɪd kəˈlɛkʃən əv ˈmaɪkroˎsko·ps, —
fiːldz ˈkɑmˎpɑʊnd, ˈhɪŋəmz, ˈspɛnsəɹz, næˈʃeɪz ˎbaɪ-
ˈnɑkjuləɹ (ðæt ˈfɑʊndɪd ɔn ðə ˈprɪnsɪplz əv ðə ˈstɛrɪəs-
ˎkoːp), ænd æt lɛŋkθ fɪkst əˈpɔn ðæt fɔːɹm noːn æz
ˈspɛnsəɹz ˈtrʌnjən ˈmaɪkroˎsko·p, æz kəmˈbɑɪnɪŋ ðə
15 ˈgreːtɪst ˈnʌmbəɹ əv ɪmˈpruːvmənts wɪð n ˈɔlˎmo·st
ˈpəɹfɪkt ˈfriːdəm frʌm ˈtrɛməɹ. əˈlɔŋ wɪð ðɪs aɪ ˈpəɹ-
tʃɪst ˈɛvrɪ ˈpɑsɪbl ækˈsɛsərɪ, — ˈdrɔː-ˎtjuːbz, ˎmaɪˈkrɑm-
ətəɹz, ə ˈkɑmərɑ-ˈlusɪdɑ, ˈliːvəɹ-ˎsteɪdʒ, ˎækroˈmæ-
tɪk kənˈdɛnsəɹz, ʍaɪt klɑʊd ɪˈluːmɪˎne·təɹz, prɪzmz,
20 ˎpærəˈbɑlɪk kənˈdɛnsəɹz, ˈpoːləˎraɪzɪŋ æpəˈrɑːtəs, ˈfɔːɹ-
sɛps, əˈkwɑtɪk ˈbɑksəz, ˈfɪʃɪŋ-ˎtjuːbz, wɪð ə hoːst əv
ˈʌðəɹ ˈɑɹtɪklz, ɔːl əv ʍɪtʃ wʊd əv bɪn ˈjusfəl ɪn ðə
hændz əv n ɪksˈpɪrɪənst maɪˈkrɑskopɪst, bʌt, æz aɪ
ˈæftəɹwəɹdz dɪsˈkʌvəɹd, wəɹ nɑt əv ðə ˈslaɪtɪst ˈprɛznt
25 ˈvælju tə miː. ɪt teːks ˈjɪəɹz əv ˈpræktɪs tə noː hɑʊ tə
juːz ə ˈkɑmplɪˎke·tɪd ˈmaɪkroˎsko·p. ðɪ ɑpˈtɪʃən lʊkt
səsˈpɪʃəslɪ æt mi æz aɪ meːd ðiːz ˈhoːl-ˎseːl ˈpəɹtʃɪsəz.
hɪ ˈɛvɪdəntlɪ wəz ʌnˈsəɹtn ˈʍɛðəɹ tə sɛt mɪ dɑʊn æz
sʌm ˎsaɪənˈtɪfɪk sɛˈlɛbrɪtɪ ɔɹ ə ˈmædˎmæn. aɪ θɪŋk hɪ
30 ɪnˈklaɪnd tə ðə ˈlætəɹ bɪˈliːf. aɪ səˈpoːz aɪ wɑz mæd.

′ɛvrɪ greːt ′dʒiːnjəs ɪz mæd ə′pɔn ðə ′sʌbdʒɛkt ɪn
ʍɪtʃ hɪ ɪz ′greːtɪst. ðɪ ′ʌnsəkˋsɛsfəl ′mædˋmæn ɪz
dɪs′greːst ænd kɔːld ə ′lunətɪk.
mæd ɔɹ nɑt, aɪ sɛt maɪ′sɛlf tə wəɹk wɪð ə ziːl ʍɪtʃ
35 fju ˋsaɪən′tɪfɪk ′stjudənts hæv ′ɛvəɹ ′iːkwəld. aɪ hæd
′ɛvrɪˋθɪŋ tə ləɹn ′rɛlətɪv tə ðə ′dɛlɪkɪt ′stʌdɪ ə′pɔn
ʍɪtʃ aɪ hæd ɪm′bɑːɹkt, — ə ′stʌdɪ ɪn′vɑlvɪŋ ðə moːst
′əɹnəst ′peːʃəns, ðə moːst ′rɪdʒɪd ænə′lɪtɪk ′pɑʊəɹz, ðə
′stɛdɪəst hænd, ðə moːst ˋʌn′taɪrɪŋ aɪ, ðə moːst rɪ-
40 ′faɪnd ænd ′sʌbˋtaɪl mæˋnɪpju′leːʃən.
fɔɹ ə lɔŋ taɪm hæf maɪ æpə′rɑːtəs leɪ ɪn′æktɪvlɪ ɔn
ðə ʃɛlvz əv maɪ ′læbərəˋtɔrɪ, ʍɪtʃ wəz nɑʊ moːst
′æmplɪ ′fəɹnɪʃt wɪð ′ɛvrɪ ′pɑsɪbl kən′traɪvəns fɔr fə-
′sɪlɪˋte·tɪŋ maɪ ɪnˋvɛstɪ′geːʃənz. ðə fækt wɑz ðæt aɪ
45 dɪd nɑt noː hɑʊ tə juːz sʌm əv maɪ ˋsaɪən′tɪfɪk ′ɪm-
pləmənts, — ′nɛvəɹ ′hævɪŋ bɪn tɔːt ˋmaɪkro′skɑpɪks,
— ænd ðoːz huz juːs aɪ ˋʌndəɹ′stʊd ˋθio′rɛtɪkəlɪ wəɹ
əv ′lɪtl ə′veːl, ən′tɪl baɪ ′præktɪs aɪ kʊd ə′teːn ðə
′nɛsəˋsɛrɪ ′dɛlɪkəsɪ əv ′hændlɪŋ. stɪl, sʌtʃ wəz ðə
50 ′fjurɪ əv maɪ æm′bɪʃən, sʌtʃ ðɪ ˋʌn′taɪrɪŋ pəɹsɪ′vɪrəns
əv maɪ ɪks′pɛrɪmənts, ðæt, ′dɪfɪkəlt əv ′krɛdɪt æz ɪt
me· biː, ɪn ðə kɔɹs əv wʌn ′jɪəɹ aɪ bɪ′keːm ˋθio′rɛtɪkəlɪ
ænd ′præktɪkəlɪ æn ə′kɑmplɪʃt maɪ′krɑskopɪst.
′djurɪŋ ðɪs ′pɪrɪəd əv maɪ ′leːbəɹz, ɪn ʍɪtʃ aɪ səb-
55 ′mɪtɪd ′spɛsɪmənz əv ′ɛvrɪ ′sʌbstəns ðæt ke·m ′ʌndəɹ
maɪ ˋɑbsəɹ′veːʃən tə ðɪ ′ækʃən əv maɪ ′lɛnzɪz, aɪ bɪ-
′keːm ə dɪs′kʌvərəɹ, — ɪn ə smɔːl weɪ, ɪt ɪz truː, fɔɹ
aɪ wəz ′vɛrɪ jʌŋ, bət stɪl ə dɪs′kʌvərəɹ. ɪt wəz aɪ hu
dɪs′trɔɪd ′ɛrənbəɹgz ′θiorɪ ðæt ðə ′vɔlvɔks glo′bɑːtor
60 wɑz æn ′ænɪməl, ænd pruːvd ðæt hɪz "′moːnædz"
wɪð ′stʌməks nd aɪz wəɹ ′mɪɹlɪ ′feːzəz əv ðə fɔɹ′meɪ-
ʃən əv ə ′vɛdʒətəbl sɛl, ænd wəɹ, ʍɛn ðe· riːtʃt ðɛɹ
mə′tjuɹ steːt, ɪn′keːpəbl əv ðɪ ækt əv ˋkɑndʒu′geːʃən,

ɔɹ ˈɛnɪ truː ˈdʒɛnəˎre·tɪv ækt, wɪðˈɑʊt ʌɪtʃ noː ˈɔɹ-
65 gənɪzm ˈraɪzɪŋ tʊ ˈɛnɪ steɪdʒ əv ɫaɪf ˈhaɪəɹ ðən ˈvɛdʒə-
təbl kæn bɪ sɛd tə bi kɑmˈpliːt. ɪt wəz aɪ hu rɪˈzɑlvd
ðə ˈsɪŋgjuləɹ ˈprɑbləm əv roˈteːʃən ɪn ðə sɛlz ænd
hɛːɹz əv plænts ˈɪntu ˈsɪlɪˎɛrɪ əˈtrækʃən, ɪn spaɪt əv ðɪ
əˈsəɹʃənz əv ˈmɪstəɹ ˈwɛnəm ænd ˈʌðəɹz, ðæt maɪ
70 ɛkspləˈneːʃən wɑz ðə rɪˈzʌlt əv ən ˈɑptɪkl ɪˈluːʒən.

## The Longing of a Man of Science

My first step of course was to find suitable apartments. These I obtained, after a couple of days' search, in Fourth Avenue; a very pretty second-floor unfurnished, containing sitting-room, bed-room, and a smaller apartment which I intended to fit up as a laboratory. I furnished my lodgings simply, but rather elegantly, and then devoted all my energies to the adornment of the temple of my worship. I visited Pike, the celebrated optician, and passed in review his splendid collection of microscopes, — Field's Compound, Hingham's, Spencer's, Nachet's Binocular (that founded on the principles of the stereoscope), and at length fixed upon that form known as Spencer's Trunnion Microscope, as combining the greatest number of improvements with an almost perfect freedom from tremor. Along with this I purchased every possible accessory, — draw-tubes, micrometers, a *camera-lucida*, lever-stage, achromatic condensers, white cloud illuminators, prisms, parabolic condensers, polarizing apparatus, forceps, aquatic boxes, fishing-tubes, with a host of other articles, all of which would have been useful in the hands of an experienced microscopist, but, as I afterwards discovered, were not of the slightest present value to me. It takes years of practice to know how to use a complicated microscope. The optician looked suspiciously at me as I made these whole-sale purchases. He evidently was uncertain whether to set me down as some scientific celebrity or a madman. I think he inclined to the latter belief. I suppose I was mad. Every great genius is mad upon the subject in which he is greatest. The unsuccessful madman is disgraced and called a lunatic.

Mad or not, I set myself to work with a zeal which few scientific students have ever equaled. I had everything to learn relative to the delicate study upon which I had embarked, — a study involving the most earnest patience, the most rigid analytic powers, the steadiest hand, the most untiring eye, the most refined and subtile manipulation.

For a long time half my apparatus lay inactively on the shelves of my laboratory, which was now most amply furnished with every possible contrivance for facilitating my investigations. The fact was that I did not know how to use some of my scientific implements, — never having been taught microscopics, — and those whose use I understood theoretically were of little avail, until by practice I could attain the necessary delicacy of handling. Still, such was the fury of my ambition, such the untiring perseverance of my experiments, that, difficult of credit as it may be, in the course of one year I became theoretically and practically an accomplished microscopist.

During this period of my labors, in which I submitted specimens of every substance that came under my observation to the action of my lenses, I became a discoverer, — in a small way, it is true, for I was very young, but still a discoverer. It was I who destroyed Ehrenberg's theory that the *Volvox globator* was an animal, and proved that his "monads" with stomachs and eyes were merely phases of the formation of a vegetable cell, and were, when they reached their mature state, incapable of the act of conjugation, or any true generative act, without which no organism rising to any stage of life higher than vegetable can be said to be complete. It was I who resolved the singular problem of rotation in the cells and hairs of plants into ciliary attraction, in spite of the assertions of Mr. Wenham and others, that my explanation was the result of an optical illusion.

## REMARKS

These paragraphs are from *The Diamond Lens* by Fitz-James O'Brien. The transcription represents the author's conception of a standard reading pronunciation, more formal than a colloquial but less formal than an oratorical style.

l. 1. [ˈsjutəbl]. But [ˈsutəbl] is also possible.

l. 5. [ɪnˈtɛndɪd]. The final syllable, in this and similar words, is quite as likely to be [-əd] as [-ɪd].

l. 9. [pæst]. Or [paːst]. The pronunciation [pɑːst] is likely to be noticeable. Neither [paːst] nor [pɑːst] are natural to the author, whose native speech was formed in Southern Ohio.

l. 13. [lɛŋkθ]. Or [lɛŋθ].

l. 16. [ˈtrɛməɹ]. Rarely [ˈtriːməɹ].

l. 18. [ˌækroˈmætɪk]. For emphasis on the etymological elements of the word, one might say [ˈeɪkroˈmætɪk].

l. 20. [æpəˈrɑːtəs]. Or [æpəˈreːtəs], scarcely [æpəˈrætəs], though this pronunciation is common popularly and is sometimes heard among physicists and other scientists.

l. 21. [əˈkwɑtɪk]. Or [əˈkwɔtɪk].

l. 26. [ɑpˈtɪʃən]. Of course [ɔpˈtɪʃən] is also possible, but in this and other words where a choice between the two is open, the form with [ɑ] is much the more general, and represents the author's habit.

l. 28. [ˈɛvɪdəntlɪ]. Or [ˈɛvɪˌdɛntlɪ].

l. 30. [wɑz]. An emphatic form of unemphatic [wəz].

l. 31. [ˈsʌbdʒɛkt]. Or [ˈsʌbdʒɪkt].

l. 32. [ðɪ]. Before a vowel, [ðə] before consonants.

[ˈʌnsəkˌsɛsfəl]. Or [ˌʌnsəkˈsɛsfəl].

l. 34. [ɔɹ]. In rapid reading more likely to be [əɹ] than [ɔɹ]. So also [ænd] may frequently be merely [nd].

l. 36. [ˈdɛlɪkɪt]. The pronunciation [ˈdɛləkət] seems scarcely permissible.

l. 37. [ɪmˈbɑːɹkt]. Or [ɛmˈbɑːɹkt].

l. 39. [ˌʌnˈtaɪrɪŋ]. Or [ənˈtaɪrɪŋ].

l. 41. [hæf]. Or [haːf].

l. 52. [bɪˈkeːm]. The vowel is distinctly long here before a slight pause.

l. 54. [ˈdjurɪŋ]. In British English a glide vowel before [r] is prominent, giving [ˈdjuərɪŋ], [ˈpɪərɪəd], l. 61 [ˈmɪəɹlɪ], etc., but in American speech this glide vowel is very slight when heard and usually is not heard at all.

l. 62. [wəɹ]. Stressed here, but usually unstressed.

l. 66. [bɪ], [bi]. The second **be** is more emphatic, hence the vowel is higher and tenser. The second syllable of **complete** is still more emphatic.

## III

### ðə ˈhəɹmɪt

wʌn naɪt, ə ˈbjutɪfəl ˈklɪəɹ ˈfrɔstɪ naɪt, hi keːm bæk tʊ hɪz sɛl, ˈæftəɹ ə ʃɔɹt rɛst. ðə stɑːɹz wəɹ ˈwʌndəɹfəl. ˈhɛvn siːmd ə ˈθaʊzənd taɪmz ˈlɑːɹdʒəɹ əz wɛl əz ˈbraɪtəɹ ðən əɹθ, nd tə lʊk wɪð ə ˈθaʊzənd aɪz ɪnˈstɛd əv
5 wʌn.

"oʊ, ˈwʌndəɹfəl," hi kraɪd, "ðət ðɛɹ ʃʊd bi mɛn hu duː kraɪmz baɪ naɪt; ænd ˈʌðəɹz skɛːɹs lɛs mæd, hu lɪv fɔɹ ðɪs ˈlɪtl wəɹld, nd nɑt fɔɹ ðæt greːt n ˈglɔːrɪəs wʌn, ʍɪtʃ ˈnaɪtlɪ, tʊ ɔːl aɪz nɑt ˈblaɪndɪd baɪ ˈkʌstəm,

10 rɪˈviːlz ɪts ˈgloːrɪŋ ˈglɔːriz. θæŋk gɑd aɪ æm ə ˈhəɹ-
mɪt."

ænd ɪn ðɪs muːd hi keːm tʊ hɪz sɛl dɔːɹ.

hi pɔːzd æt ɪt; ɪt wəz kloːzd.

"ʍaɪ, mɪˈθɔːt aɪ lɛft ɪt ˈoːpn," sɛd hi. "ðə wɪnd.
15 ðəɹ ɪz nɑt ə brɛθ əv wɪnd. ʍɑt miːnz ðɪs?"

hi stʊd wɪð ɪz hænd əˈpɔn ðə ˈrʌgɪd dɔːɹ. hi lʊkt
θru wʌn əv ðə greːt tʃɪŋks, fɔɹ ɪt wəz mʌtʃ ˈsmɔːləɹ ɪn
ˈpleːsɪz ðæn ðɪ ˈæpəɹtʃəɹ ɪt prɪˈtɛndɪd tə kloːz, ænd
sɔː hɪz ˈlɪtl ɔɪl wɪk ˈbəɹnɪŋ dʒʌst ʍɛːɹ hi hæd lɛft ɪt.

20 "haʊ ɪz ɪt wɪð mi," hi saɪd, "ʍɛn aɪ stɑːɹt n ˈtrɛmbl
æt ˈnʌθɪŋ? ˈiːðəɹ aɪ dɪd ʃʌt ɪt, ɔɹ ðə fiːnd hæθ ʃʌt ɪt
ˈæftəɹ mi tə dɪsˈtəɹb maɪ ˈhæpɪ soʊl. ˈrɛtro səˈθɑːnɑs!"

ænd hi ˈɛntəɹd hɪz keːv ˈræpɪdlɪ, nd bɪˈgæn wɪð
ˈsʌmʍɑt ˈnəɹvəs ɛkspɪˈdɪʃən tə laɪt wʌn əv hɪz ˈlɑːɹdʒ-
25 ɪst ˈteːpəɹz. ʍaɪl hi wəz ˈlaɪtɪŋ ɪt, ðɛɹ wəz ə sɔft saɪ
ɪn ðə keːv.

hi ˈstɑːɹtɪd nd drɑpt ðə ˈkændl dʒʌst əz ɪt wəz ˈlaɪtɪŋ, ænd ɪt wɛnt aʊt.

hi stuːpt fɔɹ ɪt ˈhʌrɪədlɪ nd ˈlaɪtɪd ɪt, ˈlɪsnɪŋ ɪn-
30 ˈtɛntlɪ. ʍɛn ɪt wəz ˈlaɪtɪd hi ˈʃeːdɪd ɪt wɪð ɪz hænd
frəm bɪˈhaɪnd, ænd θruː ðə feːnt laɪt ɔːl raʊnd ðə sɛl.

ɪn ðə ˈfɑːɹðɪst ˈkɔɹnəɹ ðɪ ˈaʊtlaɪn əv ðə wɔːl siːmd
ˈbroːkn.

hi tʊk ə stɛp tɔːɹdz ðə pleːs wɪð ɪz hɑːɹt ˈbiːtɪŋ.

35 ðə ˈkændl æt ðə seːm taɪm ˈgɛtɪŋ ˈbraɪtəɹ, hi sɔː ɪt
wəz ðə ˈfɪgjʊɹ əv ə ˈwʊmən.

əˈnʌðəɹ stɛp wɪð ɪz niːz ˈnɑkɪŋ təˈgɛðəɹ.

ɪt wɑz ˈmɑːɹgrɪt brænt.

## The Hermit

One night, a beautiful clear frosty night, he came back to his cell, after a short rest. The stars were wonderful. Heaven seemed a thousand times larger as well as brighter than earth, and to look with a thousand eyes instead of one.

"Oh, wonderful," he cried, "that there should be men who do crimes by night; and others scarce less mad, who live for this little world, and not for that great and glorious one, which nightly, to all eyes not blinded by custom, reveals its glowing glories. Thank God I am a hermit."

And in this mood he came to his cell door.

He paused at it; it was closed.

"Why, methought I left it open," said he. "The wind. There is not a breath of wind. What means this?"

He stood with his hand upon the rugged door. He looked through one of the great chinks, for it was much smaller in places than the aperture it pretended to close, and saw his little oil wick burning just where he had left it.

"How is it with me," he sighed, "when I start and tremble at nothing? Either I did shut it, or the fiend hath shut it after me to disturb my happy soul. Retro Sathanas!"

And he entered his cave rapidly, and began with somewhat nervous expedition to light one of his largest tapers. While he was lighting it, there was a soft sigh in the cave.

He started and dropped the candle just as it was lighting, and it went out.

He stooped for it hurriedly and lighted it, listening intently. When it was lighted he shaded it with his hand from behind, and threw the faint light all round the cell.

In the farthest corner the outline of the wall seemed broken.

He took a step towards the place with his heart beating.

The candle at the same time getting brighter, he saw it was the figure of a woman.

Another step with his knees knocking together.

It was Margaret Brandt.

## REMARKS

From Cap. XCV of Charles Reade's *The Cloister and the Hearth.*

l. 1. [wʌn naɪt]. Two distinct [n] consonants are not pronounced here, see above, § 83.

l. 10. [aɪ æm]. Less formally, [aɪm].

l. 17. [θru]. The word is very slightly stressed, hence the vowel is short.

[greːt]. As an intensive, **great** is not usually a very emphatic word. Here it is lightly stressed and the vowel is perhaps only half-long.

l. 18. [ˈpleːsɪz]. Or [ˈpleːsəz]?

l. 38. [ˈmɑːɹgrɪt]. This word would be trisyllabic only in a formal spelling-pronunciation.

## IV

### ðə ˈlʊk-ˌaʊt

"ðɛːɹ ʃi bloʊz," wəz sʌŋ ɑʊt frəm ðə ˈmæst-ˌhɛd.
"ʍɛːɹ əˈweɪ?" dɪˈmændɪd ðə ˈkæptn.
"θriː pɔɪnts ɔːf ðə liː bɑʊ, səɹ."
"reːz ʌp jəɹ ʍiːl. ˈstɛːˌdɪː!"
5 "ˈstɛdɪ, səɹ."
"ˈmæst-ˌhɛd əˈhɔɪ! djə siː ðæt ʍeɪl nɑʊ?"
"aɪ, aɪ, səɹ! ə ʃoʊl ə spəɹm ʍeɪlz! ðɛːɹ ʃi bloʊz! ðɛːɹ ʃi ˈbriːtʃəz!"
"sɪŋ ɑʊt! sɪŋ ɑʊt ɛvrɪ taɪm!"

10 "aɪ, aɪ, səɹ! ðɛːɹ ʃi bloʊz! ðɛːɹ — ðɛːɹ — ðɑːɹ ʃi bloʊz — boʊz — boːʊz!"

"haʊ fɑːɹ ɔːf?"

"tu maɪlz nd ə hæf."

"ˈθʌndr n ˈlaɪtnɪŋ! so ˈnɪəɹ! kɔːl ɔːl hændz!"

## The Look-out

"There she blows," was sung out from the mast-head.

"Where away?" demanded the captain.

"Three points off the lee bow, sir."

"Raise up your wheel. Steady!"

"Steady, sir."

"Mast-head ahoy! Do you see that whale now?"

"Ay, ay, sir! A shoal of Sperm Whales! There she blows! There she breaches!"

"Sing out! sing out every time!"

"Ay, ay, sir! There she blows! there — there — *thar* she blows — bowes — bo—o—o—s!"

"How far off?"

"Two miles and a half."

"Thunder and lightning! So near! Call all hands!"

### REMARKS

From *Extracts* at the end of Melville's *Moby Dick*. Note the prolonged quality of some of the vowels, resulting of course from the manner of speech exemplified by the passage. In line 6, [djə] might be transcribed [dʒə].

## V

### ðə fiːst

ænd stɪl ʃi slept ɪn ˈæʒəɹ-ˈlɪdɪd sliːp,
ɪn ˈblæntʃɪd ˈlɪnɪn, smuːð, ænd ˈlævənˈdəɹd,

ʌaɪl hiː fram fɔːɹθ ðə ˈklɔzɪt brɔːt ə hiːp
ɑv ˈkænˋdid ˈæpəl, kwɪns, ænd plʌm, ænd ˈgʊəɹd;
5 wɪθ ˈdʒɛliz ˈsuːðəɹ ðæn ðə ˈkriːmɪ kəɹd,
ænd ˈljuːsɛnt ˈsɪrɔps, tɪŋkt wɪθ ˈsɪnəˈmɔn;
ˈmænə ænd deːts, ɪn ˈɑːɹgoˈsi trænsˈfəɹd
fram fɛz; ænd ˈspaɪsɪd ˈdeːntiz, ˈɛvrɪ wʌn,
fram ˈsɪlkən ˈsæməɹˈkænd tu ˈsidəɹd ˈlɛbəˈnɔn.

10 ðiːz ˈdɛlɪˈkeːts hi hiːpt wɪθ ˈgloːɪŋ hænd
ɔn ˈgoːldɪn ˈdɪʃɪz ænd ɪn ˈbɑːskɪts braɪt
ɑv ˈwriːðɪd ˈsɪlvəɹ: ˈsʌmptʃuˈʌs ðe· stænd
ɪn ðə rɪˈtaɪəɹd ˈkwaɪɪt ɑv ðə naɪt,
ˈfɪlɪŋ ðə ˈtʃɪlɪ ruːm wɪθ ˈpəɹfjum laɪt. —
15 "ænd nɑʊ, maɪ lʌv, maɪ ˈsɛræf ˈfɛːəɹ, əˈweːk!
ðɑʊ ɑɹt maɪ ˈhɛvn, ænd aɪ ðaɪn ˈɛrɪˈmaɪt:
ˈoːpn ðaɪn aɪz, fɔɹ miːk se·nt ˈægnɪs seːk,
ɔɹ aɪ ʃæl drɑʊz bɪˈsaɪd ðiː, soʊ maɪ soʊl dʌθ eːk."

## The Feast

And still she slept in azure-lidded sleep,
In blanched linen, smooth, and lavender'd,
While he from forth the closet brought a heap
Of candied apple, quince, and plum, and gourd;
With jellies soother than the creamy curd,
And lucent syrops, tinct with cinnamon;
Manna and dates, in argosy transferr'd
From Fez; and spiced dainties, every one,
From silken Samarcand to cedar'd Lebanon.

These delicates he heap'd with glowing hand
On golden dishes and in baskets bright
Of wreathed silver: sumptuous they stand

In the retired quiet of the night,
Filling the chilly room with perfume light. —
"And now, my love, my seraph fair, awake!
Thou art my heaven, and I thine eremite:
Open thine eyes, for meek St. Agnes' sake,
Or I shall drowse beside thee, so my soul doth ache."

## REMARKS

These two stanzas from *The Eve of St. Agnes*, by Keats, are transcribed into a text for very formal and somewhat artificial pronunciation, such as one would employ in a slow recitation of the lines.

l. 1. ['æʒəɹ-]. Or ['eɪʒəɹ-].

l. 4. ['gʊəɹd]. The word is a poor rime to **lavender'd, curd, transferr'd**, unless one adopts an artificial pronunciation, [gəɹd], for the sake of the rime. Normally the word is pronounced ['gʊəɹd] or [gɔɹd].

l. 6. ['ljuːsɛnt 'sɪrɔps]. In colloquial style, ['luːsənt 'sɪrəps].

l. 8. [wʌn]. Should one pronounce [wɔn] for the rime, or ['sɪnə'mʌn], ['lɛbə'nʌn], or be satisfied merely with the approximate eye-rime in the spellings **cinnamon, one, Lebanon?**

l. 11. ['bɑːskɪts]. Or ['baːskɪts], ['bæskɪts], though one would not likely hear ['bæskɪts] from a professional elocutionist.

l. 12. ['sʌmptʃu'ʌs]. In colloquial style, ['sʌmptʃuəs].

## VI

### ɪmɔɹ'tælɪtɪ

soʊ wi dʒʌdʒ əv ðə hoːp əv ɪmɔɹ'tælɪtɪ. ɪt bɪ'lɔŋz
wɪð ənd fɪts 'ɪntu ə 'strʌktʃəɹ; ɪt ɪz ðæt wɪð'aʊt ʌɪtʃ
ju kən 'nɛvəɹ meːk ðə 'bjutɪ ɔɹ 'junɪtɪ lɑːst, wɪðaʊt
ʌɪtʃ 'ɔlso ðə 'strʌktʃəɹ tɛndz tə fɔːl ə'pɑːt. ðɪ ɑːtʃ ɪz
5 nɑt jɛt truː tɪl 'ɛvrɪ stoːn fɪts 'ɪntu pleːs. pʊt ðə hoːp
əv ɪmɔɹ'tælɪtɪ 'ɪntu ðə kraʊn əv ðə 'væljuz əv laɪf, ənd
ðe· ko'hɪəɹ, ənd ɔːl əv ðɛm teːk ɔn njuː sɪg'nɪfɪkəns.

iːtʃ stoːn bɪlt ˈɪntə ðə ˈstrʌktʃəɹ ɪz wʌːθ ˈmɔəɹ ðən ɪt
ɪz wʌːð baɪ ɪtˈsɛlf ɪn ðə fiːld. iːtʃ stoːn ɪz wʌːð stɪl
10 ˈmɔəɹ ʍɛn ðə ˈstrʌktʃəɹ ɪz ˈfɪnɪʃt. rɪˈfjuz ˈjʊəɹ ˈkiː-
ˌstoːn ðə pleːs fɔɹ ʍɪtʃ ɪt siːmz tə bɪ ˈfɪtɪd ɛgˈzæktlɪ,
ænd ju hæv pʊt ˈɛvrɪ ˈprɛʃəs ˈvælju æt rɪsk. ju əɹ nɑt
so ˈʃʊəɹ əv ə gʊd gɑd ˈɛnɪ ˈlɔŋgəɹ. ˈhjumən laɪf ɪz no
ˈlɔŋgəɹ so sɪgˈnɪfɪkənt əz ɪt wəz bɪˈfɔəɹ. ju həv lɔst
15 wʌːθ ɑʊt əv lʌv ənd ˈfrɛndʃɪp, ənd ˈlɛvɛld ðɛm tɔːɹd
ðə dʌst. ju həv rɪˈdust ˈpe·trɪətɪzm ənd fɪlˈænθrəpɪ tʊ
ˈfaɪˌnaɪt ˈvæljuz, iːtʃ wɪð ɪts praɪs. ju həv te·kn
ˈbʊɪjənt dʒɔɪ ənd ɛnˈθuzɪæzm ɑʊt əv ɔːl məˈtʊɹ mɛnz
laɪf, ənd ˈθrɛtnd ðɛm wɪð ən ˈəɹlɪəɹ oːld eːdʒ. ju həv
20 ˈʃeːkn ðə ˈbeːsəz əv moˈrælɪtɪ ənd pʊt ˈraɪtʃəsnəs ˈɪntu
təɹmz əv ˈkʌmfət ənd ˈpɑlɪsɪ. ju həv ˈbɪdn ðɪ ˈɑːtɪst,
ðə ˈpoɛt, ənd ðə ˈprɑfɛt lɑːf ət ðɛɹ ˈvɪʒənz ənd daʊt
ðɛɹ vəˈlɪdɪtɪ. ju həv dɪsˈtɪŋktlɪ ˈʃeːkn mænz feːθ ɪn
ˈlɑdʒɪk ənd ˈriːzən, ənd brɔːt ɔːl ɪntəˈlɛktʃʊəl ˈprɑsəsəz
25 ˈɪntu dɪsˈkrɛdɪt. fɔɹ ɔːl ðət ˈlɑdʒɪk ɪz ˈfɔːə ɪz tə baɪnd
θɪŋz ˈɪntu koˈhɪrəns ənd ˈjunɪtɪ. ɔːl ˈvæljuz, ɪn fækt,
bɪˈlɔŋ ɪn ðɪ aɪˈdɪəl ˈrɛlm; ðe· goː təˈgɛðəɹ ənd meːk ə
ˈjunɪtɪ, əɹ ɛls ðe· fɔːl təˈgɛðəɹ.

fɔːl təˈgɛðəɹ? noʊ! no mæn kæn meːk ðə greːt
30 ˈvæljuz fɔːl, ɔ teːk ðɛm əˈpɑːt, ɔ həɹt wʌn əv ðɛm. ə
mæn kæn həɹt ənd mɑː hɪz oʊn laɪf baɪ hɪz dɪsˈtrʌst,
bət hɪ kən mɑː noʊ rɪˈælɪtɪ. no mænz daʊt kən meːk
ˈdʒʌstɪs, ˈbjutɪ, truːθ, lʌv, lɛs ðən ˈrɪəl. ðiːz θɪŋz ɑ
ɪnˈgreːnd ɪn ɑ ˈneːtʃə. wɪ niːd ˈoːnlɪ tə trʌst ðɛm.
35 ðe· ˈkɑnstɪˌtʊt æn ˈɪnfɪnɪt ˈɔɹdəɹ. ðe· ˈvælɪˌde·t ðɛm-
ˈsɛlvz ðə ˈmɔəɹ wɪ θroʊ ɑʊɚ weːt əˈpɔn ðɛm. ðə hoːp
əv ɪmɔɹˈtælɪtɪ ɪz ˈsɪmplɪ ðə ˈkiːˌstoːn, ʍɪtʃ ˈɔlwez
stændz fɑːst, bɪˈjɔnd ˈɛnɪ mænz daʊt, æt ðə kraʊn əv
ðə ˈstrʌktʃəɹ. ɪt fɪts ɪts kəmˈpænjən ˈvæljuz, ənd ðe·
40 klɑːsp ɪt wɪð ðɛɹ ɑːmz ˈɪntu ə sɪˈriːn ɪnˈtɛgrɪtɪ. ðe·

bɪd ʌs trʌst ɑʊə laɪvz ə'pɔn ðɪ 'ɑɪtʃˌweɪ, ʍɪtʃ 'ɛvrɪ 'vælju ɪn ðə 'junɪˌvʌɪs hæz dʒɔɪnd tə kən'strʌkt. wiː dɪd nɑt bɪld ðə 'bjutɪfəl 'strʌktʃəɹ: wɪ 'oːnlɪ fɑʊnd ɪt.

ʍɑt ɪz 'ɛksələnt,
45 æz gɑd lɪvz, ɪz 'pʌːmənənt.

## Immortality

So we judge of the hope of immortality. It belongs with and fits into a structure; it is that without which you can never make the beauty or unity last, without which also the structure tends to fall apart. The arch is not yet *true* till every stone fits into place. Put the hope of immortality into the crown of the values of life, and they cohere, and all of them take on new significance. Each stone built into the structure is worth more than it is worth by itself in the field. Each stone is worth still more when the structure is finished. Refuse your keystone the place for which it seems to be fitted exactly, and you have put every precious value at risk. You are not so sure of a good God any longer. Human life is no longer so significant as it was before. You have lost worth out of love and friendship, and leveled them toward the dust. You have reduced patriotism and philanthropy to finite values, each with its price. You have taken buoyant joy and enthusiasm out of all mature men's life, and threatened them with an earlier old age. You have shaken the bases of morality and put righteousness into terms of comfort and policy. You have bidden the artist, the poet, and the prophet laugh at their visions and doubt their validity. You have distinctly shaken man's faith in logic and reason, and brought all intellectual processes into discredit. For all that logic is for is to bind things into coherence and unity. All values, in fact, belong in the ideal realm; they go together and make a unity, or else they fall together.

Fall together? No! No man can make the great values fall, or take them apart, or hurt one of them. A man can hurt and mar his own life by his distrust, but he can mar no reality. No man's doubt can make justice, beauty, truth, love, less than real. These things are ingrained in our nature. We need only to trust them. They constitute an infinite order. They validate themselves the more we throw our weight upon them. The hope of immortality is simply the keystone, which always stands fast, beyond any man's doubt, at the crown of the structure. It fits its companion values, and they clasp it with their arms into a serene integrity. They bid us trust our lives upon the archway, which every value in the universe has joined to construct. We did not build the beautiful structure: we only found it.

What is excellent,
As God lives, is permanent.

## REMARKS

This passage, from *Truth and Immortality*, an essay by Charles Fletcher Dole, represents the pronunciation of Mr. W. W. Lawrence who was born in Portland, Maine, and spent his early life there. After the usual college training at Bowdoin, and graduate discipline, especially in English and German at Harvard, he spent several years in Kansas, but for the past dozen or fifteen years he has lived in New York, regularly returning, however, for three or four months of each year to his native New England. His pronunciation represents not an extreme local New England speech, but what may be taken as a fair example of cultivated standard New England speech. Perhaps its most interesting feature is its mixed character. This is evident, for example, in the treatment of [ɹ]. Final unstressed or lightly stressed [ɹ] is regularly present, but disappears in a heavily stressed syllable like [fɔːə], l. 25, or [mɑː], l. 31. Before consonants no [ɹ] is present in [ə'pɑːt], l. 30, [ɑːmz], l. 40, [ɑːtʃ–], l. 41, but is present in [həɹt], l. 30, the acoustic test being positively confirmed by the organic analysis. Yet no [ɹ] is present in [wʌːθ], l. 15, or in ['junɪˌvʌːs], l. 42, ['pʌːmənənt], l. 45. In ll. 33, 34, the pronunciation [ɑ] for **are, our,** evidently represents an occasional and unsettled, not a fixed and permanent habit, see ll. 36, 41. The loss of [ɹ] in ['kʌmfət], l. 21, is a very wide spread phenomenon, noticeable even in the speech of those who commonly retain [ɹ] before consonants; cf. the pronunciation ['kʌmftəbl] for **comfortable.**

The pronunciation [lɑːf], l. 22, [fɑːst], l. 38, [klɑːsp], l. 40, is consistent for this passage, but Mr. Lawrence declares that in an informal pronunciation, say if he went into a stationery store and asked for paper-clasps, he would say [klæsps]. Further examination showed that in words of this type he sometimes pronounced [ɑː], sometimes [æ].

The pronunciations ['kɑnstɪˌtʊt], l. 35, [mə'tʊɹ], l. 18, [ɛn'θuzɪæzm], l. 18, cannot be taken as indicating a constant preference of [ʊ], [u] for [ju] after [t], [d], etc., for sometimes, especially under full stress, the pronunciation is [ju], as in [njuː], l. 7.

The diphthongal vowel in [soʊ], l. 1, is due to an exceptionally strong stress in this word, and so also in other cases of [oʊ].

For the vowel of **not, God, what,** etc., the pronunciation [ɑ] is constant. Observe that for the accented vowel in **make, take, patriotism, they,** etc., a diphthong was not present, even under strong stress. As to final unstressed syllables, note ['beːsəz], l. 20, ['raɪtʃəsnəs], l. 20, etc., beside ['fɪtɪd], l. 11, ['lɛvɛld], l. 15. The mixed character of this pronunciation is not an individual peculiarity but is quite generally characteristic of cultivated American speech.

## VII

### 'wɔːkɪŋ

ðə 'plɛʒəɹ əv 'ɛksəsaɪz ɪz duː fʌɪst tʊ ə 'pjʊəlɪ 'fɪzɪkl ɪm'prɛʃən, ænd 'sɛkəndlɪ tʊ ə sɛns əv 'paʊəɹ ɪn 'ækʃən.

ðə fʌɪst sɔːs əv ˈplɛʒəɹ, ˈvɛːrɪz əv kɔːs wɪð ɑʊə kənˈdɪ-
ʃən ænd ðə steːt əv ðə səˈrɑʊndɪŋ ˈsʌːkəmˈstænsəz; ðə
5 ˈsɛkənd wɪ ðɪ əˈmɑʊnt ænd kaɪnd əv ˈpɑʊə, ænd ðɪ
ɛkˈstɛnt ænd kaɪnd əv ˈækʃən. ɪn ɔːl fɔːmz əv ˈæktɪv
ˈɛksəsaɪz, ðəɹ ɑ θriː ˈpɑʊəz ˌsaɪməlˈte·nɪəslɪ ɪn ˈækʃən,
— ðə wɪl, ðə ˈmʌslz nd ðɪ ˈɪntɛlɛkt. iːtʃ əv ðiːz prɪ-
ˈdɑmɪˌne·ts ɪn ˈdɪfrənt kaɪndz əv ˈɛksəsaɪz. ɪn ˈwɔː-
10 kɪŋ, ðə wɪl n ˈmʌslz ə so əˈkʌstəmd tə wʌːk təˈgɛðəɹ, n
pəˈfɔːm ðɛə tæsk wɪð so ˈlɪtl ɛkˈspɛndɪtʃʊɹ əv fɔːs ðæt
ðɪ ˈɪntɛlɛkt ɪz lɛft kəmˈpærɪtɪvlɪ friː. ðə ˈmɛntl ˈplɛʒəɹ
ɪn ˈwɔːkɪŋ, əz sʌtʃ, ɪz ɪn ðə sɛns əv ˈpɑʊəɹ ˈovəɹ ɔːl ɑʊə
ˈmuːvɪŋ məˈʃinərɪ . . .
15 ˈhɪəɹ ənd ðæːɹ, ðə fiːld w z ˈdɑtɪd wɪð smɔːl ˈflɑʊəz.
ʍɛrˈɛvə ju lʊkt, ju sɔː ðɛə ˈgoːldn hɛdz ˈnɑdɪŋ ɪn ðə
briːz. ðe· fɪld ðɪ æː wɪð ðɛə ˈrɪtʃ ˈoːdə. ɪt wəz ə
ˈmɑːvəl ðət sʌtʃ ˈtaɪnɪ ˈblɑsəmz ʃʊd hæv so ˈvɛrɪ ˈhɛvɪ
ə pəˈfjum. ɪn ˈkʌlə ðe· ˈvɛːrid frəm rɪtʃ ˈɑrɪndʒ tə
20 ˈpeːlɪst ˈjɛlo. wʌn wɔːkt ˈwɛːr lɪ fɔ ˈfɪəɹ əv ˈkrʌʃɪŋ
ðɛm ˈʌndə fʊt.

## Walking

The pleasure of exercise is due first to a purely physical impression, and secondly to a sense of power in action. The first source of pleasure varies of course with our condition and the state of the surrounding circumstances; the second with the amount and kind of power; and the extent and kind of action. In all forms of active exercise there are three powers simultaneously in action, — the will, the muscles and the intellect. Each of these predominates in different kinds of exercise. In walking, the will and muscles are so accustomed to work together, and perform their task with so little expenditure of force, that the intellect is left comparatively free. The mental pleasure in walking, as such, is in the sense of power over all our moving machinery . . .

Here and there, the field was dotted with small flowers. Wherever you looked, you saw their golden heads nodding in the breeze. They filled the air with their rich odor. It was a marvel that such tiny blossoms should have so very heavy a perfume. In color they varied from rich orange to palest yellow. One walked warily for fear of crushing them under foot.

## REMARKS

Down to the break, this passage is from Holmes' *Autocrat*. The concluding sentences were made up for the purpose of transcription. The pronunciation is that of Mr. H. W. Wells, who has always lived in New York City, with occasional short periods of residence in New England. Final [ɹ] appears in Mr. Wells's pronunciation in unstressed syllables before vowels, and usually, though not always, before pauses. In l. 5, the two words **with the** are run together, with only one consonant between them. In l. 10, **are** is made very unemphatic, the sound being recorded as [ə], though it is better described as a weakened form of [ɑ]. Nasalization of vowels is marked in Mr. Wells's pronunciation. In strongly stressed syllables or words like **there**, l. 15, **air**, l. 17, the vowel is [æː], but not in weak syllables, as in **there**, l. 7, **their**, ll. 16, 17, or in **varies**, l. 3, **varied**, l. 19, **warily**, l. 20. The stress in **perfume**, l. 19, as a noun, is usually on the first syllable.

## VIII

### dɑʊt

ʌn'fɔːtʃənətlɪ dʒʌst əz aɪ wəz traɪ'ʌmfntlɪ 'ænsərɪŋ, "'sʌɪtnlɪ nɑt," ə'nʌðə 'kwɛstʃən mɑːtʃt 'ɪntə maɪ maɪnd, ɪs'kɔːtəd baɪ ə 'vɛrɪ dɪ'faɪənt "ɔːt."

"ɔːt aɪ tə goʊ, ʍɛn aɪ hæv sʌtʃ ə dɪ'beːt ə'baʊt ət?"

5 bət ʍaɪl aɪ wəz pəˈplɛkst, nd ˈskɑfɪŋ æt maɪ oʊn ˈskruplz, ðə ˈfɛrɪ-ˌbɛl ˈsʌdnlɪ ræŋ, nd ˈænsəd ɔːl maɪ ˈkwɛstʃənz. ɪnˌvɑlənˈtɛrɪlɪ aɪ ˈhʌrəd ɔn bɔəd. ðə boːt slɪpt frəm ðə dɑk. aɪ wɛnt ʌp ɔn dɛk tʊ ɪnˈdʒɔɪ ðə vjuː əv ðə ˈsɪtɪ frəm ðə beɪ, bət dʒʌst əz aɪ sæt dɑʊn,
10 n mɛnt tʊ hɛv sɛd, "hɑʊ ˈbjutəfəl," ə fɑʊnd məˈsɛlf ˈæskɪŋ, "ɔːt aɪ tʊ hɛv kʌm?"

lɔst ɪn pəˈplɛksɪŋ dɪˈbeːt, aɪ sɔː ˈlɪtl əv ðə ˈsɪnərɪ əv ðə beɪ; bət ðə rɪˈmɛmbrəns əv prʊu nd ðə ˈdʒɛntl ˈɪnfluəns əv ðə ˈdeɪ ˈplʌndʒd mɪ ˈɪntə ə mʊːd əv ˈpɛnsɪv
15 ˈrɛvərɪ ʍɪtʃ ˈnʌθɪŋ ˈtɛndəd tə dɪsˈtrɔɪ, ənˈtɪl wɪ ˈsʌdnlɪ əˈraɪvd ət ðə ˈlændɪŋ.

## Doubt

Unfortunately, just as I was triumphantly answering "Certainly not!" another question marched into my mind, escorted by a very defiant *ought*.

"Ought I to go when I have such a debate about it?"

But while I was perplexed, and scoffing at my own scruples, the ferry-bell suddenly rang, and answered all my questions. Involuntarily I hurried on board. The boat slipped from the dock. I went up on deck to enjoy the view of the city from the bay, but just as I sat down, and meant to have said "how beautiful!" I found myself asking:

"Ought I to have come?"

Lost in perplexing debate, I saw little of the scenery of the bay; but the remembrance of Prue and the gentle influence of the day plunged me into a mood of pensive reverie which nothing tended to destroy, until we suddenly arrived at the landing.

## REMARKS

The passage is from George William Curtis, *Prue and I*, and the transcription is the reading pronunciation of Mr. George Summey, Jr., a native of Kentucky, of North Carolina parentage, who has lived in South Carolina, Tennessee, and since the age of twenty-three in North Carolina. His manner of speech would strike any attentive observer as Southern, but not markedly so. His speech is slow, and more attention is given to unstressed syllables than is customary, though the vowels are not necessarily made clearer.

l. 1. [ʌn'fɔːtʃənətlɪ]. There is no trace of a consonant for **r** before consonants and finally.

l. 4. [ət]. Very lightly stressed.

l. 5. ['skɑfɪŋ]. The more usual pronunciation is ['skɔfɪŋ].

l. 7. ['hʌrəd]. A more common standard pronunciation would be ['hʌrɪd], or ['hʌrid], the latter to be preferred.

[bɔəd]. The vowel is distinctly short.

[boːt]. No trace of diphthongal quality, but when final, as in [goʊ], l. 4, the diphthong is present.

l. 10. ['bjutəfəl]. In a word like this, if one had a mark for accent indicating a degree between half-stress and unstressed, one would employ it on the second and third syllables to suggest Mr. Summey's pronunciation. More commonly pronounced ['bjutɪfəl].

l. 12. ['sɪnərɪ]. The vowel of the first syllable is not usually lowered.

l. 13. [prʊu]. The diphthong very distinct, perhaps because of the slow tempo.

['ɪnfluəns]. More commonly, ['ɪnflʊəns].

l. 14. [mʊːd]. For common standard [muːd].

## IX

### ˌθænə'tɑpsəs

tu hɪm hu ɪn ðə lʌv əv 'neɪtʃəɹ hoːldz
kə'mjunjən wɪθ həɹ 'vɪzɪbl fɔːɹmz, ʃɪ spiːks
ə 'vɛːrɪəs 'læŋgwɪdʒ; fɔɹ ɪz 'geːəɹ 'ɑʊəɹz
ʃɪ hæz ə vɔɪs əv 'glædnəs, nd ə smaɪl

5 nd ˈɛləkwəns əv ˈbjutɪ, nd ʃɪ glaɪdz
ɪntu hɪz ˈdɑːɹkəɹ ˈmjuzɪŋz, wɪθ ə maɪld
nd ˈhiːlɪŋ ˈsɪmpəθɪ ðət stiːlz əˈweɪ
ðɛɹ ˈʃɑːɹpnəs, ɛːɹ hi ɪz əˈwɛːɹ. ʍɛn θɔːts
əv ðə læst ˈbɪtəɹ ˈɑʊəɹ kʌm laɪk ə blaɪt
10 ˈovəɹ ðaɪ ˈspɪrət, nd sæd ˈɪmɪdʒəz
əv ðə stəɹn ˈægənɪ, nd ʃrɑʊd, nd pɔːl,
nd ˈbrɛθləs ˈdɑːɹknəs, nd ðə ˈnæro hɑʊs,
meɪk ði tə ˈʃʌdəɹ, nd groː sɪk æt hɑːɹt; —
goː fɔːɹθ ˈʌndəɹ ðɪ ˈoːpn skaɪ, nd lɪst
15 tə ˈneɪtʃəɹz ˈtiːtʃɪŋz, ʍaɪl frəm ɔːl əˈrɑʊnd —
əɹθ nd həɹ ˈwɑtəɹz nd ðə dɛpθs əv ɛːɹ —
kʌmz ə stɪl vɔɪs.

## Thanatopsis

To him who in the love of Nature holds
Communion with her visible forms, she speaks
A various language; for his gayer hours
She has a voice of gladness, and a smile
And eloquence of beauty, and she glides
Into his darker musings, with a mild
And healing sympathy, that steals away
Their sharpness, ere he is aware. When thoughts
Of the last bitter hour come like a blight
Over thy spirit, and sad images
Of the stern agony, and shroud, and pall,
And breathless darkness, and the narrow house,
Make thee to shudder, and grow sick at heart; —
Go forth, under the open sky, and list
To Nature's teachings, while from all around —
Earth and her waters, and the depths of air —
Comes a still voice.

## REMARKS

This passage represents the informal reading pronunciation of Mr. F. L. Mott, a native and resident of Iowa. The only pronunciations which call for comment are [θɔːts], l. 8, which has been recorded with [ɔː], but which has a sound between [ɑː] and [ɔː]; in l. 16 [ˈwɑtəɹz] has distinctly [ɑ]; in ll. 2, 6, **with** has a voiceless final consonant. For **r** final and before consonants the transcription [ɹ] has been used, though perhaps the sound is nearer [r].

## X

### æn ˈɛləˋve·təd ˋkɑnvərˈseːʃən

aɪ wəz ˈgoːɪŋ dɑʊn tɑʊn ɔn ðɪ ˈɛləˋve·təd ðɪs ˈæftər-
ˋnuːn nd pæst ðə taɪm baɪ ˈlɪsnɪŋ tə ðə ˋkɑnvərˈseːʃən
əv ə ˈnʌmbər əv ˈskuːl-ˋgərlz. ðə· wər frəm wʌn əv
ðə ˈsɪtɪ ˈhaɪ-ˋskuːlz, n wər drɛst laɪk ðə ˈdɔːtərz əv
5 ˈwɛl-tə-ˈduː ˈpɛːrənts. ðe· wər ɔːl ˈvɛrɪ mʌtʃ ɪkˈsaɪtəd
ˈovər n ɪgzæmɪˈneːʃən ɪn ˈɪŋglɪʃ ˈlɪtərəˈtʃʊr ʍɪtʃ əd bɪn
hɛld ɪn ðə skuːl ðæt ˈmɔːrnɪŋ. wʌn əv ðə gərlz siːmd
ˈvɛrɪ mʌtʃ dɪsˈtərbd ˈovər ðɪ ˈænsər tə wʌn əv ðə ˈkwɛstʃənz. "o gərlz," ʃɪ sɛd, "aɪ wɑnt ə noʊ əˈbɑʊt ðoːz
10 oʊdz. aɪ noː wʌn wəz baɪ kiːts n wʌn wəz baɪ ˈʃɛlɪ, n
aɪ noː wʌn wəz əˈbɑʊt ə ˈskaɪ-ˋlɑːrk n wʌn wəz əˈbɑʊt
ə ˈnaɪtənˋgeːl, bət aɪ doːnt noː ˈʍɛðər aɪ gɑt ðəm
streːt." "ʍaɪ," ˈænsərd wʌn əv hər kəmˈpænjənz,
"ˈʃɛlɪ roːt ðə wʌn əˈbɑʊt ðə ˈnaɪtənˋgeːl n kiːts ðə wʌn
15 əˈbɑʊt ðə ˈskaɪ-ˋlɑːrk." "ðɛːr nɑʊ," moːnd ðə gərl
huː hæd æskt ðə ˈkwɛstʃən, "ɪznt ðæt tuː bæd! aɪ
dʒʌst nuː aɪd gɛt ðoːz bəɪdz mɪkst, n aɪ dɪd."

### An Elevated Conversation

I was going down town on the Elevated this afternoon and passed the time by listening to the conversation of a number of school-girls. They were from one of the city high-schools, and were dressed like the daughters of well-to-do parents. They were all very much excited over an examination in English literature which had been held in the school that morning. One of the girls seemed very much disturbed over the answer to one of the questions. "O girls," she said, "I want to know about these odes. I know one was by Shelley and one was by Keats, and I know one was about a sky-lark and one was about a nightingale, but I don't know whether I get them straight." "Why," answered one of her companions, "Shelley wrote the one about the nightingale and Keats the one about the sky-lark." "There now," moaned the girl who had asked the question, "isn't that too bad! I just knew I'd get those boids mixed, and I did."

## REMARKS

This represents the conversational pronunciation of Mr. G. W. Mead, practically all of whose life has been passed in the Middle West. There is no [ɹ] in Mr. Mead's pronunciation, except occasionally in unstressed final syllables. In l. 6 [ˈlɪtərəˈtʃʊr] is a somewhat formal pronunciation for informal [ˈlɪtərətʃəɹ]. For **want**, the transcription is [wɑnt], l. 9, and so it would be generally in this pronunciation for words like **watch**, **water**, **swan**, etc. A rather slow tempo accounts for the diphthongs in [noʊ], l. 9, [oʊdz], l. 10, both stressed. But [noː], l. 10, is only relatively lightly stressed. For [ˈnaɪtənˌgeːl], l. 12, [ˈnaɪtnˌgeːl] might have been written. In l. 17 [bɜɪdz] is New York dialect for **birds**.

## XI

### rɪp væn ˈwɪŋkl

æz hɪ wəz əˈbæʊt tə dɪˈsɛnd, hɪ hʌːd ə vɔɪs frəm ə ˈdɪstəns ˈhælʊɪŋ, "rɪp væn ˈwɪŋkl! rɪp væn ˈwɪŋkl!"

hɪ lʊkt ræʊnd, bət kʊd siː ˈnʌθɪŋ bət ə kroʊ, ˈwɪŋɪŋ
ɪts ˈsɑlɪˌtɛrɪ flaɪt əˈkrɔs ðə ˈmæʊntn. hɪ θɔːt ɪz ˈfænsɪ
5 mʌst əv dɪˈsiːvd ɪm, nd tᴀɪnd əˈgɛn tʊ dɪˈsɛnd, ʍɛn
hɪ hᴀɪd ðə seɪm kraɪ rɪŋ θrʊɪ ðə stɪl ˈiːvnɪŋ ɛɪə; "rɪp
væn ˈwɪŋkl! rɪp væn ˈwɪŋkl!" — æt ðə seɪm taɪm wʊlf
ˈbrɪsld ʌp hɪz bæk, nd ˈgɪvɪŋ ə loʊ ˈgræʊəl, skʌlkt tʊ
hɪz ˈmæstəz saɪd, ˈlʊkɪŋ ˈfɪəflɪ dæʊn ˈɪntʊ ðə glɛn.
10 rɪp næʊ fɛlt ə veɪg æprɪˈhɛnʃən ˈstiːlɪŋ ˈovə hɪm; hɪ
lʊkt ˈæŋʃəslɪ ɪn ðə seɪm dɪˈrɛkʃən, nd pəˈsiːvd ə
streɪndʒ ˈfɪgjə ˈsloʊlɪ ˈtɔɪlɪŋ ʌp ðə rɑks, nd ˈbɛndɪŋ
ˈʌndə ðə weɪt əv ˈsʌmθɪŋ hɪ ˈkærid ɔn hɪz bæk. hɪ wəz
səˈpraɪzd tə siː ˈɛnɪ ˈhjumən ˈbiːɪŋ ɪn ðɪs ˈloʊnlɪ nd
15 ʌnˈfrikwɛntɪd pleɪs; bət səˈpoɪzɪŋ ɪt tə bi ˈsʌmˌwʌn əv
ðə ˈneɪbəˌhʊd ɪn niːd əv hɪz əˈsɪstəns, hɪ ˈheɪsnd dæʊn
tə jiːld ɪt.

ɔn ˈnɪrə əˈproɪtʃ hɪ wəz stɪl mɔː səˈpraɪzd æt ðə
sɪŋgjuˈlɛrɪtɪ əv ðə ˈstreɪndʒəz əˈpɪrəns. hɪ wəz ə ʃɔːt
20 ˈskwɛə-ˌbɪlt old ˈfɛlo, wɪð θɪk ˈbʊʃɪ ˈhɛɪə nd ə ˈgrɪzld
ˈbɪəd. hɪz drɛs wəz əv ðɪ ænˈtiːk dʌtʃ ˈfæʃn: ə klɔθ
ˈdʒəɹkn stræpt ræʊnd ðə weɪst, ˈsɛvrəl ˈpɛɪə əv ˈbrɪtʃɪz,
ðə ˈæʊtə wʌn əv ˈæmpl ˈvɑljəm, ˈdɛkəˌre·tɪd wɪð roʊz
əv ˈbʌtnz dæʊn ðə saɪdz, nd ˈbʌntʃəz æt ðə niːz. hɪ
25 bɔːr ɔn hɪz ˈʃoːldə ə stæʊt kɛg, ðæt siːmd fʌl əv ˈlɪkə,
nd me·d saɪnz fə rɪp tə əˈproɪtʃ nd əˈsɪst ɪm wɪθ ðə
loʊd. ðo ˈræðə ʃaɪ nd dɪsˈtrʌstfəl əv ðɪs nju əˈkwe·ntns,
rɪp kəmˈplaɪd wɪð ɪz ˈjuʒjəl əˈlækrɪtɪ; nd ˈmjutʃuəlɪ
rɪˈliːvɪŋ wʌn əˈnʌðə, ðe· ˈklæmbəd ʌp ə ˈnæro ˈgʌlɪ,
30 əˈpɛɪrəntlɪ ðə draɪ bɛd əv ə ˈmæʊntn ˈtɔrənt.

. . .

jɛs, ðæt ˈɛldəlɪ ˈle·dɪ ɪz ˈmɪzəz wᴀɪθ. ʃi lɪvz ɪn
ˈtʃɑːlstn. ðə tu gᴀɪlz ɑː hə ˈdɔːtəz, ðə ˈmɪsɪs wᴀɪθ.
ˈmɪzəz wᴀɪθ ɪz ə gre·t ˈlʌvə əv ˈmjuzɪk, nd ˈræɪlɪ ˈɛvə

ˈmɪsəz ə ˈsɪmfənɪ ˈkɑnˈsʌːt. ɪn ðə ˈsʌmə ʃi spɛndz ə
35 gre·t diːl əv hə taɪm ɪn ðə ˈgɑːdn, ˈwɔtərɪŋ nd ˈtrɪmɪŋ
hə plænts. ʃi ɪz pəˈtɪkjəlɪ fɔnd əv pəˈtuːnjəz.

## Rip Van Winkle

As he was about to descend, he heard a voice from a distance, hallooing, "Rip Van Winkle! Rip Van Winkle!" He looked round, but could see nothing but a crow winging its solitary flight across the mountain. He thought his fancy must have deceived him, and turned again to descend, when he heard the same cry ring through the still evening air; "Rip Van Winkle! Rip Van Winkle!" — at the same time Wolf bristled up his back, and giving a low growl, skulked to his master's side, looking fearfully down into the glen. Rip now felt a vague apprehension stealing over him; he looked anxiously in the same direction, and perceived a strange figure slowly toiling up the rocks, and bending under the weight of something he carried on his back. He was surprised to see any human being in this lonely and unfrequented place; but supposing it to be someone of the neighborhood in need of his assistance, he hastened down to yield it.

On nearer approach he was still more surprised at the singularity of the stranger's appearance. He was a short, square-built old fellow, with thick bushy hair, and a grizzled beard. His dress was of the antique Dutch fashion: a cloth jerkin strapped round the waist, several pair of breeches, the outer one of ample volume, decorated with rows of buttons down the sides, and bunches at the knees. He bore on his shoulder a stout keg, that seemed full of liquor, and made signs for Rip to approach and assist him with the load. Though rather shy and distrustful of this new acquaintance, Rip complied with his usual alacrity; and mutually relieving one another, they clambered up a narrow gully, apparently the dry bed of a mountain torrent.

. . .

Yes, that elderly lady is Mrs. Worth. She lives in Charleston. The two girls are her daughters, the Misses Worth. Mrs. Worth is a great lover of music, and rarely ever misses a symphony concert. In the summer she spends a great deal of time in her garden, watering and trimming her plants. She is particularly fond of petunias.

## REMARKS

This passage down to the break represents the slightly formal reading pronunciation of a paragraph or two from Irving's *Rip Van Winkle* as read by Miss Susan Lewis, a native and always a resident of Texas. After the break come several made-up sentences of somewhat less formal character. The tempo was rather slow, the diphthongal quality of some sounds being thus more marked than ordinarily. For **jerkin**, l. 22, a somewhat literary and unfamiliar word, we have [ˈdʒəɹkn], probably as a spelling-pronunciation, since **r** is regularly omitted by Miss Lewis before consonants. In final position, **r** is also silent, even before words beginning with a vowel, except [bɔːr], l. 25, where the [r] is perhaps due to the [ɔː], see above, § 305. In the concluding passage, compare the pronunciation of **Mrs.**, **Misses** and **misses**, and for **Mrs.**, see above, § 320. As Miss Lewis pronounces **Mrs.**, the word is almost a monosyllable with a long final consonant. For **rarely**, l. 33, perhaps the transcription should be [ˈræːəlɪ]. The stressing of **concert** [ˈkɑnˈsʌːt], l. 34, is noteworthy. In general the vowel [ʌː] is only slightly tense in Miss Lewis's pronunciation. In l. 26 [wɪθ ðə] is a good example of phonetic differentiation, the voiceless consonant in [wɪθ] being evidently assumed to keep the word separate from [ðə].

## XII

### ˈhæmlɪts spiːtʃ

spiːk ðə spiːtʃ, aɪ preɪ ju, æz aɪ prəˈnaʊnst ɪt tʊ ju, ˈtrɪpɪŋlɪ ɔn ðə tʌŋ; bət ɪf ju maʊð ɪt, æz ˈmɛnɪ əv jʊə ˈpleɪəz duː, aɪ hæd æz liːf ðə taʊn ˈkraɪə spoːk maɪ laɪnz. nɔ du nɔt sɔː ðɪ ɛːə tuː mʌtʃ wɪð jʊə hænd,
5 ðʌs, bət juz ɔːl ˈdʒɛntlɪ; fɔɹ ɪn ðə ˈvɛrɪ ˈtɔrɛnt, ˈtɛmpɪst, ænd æz aɪ meɪ seɪ, ðə ˈʍɛːlˌwɪnd əv ˈpæʃən, ju mʌst əˈkwaɪəɹ ənd bɪˈgɛt ə ˈtɛmpərəns ðæt me· gɪv ɪt ˈsmuːðnəs. o ɪt əˈfɛndz mi tə ðə soʊl tʊ hɪɹ ə roˈbʌstʃəs ˈpɛrɪˌwɪg-ˈpeːtəd ˈfɛlo tɛːɹ ə ˈpæʃən tʊ ˈtætəz,
10 tʊ ˈvɛrɪ rægz, tʊ splɪt ðɪ ˈɪəz əv ðə ˈgraʊndlɪŋz, huː fɔ ðə most paːt ɑː ˈkeːpəbl əv ˈnʌθɪŋ bʌt ɪnˈɛksplɪkəbl ˈdʌm-ˈʃoʊz ænd nɔɪz. aɪ kʊd hæv sʌtʃ ə ˈfɛlo ʍɪpt fɔɹ ˌɔːˈduːɪŋ ˈtɛːməgənt; ɪt ˌɑʊtˈhɛrədz ˈhɛrəd; preɪ ju əˈvɔɪd ɪt.
15 biː nɔt tʊ teɪm ˈniːðəɹ, bət lɛt jʊəɹ oʊn dɪsˈkrɛʃən bɪ jʊə ˈtjutəɹ; sjut ðɪ ˈækʃən tʊ ðə wɛːd, ðə wɛːd tə ðɪ ˈækʃən; wɪð ðɪs ˈspɛʃəl əbˈzɛːvəns, ðætʃʊ ˌɔːˈstɛp nɔt ðə ˈmɔdəstɪ əv ˈneːtʃəɹ; fɔɹ ˈɛnɪˌθɪŋ so ˌovəˈdʌn ɪz frɔm ðə ˈpɛːpəs əv ˈpleɪɪŋ, huz ɛnd, boθ æt ðə fɛːst
20 ænd naʊ, wɔz ænd ɪz, tʊ hoʊld, æz twɛːɹ, ðə ˈmɪrəɹ ʌp tʊ ˈneːtʃəɹ; tʊ ʃoʊ ˈvɛːtʃʊ həɹ oʊn ˈfiːtʃəɹ, skɔːn həɹ oʊn ˈɪmɪdʒ, ænd ðə ˈvɛrɪ eɪdʒ ənd ˈbɔdɪ əv ðə taɪm, hɪz fɔːm ənd ˈprɛʃəɹ. naʊ ðɪs ˌovəˈdʌn, ɔ kʌm ˈtɑːdɪ ɔːf, ðo ɪt me·k ðɪ ʌnˈskɪlfəl lɑːf, ˈkæˌnɔt bət me·k
25 ðə dʒuˈdɪʃəs griːv; ðə ˈsɛnʃəɹ əv ðə ʍɪtʃ wʌn mʌst ɪn jʊəɹ əˈlaʊəns, ˌɔːˈweɪ ə hoʊl ˈθɪətəɹ əv ˈʌðəz.

### Hamlet's Speech

Speak the speech, I pray you, as I pronounced it to you, trippingly on the tongue; but if you mouth it, as many of your players do, I had as lief the town-crier spoke my lines. Nor do not saw the air too much with your hand, thus, but use all gently; for in the very torrent, tempest, and, as I may say, the whirlwind of passion, you must acquire and beget a temperance that may give it smoothness. O, it offends me to the soul to hear a robustious periwig-pated fellow tear a passion to tatters, to very rags, to split the ears of the groundlings, who for the most part are capable of nothing but inexplicable dumb-shows and noise. I would have such a fellow whipped for o'erdoing Termagant; it outherods Herod; pray you, avoid it.

Be not too tame neither, but let your own discretion be your tutor; suit the action to the word, the word to the action; with this special observance, that you o'erstep not the modesty of nature; for anything so overdone is from the purpose of playing, whose end, both at first and now, was and is, to hold, as 't were, the mirror up to nature; to show virtue her own feature, scorn her own image, and the very age and body of the time his form and pressure. Now this overdone, or come tardy off, though it make the unskilful laugh, cannot but make the judicious grieve; the censure of the which one must in your allowance o'erweigh a whole theater of others.

## REMARKS

The transcription of this passage from *Hamlet*, Act III, Scene II, represents the pronunciation of Miss Theodora Ursula Irvine, a professional teacher of public speaking, who has given particular attention to training students for the stage. The passage is not rendered in a highly formal, dramatic style, but as the sense of it would seem to demand, in what might be called a formal natural style. The tempo is somewhat slower than conversation, and some sounds are given clearer and different values than they would have in familiar style. Long [e] and [o] are more diphthongal than they customarily are in American speech.

l. 2. [jʊə]. A final [ɹ] is distinctly present when the succeeding word begins with a vowel, or in logically prominent words followed by a pause. When final before immediately following words with a consonant, no **r** is audible in Miss Irvine's pronunciation, though internally **r** before a consonant is sometimes given audible value, sometimes not. This is so slight, however, that it seemed better not to record it in the transcription. Intervocalic **r** is commonly trilled by Miss Irvine, though not strongly, but **r** after a consonant, as in [ˈtrɪpɪŋlɪ], l. 2, is not trilled. The most notable feature of Miss Irvine's pronunciation is the value given to vowels **e**, **i** in stressed syllables before **r** followed by a consonant. This has been transcribed as [ɛː], as in ll. 6, 13, 16, 19, 21. The symbol is not adequate, however, since the sound is not the same as the vowel of **there, where,** etc., but may be described as a mid front tense neutral vowel, which is kept distinct from both [ʌː] and [ə].

Miss Irvine pronounces **your** as [jʊə] or [jɔə] indifferently. Words with 'long **o**' are not always strongly diphthongal, sometimes not at all, as in [spoːk], l. 3. In l. 8 the exclamation [o] is short and not strongly stressed.

For **o** in **not**, l. 4, **modesty**, l. 18, **body**, l. 22, etc., Miss Irvine's sound is closer to [ɔ] than to [ɑ].

## XIII

### ˈgroːɪŋ oːld

fəɹ ˈfɔɹtɪ ˈjɪəɹz nɛkst ˈi·stəɹ deɪ,
hɪm n miː ɪn wɪnd n ˈwɛðəɹ
həv bɪn ə-ˈgɪtn bɛnt n greɪ
ˈmɔgn əˈlɔŋ təˈgɛðəɹ.

5 wɪɹ nɑt so ˈvɛrɪ oːld, əv kɔɹs!
bət stɪl, wɪ eːnt so ˈɔːfəl spraɪ
əz ʍɛn wɪ wɛnt tə ˈsɪŋən-ˌskuːl

əˈfʊt n krɔs lɑts, hɪm n aɪ —
n wɔːkt bæk hoːm ðə ˈlɔŋgəst weɪ —
10 n ðə muːn ə-ʃaɪnən ɔn ðə snoʊ,
ˈmeːkn ðə roːd əz braɪt əz deɪ
n hɪz vɔɪs ˈtɔːkn loʊ.

lænd seːks! dʒɛst ˈhɪəɹ mɪ tɔːk —
fəɹ ɔːl ðə wəɹld, dʒɛst laɪk ə gəɹl,
15 miː — nɪɹlɪ ˈsɪkstɪ! — ˈwɛl — ə — ˈwɛl!
aɪ wʌz so tɔːl n strɔŋ, ðə kəɹl
ɪn maɪ ˈhɛːəɹ, sɪm sɛd, wəz laɪk
ðə ˈkrɪŋklz ɪn ə ˈmɛdəɹ brʊk,
so brɑʊn n braɪt! bət ˈðɛːəɹ!

20 aɪ gɛs hɪ gɑt ət frʌm ə bʊk.
hɪz tɔːk ɪn ðɛm ðɛɹ deɪz wəz fʊl
əv dʒɛst sɛtʃ ˈnɑnˌsɛns — ˈdo·ntʃu θɪŋk
aɪ ˈdɪdnt laɪk ət, fəɹ aɪ dɪd!
aɪ wɔːkt əˈlɔŋ ðɛːɹ glæd tə drɪŋk
25 hɪz wəɹdz ɪn laɪk ðə brɛθ ə laɪf —
ˈhɛvənz n əɹθ, ʍɑt fuːlz wi ˈwɪmən biː!
n ʍɛn hɪ æst mɪ fəɹ ɪz waɪf,
aɪ ˈænsəɹd ‘jɛs,’ əv kɔɹs, jə siː.

n ðɛn kʌm wəɹk, n ˈtrʌbl bɪt —
30 nɑt mʌtʃ taɪm fəɹ ˈlʌvˌtɔːk ðɛn!
wɪ bɔːt ə fɑːɹm n ˈmɔɹgɪdʒd ɪt,
n wəɹkt n sleːvd laɪk ɔːl pəˈsɛst
tə lɪft ðæt ˈtərəbl ˈgraɪndn weːt.

aɪ wɔːʃt n tʃəɹnd n soʊd —
35 n ˈtʃɪldəɹn kʌm, tɪl wɪ hæd eːt

əz ˈhænsəm beːbz əz ˈɛvəɹ groʊd
tə woːk bəˈsaɪd ə ˈmʌðəɹz niː.
ðe· hɛlpt mɪ bɛːɹ ɪt ɔːl, jə siː.

ɪt eːnt bɪn ˈnʌθən ɛls bət skrʌb
40 n rʌb n beːk n stuː
ðə hʌl, hʌl taɪm, ovəɹ stoːv əɹ tʌb —
no taɪm tə rɛst əz mɛn foːks duː. —
aɪ tɛl jə, səmˈtaɪmz aɪ sɪt n θɪŋk
haʊ naɪs ðə greːv l biː, dʒɛst
45 wʌn naɪs, swiːt, ˈɛvəɹˈlæstn rɛst!

o doːnt lʊk ˈskɛəɹt! aɪ miːn
dʒɛst ʍæt aɪ seɪ. eːnt ˈkreːzɪ jɛt,
bət ɪts əˈnʌf tə meːk mɪ soʊ —
əv kɔɹs ɪt eːnt no jus tə frɛt —
50 hu sɛd ɪt wʌz? ɪts ˈnætʃəɹl, ðoʊ,
bət oʊ, ɪf aɪ wəz ˈoːnlɪ ˈðɛːəɹ —
ɪn ðə pæst, n jʌŋ wʌns ˈmɔːəɹ —
n hæd ðə ˈkrɪŋklz ɪn maɪ ˈhɛːəɹ —
n ɑːɹmz əz raʊnd n strɔŋ, n saɪd
55 əz ɪt wəz ðɛn! — aɪd — aɪd —

aɪd duː ət ɔːl ˈovəɹ əˈgɛn, laɪk ə fuːl,
aɪ spoːz! aɪd teːk ðə peːn
n wəɹk n ˈwʌrɪ, beːbz n ɔːl.
aɪ spoːz θɪŋz goʊ baɪ sʌm bɪg ruːl
60 əv gɑdz oʊn bʊk, bət maɪ oʊl breːn
kænt fɪks əm ʌp, so aɪl dʒɛst weːt
n duː maɪ dutɪ ʍɛn ɪts ˈklɪəɹ,
n trʌst tə hɪm tə meːk ət streːt.
— — — ˈgʊdnəs! nuːn ɪz ˈɔlmo·st ˈhɪəɹ
65 n ðɛɹ ðə mɛn kʌm θruː ðə geːt!

### Growing Old

F'r forty years next Easter day,
Him and me in wind and weather
Have been a-gittin' bent 'n' gray
Moggin' along together.

We're not so *very* old, of course!
But still, we ain't so awful spry
As when we went to singin'-school
Afoot and 'cross lots, him and I —
And walked back home the longest way —
An' the moon a-shinin' on the snow,
Makin' the road as bright as day
An' his voice talkin' low.

Land sakes! Jest hear me talk —
F'r all the world, jest like a girl,
Me — nearly sixty! — Well — a — well!
I *was* so tall and strong, the curl
In my hair, Sim said, was like
The crinkles in a medder brook,
So brown and bright! but there!
I guess he got it from a book.

His talk in them there days was full
Of jest sech nonsense — Don't you think
I didn't like it, for I did!
I walked along there, glad to drink
His words in like the breath o' life —
Heavens and earth, what fools we women be!
And when he asked me for his wife,
I answered 'yes,' of course, y' see.

And then come work, and trouble bit —
Not much time for love talk then!
We bought a farm and mortgaged it,
And worked and slaved like all possessed
To lift that turrible grindin' weight.

I washed and churned and sewed —
An' childurn come, till we had eight
As han'some babes as ever growed
To walk beside a mother's knee.
They helped me bear it all, y' see.

It ain't been nothin' else but scrub
An' rub and bake and stew
The hull, hull time, over stove or tub —
No time to rest as men folks do. —
I tell yeh, sometimes I sit and think
*How nice the grave 'll be, jest*
*One nice, sweet, everlastin' rest.*

O don't look scart! I mean
Jest what I say. Ain't crazy yet,
But its enough to make me so —
Of course it ain't no use to fret —
Who said it was? It's nacherl, though,
But O, if I was only there —
In the past, and young once more —
An' had the crinkles in my hair —
An' arms as round and strong, and side
As it was then! — I'd — I'd —

I'd do it all over again, like a fool,
I s'pose! I'd take the pain

An' work an' worry, babes and all.
I s'pose things go by some big rule
Of God's own book, but my ol' brain
Can't fix 'um up, so I'll just wait
An' do my duty when it's clear,
An' trust to Him to make it straight.
— — — Goodness! noon is almost here,
And there the men come through the gate!

## REMARKS

From *Prairie Songs*, by Hamlin Garland, pp. 142–144. The volume was published in 1893, and the poem represents a rustic dialect of the Middle West, specifically Iowa, as spoken by the pioneer settlers. It has now passed out of existence, except for sporadic survivals in country districts which have been only slightly affected by the leveling influences of public school instruction.

In this and the following dialect passages, the author's method has been to transcribe as dialectal only what it seems to have been the intention of the original writers of the passages to indicate by means of spelling as dialectal. Otherwise the passages have been transcribed in familiar colloquial style, appropriate to the general tone of the writings, but not necessarily peculiar to any particular dialect. It should be remembered that writers of dialect literature seldom endeavor to indicate dialect features either exhaustively or systematically. Mr. Garland has made no attempt to indicate different kinds of **r** in this poem, but **r** before consonants and finally is usually [r] in Iowa speech, both dialect and cultivated, or even at times back **ɹ**, see § 44.

## XIV

### ˈjæŋkɪ spiɪtʃ

næʊ ɪz ðə ˈwɪntə əv ˈæʊə ˈdɪskənˈtɛnt
mɛd ˈglorɪəs ˈsʌmə baɪ ðɪs sʌn ə jɔːk,
n ɔːl ðə ˈklæʊdz ðət læʊəd əˈpʌn æʊə hæʊs
ɪn ðə diːp ˈbʌzəm ə ðɪ ˈoːʃɪn ˈbɛrid;

5 næʊ ɛə æʊə bræʊz bæʊnd ɪð vɪk'torɪəs riːðz;
æʊə 'brjuːzɪd ɑːmz hʌŋ ʌp fə 'mɔnɪ'mɛns;
æʊə stɑːn ə'lɑrəmz 'tʃændʒd tə'mɛrɪ 'miːtɪŋz,
æʊə 'drɛfl 'mɑːtʃɪz tə də'laɪfl 'meːʒəz.
'grɪm-ˌvɪzɪdʒd wɔː hɛθ 'smjuːðd hɪz 'rɪŋkld frʌnt,
10 n næʊ, ɪn'stɪd ə 'mæʊntɪn 'bɛəbɪd stiːdz
tə fraɪt ðə soʊlz ə 'fʌːfl 'ɛdvə'sɛriz,
hi 'keːpəz 'nɪmlɪ ɪn ə 'leːdɪz 'tʃæmbə,
tə ðə lə'sɪvɪəs 'pliːzɪŋ əv ə luːt.

## Yankee Speech

Neow is the winta uv eour discontent
Med glorious summa by this sun o' Yock,
An' all the cleouds thet leowered upun eour heouse
In the deep buzzum o' the oshin buried;
Neow air eour breows beound 'ith victorious wreaths;
Eour breused arms hung up fer monimunce;
Eour starn alarums changed to merry meetins,
Eour dreffle marches to delighfle masures.
Grim-visaged war heth smeuthed his wrinkled front,
An' neow, instid o' mountin' barebid steeds
To fright the souls o' ferfle edverseries,
He capers nimly in a lady's chămber,
To the lascivious pleasin' uv a loot.

Now is the winter of our discontent
Made glorious summer by this sun of York,
And all the clouds that lour'd upon our house
In the deep bosom of the ocean buried;
Now are our brows bound with victorious wreaths;
Our bruised arms hung up for monuments;
Our stern alarums changed to merry meetings,

Our dreadful marches to delightful measures.
Grim-visaged war hath smooth'd his wrinkled front,
And now, instead of mounting barbed steeds
To fright the souls of fearful adversaries,
He capers nimbly in a lady's chamber,
To the lascivious pleasing of a lute.

## REMARKS

In the introduction to the First Series of the *Biglow Papers,* Lowell gave a version of the opening lines of *Richard III,* using the ordinary spelling to indicate as exactly as he could the pronunciation of the rustic Yankee of his day. Lowell's spelling is given here for the sake of comparison with the phonetic transcription of it which precedes it. The passage represents dialect New England speech of the middle of the last century, but many of the characteristics indicated by Lowell still survive. The author has profited by a phonetic transcription of the passage made by Professor Grandgent, in *From Franklin to Lowell, A Century of New England Pronunciation,* Publications of the Modern Language Association, Vol. VII (New Series), p. 239 (1899).

After having given a description of New England dialect speech, Lowell adds, "To the dish thus seasoned, add a drawl *ad libitum,*" but he does not try to represent the drawl.

l. 1. [næʊ]. As the first element in the diphthong, [æ] for [ɑ] is still heard in New England and in certain regions of the South.

l. 3. [əˈpʌn]. Still current dialectally.

l. 6. [ˈbrjuːzɪd]. See also [ˈsmjuːðd], l. 9. Grandgent, in the article cited above, pp. 224–226, notes a confusion in the use of [u] and [ju] in New England speech which was at its height about 1820 and which affected both polite and dialect speech. As a result a pronunciation [ju] was often transferred to words where it was organically difficult to pronounce, as in [ˈbrjuːzɪd] or where it did not historically belong, as in [ˈsmjuːðd].

l. 7. [stɑːn]. The pronunciation of **e** followed by **r** and a consonant as [ɑː], which still persists in England, e.g., in **clerk** [klɑːk], **Derby** [ˈdɑːbɪ], etc., is nowhere current in cultivated American speech and has almost if not completely disappeared from the dialects. New England words which are pronounced with [ɑː] are written with **a**, as in **Marcy** from older **Mercy**, **darn**, the expletive, from older **dern** (which of course also persists as [dəɹn, dʌːn]), **tarnal** probably from **eternal**.

## XV

### 'ɑːɹtɪ ənd 'klɔːdɪ

"'ʍɛɹsɪː æt?" rɪ'pitəd ðə 'mɛsɪndʒəɹ bɔɪ . . . ʍɛn hɪ æskt "'ʍɛɹsɪː æt?" hɪ prə'nɑʊnst ɪt "'ʍɛɹsɪː," ənd ɪn ɔːl hɪz 'sʌbsɪkwənt tɔːk, hɪ geːv ðə "s" ə sɔft ənd 'hɪsɪŋ sɑʊnd wɛl prə'lɔŋd, tu ðə 'ɛvədənt ɪn'dʒɔɪmənt
5 əv 'ɑːɹtɪ ənd ðə maɪld 'wʌndəːmənt əv 'mɪləɹ.

"ʍɛɹz huː æt?" dɪ'mændəd 'ɑːɹtɪ, ə'dɑptɪŋ ə frɑʊn ənd ə hɑːɹʃ 'mænəɹ.

"waɪ, tə 'fɔːɹ-ˋaɪd nɑbz dæt sɛnt mɪ ɑʊt ɔn tə sɑʊt saɪd."

10 "ɑɹ ju ðə seːm 'lɪtl bɔɪ? 'wʊdnt ðæt frɔst jə, ðoʊ, 'mɪləɹ? ðɪs əz 'lɪtl 'braɪt-ˋaɪz ðət tʊk ðə noːt fəɹ hɔːl."

"ɔɪ, ʍəts 'iːtn jə?" æskt ðə bɔɪ, 'gɪvɪŋ ə 'wɔːɹˋlaɪk kəɹl tə ðə 'kɔɹnəɹz əv hɪz mɑʊθ.

"oːʊ, ɑːʊ! 'lɪsn tə ðæt. aɪl 'bɛtʃəɹ ðə 'tʌfəst bɔɪ
15 ðət 'ɛvəɹ 'hæpnd. 'ʍɑtʃu bɪn 'duən ɔːl deɪ, 'pleːən 'mɑːɹblz fəɹ kiːps əɹ 'stændn ɪn frʌnt ə wʌn ə ðɛm daɪm mju'ziəmz?"

"ɔɪ, seɪː; jə tɪŋk jəɹ flaɪ. dæt jʌŋ 'fɛləɹ sɛnt mɪ ɔːl tə weɪ tə 'fɔɹtɪ-ˋtriː 'naɪntɪ-ˋtriː 'kæləmɛt 'ævnuː. aɪ
20 'kʊdnt gɪt bæk no· 'sʊnəɹ."

"hu wʌz ɪt ðə noːt wəz tuː?"

"hɪz ræg, ə gɛs."

"oːʊ! hɪz ræg! 'ʍɑdʒə θɪŋk ə ðæt, 'mɪləɹ? eɪnt ðɪs bɔɪ ə bəɹd! kn jə biːt ɪm? kn jə taɪ ɪm? bɔɪ,
25 jʊɹ ɔːl raɪt."

"so· əɹ ju — dæt ɪz, frʌm jəɹ hɛd ʌp."

“n ðə fiːt daʊn, hʌ? jʊɹ wʌn ə ðɛm ‘'hʌlɪ tʃiː, 'tʃɑnɪ’ bɔɪz, 'eɪntʃə? jəɹ so tʌf ðə· 'kʊdnt 'dɛntʃə wɪð n æks.”

30 “ɪz dæt sɪoɪʊ?” æskt ðə bɔɪ, wɪð ə 'fraɪtfəl ɪs'keɪp əv “s,” ənd ə 'glɛəɹ sʌtʃ əz hɪ mʌst əv juːzd tə 'tɛrɪˏfaɪ ɔːl ðə 'smɔːləɹ bɔɪz æt ðə 'kɔɪl ˏste·ʃən.

“ɪf aɪ wəz əz tʌf əz ju ɑɹ, aɪd bɪ ə'freɪd ə maɪ'sɛlf, ɔn ðə 'lɛvəl.”

35 “jə tɪŋk jəɹ 'hævn spɔɹt wɪt mɪ, 'do·ntʃə? aɪ siːn ə lɑt ə dɛm 'fʌnɪ mʌgz bə'fɔːɹ dɪs.”

“waɪ, 'klɔːdɪ, aɪ 'wʊdnt traɪ tə dʒɔːʃ jə. aɪ θɪŋk jəɹ ə naɪs, kliːn bɔɪ. 'eɪntʃə 'gɔnə teɪk ɔːf jəɹ glʌvz?”

'mɪləɹ liːnd bæk ɪn hɪz tʃɛːɹ ənd hɑʊld wɪð 'læftəɹ.

40 “aɪ bɛg jəɹ 'pɑːɹdn,' klɔːdɪ,” kən'tɪnjud 'ɑːɹtɪ. “aɪ θɔːt ðɛm wəz glʌvz jə hæd ɔn. dʒɪi, ɪz ðɛm jəɹ mɪts? jəɹ ə bru'nɛt, 'eɪntʃə?”

ðə 'mɛsɪndʒəɹ bɔɪ hæd bɪn 'sʌmˏʍɑt 'teɪkn ə'bæk baɪ ðɪ ə'luʒən tʊ hɪz “glʌvz,” bət hɪ rɪ'kʌvəɹd ənd sɛd,

45 stɪl 'geːzɪŋ æt ɑːɹtɪ: “sɪeːɪ, jəɹ 'hævn ɔːl kaɪndz ə fʌn wɪt mɪ, 'eɪntʃə? wɛl, 'wɑtʃu — 'ɛnɪˏtɪŋ ju seɪ kʌts no aɪs wɪt miːɪ.”

## Artie and Claudie

“Where’s he at?” repeated the messenger boy . . . When he asked “Where’s he at?” he pronounced it “where ’ce,” and in all his subsequent talk he gave the “s” a soft and hissing sound well prolonged, to the evident enjoyment of Artie and the mild wonderment of Miller.

“Where’s who at?” demanded Artie, adopting a frown and a harsh manner.

“W’y, t’e four-eyed nobs dat sent me out on t’e Sout’ Side.”

"Are you the same little boy? Wouldn't that frost you, though, Miller? This is little Bright-eyes that took the note for Hall."

"Aw, what's eatin' you?" asked the boy, giving a warlike curl to the corner of his mouth.

"Oh, ow! listen to that. I'll bet you're the toughest boy that ever happened. What you been doin' all day — playin' marbles for keeps or standin' in front o' one o' them dime museeums?"

"Aw, say; you t'ink you're fly. Dat young feller sent me all t'e way to forty-t'ree ninety-t'ree Callamet av'noo. I couldn't get back no sooner."

"Who was it the note was to?"

"His rag, I guess."

"Oh—h—h—h! His rag! What do you think o' that, Miller? Ain't this boy a bird! Can you beat him? Can you *tie* him? Boy, you're all right."

"So are you — dat is, from y'r head up."

"An' the feet down, huh? You're one o' them 'Hully chee, Chonny,' boys, ain't you? You're so tough they couldn't dent you with an axe."

"Is dat so—o—o—o?" asked the boy, with a frightful escape of "s" and a glare such as he must have used to terrify all the smaller boys at the call station.

"If I was as tough as you are I'd be afraid o' myself, on the level."

"You t'ink you're havin' sport wit' me, don't you? I seen a lot o' dem funny mugs before dis."

"W'y, Claudie, I wouldn't try to josh you. I think you're a nice, clean boy. Ain't you goin' to take off your gloves?"

Miller leaned back in his chair and howled with laughter.

"I beg y'r pardon, Claudie," continued Artie. "I thought them was gloves you had on. Gee, is them your mits? You're a brunette, ain't you?"

The messenger boy had been somewhat taken aback by the allusion to his "gloves," but he recovered and said, still gazing at Artie: "S—s—ay, you're havin' all kinds o' fun wit' me, ain't you? Well, w'at you — anyt'ing you say cuts no ice wit' me."

REMARKS

From *Artie, A Story of the Streets and Town*, by George Ade, Chicago, 1897. Artie exemplifies a dialect of Chicago as spoken by a free and easy office clerk, the messenger boy a somewhat lower dialect of the streets. The dialect is of course only partially indicated by the author's spellings. In l. 1, the author records a voiceless [ʍ] in **where**, and this has been allowed to stand, and so also in **what**, l. 12, though these are probably inadvertencies, the boy's dialect apparently having only [w]. For [æskt], l. 2, see above, § 346.

## XVI

### ˈtʃɪmɪ ˈfædn

lɔŋ taɪm sɪns jə siːn mɪ? səɹt. ˈdo·ntʃə noɪ də ˈriːzn? ʍaɪ, aɪ wəz ˈmærid. ˈʃʊəɹ. aɪ noːd jəd daɪ ʍɛn aɪ toːl jə. jɛs, ɪt wəz də ˈdʌtʃəs; aɪ gɛs jə noːd dæt. wɛl, ˈlɛmɪ tɛl jə. ɪt wəz də ˈkɔɹkənəst ˈwɛdn dəɹ
5 ˈɛvəɹ wəz, wɪd sʌtʃ mʌgz əz miː n də ˈdʌtʃəs ˈduən də ˈprɪnsɪpl ɪˈvɛnt ə də ˈiːvnən.

seɪ, aɪ ˈnɛvəɹ tɔːt dəɹ wəz so mʌtʃ ˈflɪm-ˌflæm baʊt ˈgɛtn ˈrɛdɪ tə bɪ ˈmærid. aɪ ˈnɪəɹ gɑt də ˈrætlz wʌnst, n wəz ˈgoːɪn tə meːk də græn sniːk; bət aɪ tʊk ə breːs,
10 kɔːz aɪ wəz ˈtɪŋkn dæt ɪf aɪ snuːk, dæt ɪt wʊd ˈkwɪəɹ mɪs ˈfæniz geːm, n aɪ ˈwʊdnt ˈkwɪəɹ mɪs ˈfæniz geːm ɪf aɪ hæd tə sɛt ʌp ə ˈfjunərəl stɪd ə ə ˈwɛdn.

wɛl, də fəɹst feːk wɔt ˈpærəlaɪzd miː wəz də ˈdʌtʃəs

ˈse·ən dəɹ mʌst biː wɔt ʃiː kɔːld ə ˈmærɪdʒ ˈkɑntrækt.
15 seɪ, ɪt wəz wəɹs dən ˈgɛtn ɑʊt ə dʒeːl ɔn beːl. aɪ gɛs wiːz ˈwʊdnt bɪ ˈmærid jɛt, ɪf ɪt wəznt fəɹ ˈmɪstəɹ ˈbəɹtn, wɔts mɪs ˈfæniz ˈfɛlɪ. iː n mɪs ˈfænɪ, de· wəz boːt ˈnɪəɹ ˈkreːzɪ bɑʊt ˈɑʊəɹ ˈwɛdn, n wəz ˈfʌsɪn bɑʊt ɪt mɔːɹ dən de· ɪz bɑʊt dəɹ oʊn.
20 wɛl, ˈmɪstəɹ ˈbəɹtn, iː sɛnt fəɹ mi, n tɛlz mi tə kʌm tə ɪz ˈtʃeːmbəɹz. iː sɛz tə miː, sɛz iː, 'tʃeːmz,' ɪ sɛz, 'kʌm dɪs ˈiːvnən tə mɪ ˈtʃeːmbəɹz. aɪ kɔːlz mɪ ˈpɑːɹtmənts mɪ ˈtʃeːmbəɹz fəɹ dɪs ˈkeːʒən ˈoːnlɪ,' sɛz iː, ˈgɪvn mi də wɪŋk, 'kɔːz dɪs ɪz ə ˈliːgəl ˈmætəɹ, n ɪn
25 də tɛn ˈjɪəɹz aɪv bɪn ˈmɪtəd tə də bɑːɹ,' sɛz iː, 'dɪs ɪz də fəɹst taɪm aɪ ˈɛvəɹ hæd ə keːs.'

## Chimmie Fadden

Long time since ye seen me? Cert. Don't ye know de reason? Why, I was married. Sure. I knowed ye'd die when I tole ye. Yes, it was de Duchess; I guess ye knowed dat. Well, lemme tell ye. It was de corkin'est weddin' dere ever was, wid such mugs as me an' de Duchess doin' de principal event er de evenin'.

Say, I never taut dere was so much flim-flam 'bout gettin' ready to be married. I near got de rattles onct, an' was goin' t' make de gran' sneak; but I took er brace, 'cause I was tinkin' dat if I snook, dat it would queer Miss Fannie's game, an' I wouldn't queer Miss Fannie's game if I had t' set up er funeral 'stid er a weddin'.

Well, de first fake wot paralyzed me was de Duchess sayin' dere must be wot she called er marriage contract. Say, it was worse dan gettin' outter jail on bail. I guess wese wouldn't be married yet if it wasn't fer Mr. Burton, wot's Miss Fannie's felly. 'E an' Miss Fannie, dey was bote near crazy 'bout our weddin', an' was fussin' 'bout it more dan dey is 'bout dere own.

Well, Mr. Burton, 'e sent fer me an' tells me t' come t' 'is chambers. 'E says t' me, says 'e, 'Chames,' 'e says, 'come dis evenin' t' me chambers. I calls me 'partments me chambers fer dis 'casion only,' says 'e, givin' me de wink, ''cause dis is er legal matter, an' in de ten years I've been 'mitted t' de bar,' says 'e, 'dis is de first time I ever had er case.'

## REMARKS

This passage, from the Chimmie Fadden stories of Mr. E. W. Townsend, represents a Bowery dialect of New York City. The author of the stories made greater effort than is usual with writers of dialect stories to record a considerable body of detail derived from direct observation. The student will see, however, that even here the dialect is sometimes only suggested, e.g., l. 9 [ˈgoːɪn tə meːk] in popular speech like this would be [ˈgɔnə meːk] or [ˈgʌnə meːk], and [hæd tə], l. 12, would more likely be [ˈhætə], etc. It is suggested that students make a new transcription of the passage not merely on the basis of Mr. Townsend's text but taking account of features of illiterate dialect speech which Mr. Townsend has not recorded. Some of the respects in which this dialect differs from ordinary colloquial English are (*a*) the replacing of [θ] and [ð] by [t] and [d] respectively; (*b*) [dʒ] becoming [tʃ]; (*c*) loss of final dentals, as in [toːl], l. 3, [græn], l. 9; final [n] for [ŋ] in the ending **-ing**, though this is very general in all colloquial speech; [w] for [ʍ]. Writings like **t' come** for **to come, t' me** for **to me**, etc., are transcribed as [tə kʌm], [tə mi], etc., though in this dialect there is practically no vowel after [t] in these phrases, and it might be omitted. The occasional spelling **er**, for example, **dis is er legal matter**, is probably intended to indicate only [ə]. The spelling **why**, l. 2, is probably an inadvertence for dialect [waɪ]. A feature of this dialect which is not recorded either in the conventional spelling of the passage or the phonetic transcription is the very strongly aspirated character of stop consonants, see above, § 13.

## XVII

### ðə vɔɪs

ˈɔːl ðə ˈhɑʊs wəz ˈstɪl; fər aɪ bɪliːv ɔːl, ɪksɛpt ˈsɪndʒən
ənd maɪˈsɛlf, wə ˈnɑʊ rɪˈtaɪəd tə ˈrɛst. ðə ˈwʌn ˈkændl
wəz ˈdaɪɪŋ ˈɑʊt; ðə ˈrʊm wəz ˈfʊl əv ˈmuːnlaɪt. maɪ
ˈhɑːt biːt ˈfɑːst ənd ˈθɪk; aɪ ˈhəːd ɪts ˈθrɔb. ˈsʌdnlɪ ɪt
5 ˈstʊd ˈstɪl tʊ ən ɪnɪksˈprɛsɪbl ˈfiːlɪŋ ðət θˈrɪld ɪt ˈθruː
ənd ˈpɑːst ət ˈwʌns tə maɪ ˈhɛd ənd ɪksˈtrɛmɪtɪz. ðə
fiːlɪŋ wəz ˈnɔt laɪk ən ɪˈlɛktrɪk ˈʃɔk, bət ɪt wəz ˈkwaɪt
əz ˈʃɑːp, əz ˈstrɛɪndʒ, əz ˈstɑːtlɪŋ; ɪt ˈæktɪd ɔn maɪ
ˈsɛnsɪz əz ɪf ðɛər ʌtmoʊst ækˈtɪvɪtɪ hɪðəˈtuː həd biːn
10 bət ˈtɔːpə, frəm wɪtʃ (or ʍɪtʃ) ðɛɪ wə ˈnɑʊ ˈsʌmənd
ənd ˈfɔːst tʊ ˈwɛɪk. ðɛɪ ˈroʊz ɪksˈpɛktənt; ˈaɪ ənd ˈɪə
ˈwɛɪtɪd waɪl (or ʍaɪl) ðə ˈflɛʃ ˈkwɪvəd ɔn maɪ ˈboʊnz.

"ˈwɔt (or ʍɔt) əv (or həv) juː ˈhəːd? wɔt (or ʍɔt)
d (or də) juː ˈsiː?" ɑːskt ˈsɪndʒən. aɪ ˈsɔː ˈnʌðɪŋ, bət
15 aɪ ˈhəːd ə ˈvɔɪs ˈsʌmwɛə (or ˈsʌmʍɛə) kraɪ —

"ˈdʒɛɪn, ˈdʒɛɪn, ˈdʒɛɪn!" — ˈnʌðɪŋ ˈmɔː.

"ˈoʊ ˈgɔd! ˈwɔt (or ˈʍɔt) ɪz ɪt?" aɪ ˈgɑːspt.

ai ˈmaɪt əv (or həv) sɛd, "ˈwɛər (or ˈʍɛər) ɪz ɪt?"
fər ɪt ˈdɪd nɔt siːm ɪn ðə ˈrʊm, nɔːr ɪn ðə ˈhɑʊs, nɔːr
20 ɪn ðə ˈgɑːdn; ɪt ˈdɪd nɔt kʌm ɑʊt əv ðɪ ˈɛə, nɔː frəm
ʌndə ðɪ ˈəːθ, nɔː frəm oʊvəˈhɛd. aɪ əd (or həd) ˈhəːd
ɪt — ˈwɛə (or ˈʍɛə), ɔː ˈwɛns (or ˈʍɛns), fər ˈɛvə (or
ˈɛvər) ɪmˈpɔsɪbl tə ˈnoʊ! ənd ɪt wəz ðə vɔɪs əv ə ˈhjuː-
mən ˈbiːɪŋ — ə ˈnoʊn, ˈlʌvd, ˈwɛl rɪˈmɛmbəd ˈvɔɪs —
25 ˈðæt əv ˈɛdwəd ˈfɛəfæks ˈrɔtʃɪstə; ənd ɪt spoʊk ɪn
ˈpɛɪn ənd ˈwoʊ, ˈwaɪldlɪ, ˈɪərɪlɪ, ˈəːdʒəntlɪ.

"ˈaɪ əm ˈkʌmɪŋ!" aɪ kraɪd, "ˈwɛɪt fə miː! ˈoʊ, aɪ
wɪl ˈkʌm!" aɪ ˈfluː tə ðə ˈdɔː, ənd ˈlʊkt ɪntə ðə ˈpæ-
sɪdʒ; ɪt wəz ˈdɑːk. aɪ ˈræn ˈɑʊt ɪntə ðə ˈgɑːdn; ɪt wəz
30 ˈvɔɪd.

"'wɛər (or 'ʍɛər) 'ɑːɪ juːɪ?" aɪ ɪks'kleɪmd.

ðə 'hɪlz bɪ'jɔnd 'mɑːɪʃ 'glɛn 'sɛnt ðɪ 'ɑːɪnsə 'feɪntlɪ bæk, "'wɛər (or 'ʍɛər) 'ɑːɪ juːɪ?" aɪ 'lɪsnd. ðə 'wɪnd 'saɪd 'loʊ ɪn ðə 'fəːɪz; 'ɔːɪl wəz 'mʊələnd, 'loʊnlɪnɪs ənd 35 'mɪdnaɪt hʌʃ.

## The Voice

All the house was still; for I believe all, except St. John and myself, were now retired to rest. The one candle was dying out; the room was full of moonlight. My heart beat fast and thick; I heard its throb. Suddenly it stood still to an inexpressible feeling that thrilled it through, and passed at once to my head and extremities. The feeling was not like an electric shock, but it was quite as sharp, as strange, as startling; it acted on my senses as if their utmost activity hitherto had been but torper, from which they were now summoned and forced to wake. They rose expectant; eye and ear waited while the flesh quivered on my bones.

"What have you heard? What do you see?" asked St. John. I saw nothing, but I heard a voice somewhere cry —

"Jane! Jane! Jane!" — nothing more.

"O God! what is it?" I gasped.

I might have said, "Where is it?" for it did not seem in the room, nor in the house, nor in the garden; it did not come out of the air, nor from under the earth, nor from overhead. I had heard it — where, or whence, for ever impossible to know! And it was the voice of a human being — a known, loved, well-remembered voice — that of Edward Fairfax Rochester; and it spoke in pain and woe, wildly, eerily, urgently.

"I am coming!" I cried. "Wait for me! Oh, I will come!" I flew to the door and looked into the passage; it was dark. I ran out into the garden; it was void.

"Where are you?" I exclaimed.

The hills beyond Marsh Glen sent the answer faintly back, "Where are you?" I listened. The wind sighed low in the firs; all was moorland loneliness and midnight hush.

## REMARKS

This passage is adapted from Jones, *Pronunciation of English*, pp. 73–74. It is supposed to be standard British pronunciation in a careful conversational style. The passage is from *Jane Eyre*, Chapter XXXV. The only changes that have been made in Mr. Jones's notation have been the use of [ɪ] for his [i], [ʊ] for his [u], and [ɛ] for his [e] to indicate respectively the slack qualities of the several sounds as short vowels. Mr. Jones regularly uses the symbol [e] for the vowel of **rest**, **flesh**, etc., and [ɛ], he says, occurs in standard pronunciation only in the diphthong [ɛə], as in **there**, **their** [ðɛə], etc. This latter sound is slightly lower (or in Mr. Jones's terminology, more open) than his [e], as in **rest**, **set**, etc. Since in this volume the same symbol, [ɛ], has been used for the vowel of **set** and the vowel of **their**, the distinction made by Mr. Jones is not recorded in the above transcription. With this exception, the author thinks he has given a faithful reproduction of Mr. Jones's pronunciation. The accents are those given by Mr. Jones.

l. 1. [hɑʊs]. Mr. Jones records the diphthong regularly in this transcription as [ɑʊ] and this accords with American pronunciation; but in Michaelis-Jones, *A Phonetic Dictionary*, the diphthong is given as [aʊ].

[fər]. The [r] here is intervocalic in context.

l. 4. [həːd]. The sound [əː] is represented in our alphabet by [ʌː], but it seemed best to retain Mr. Jones's symbol for the sound, which he describes as half-open (that is, half-low), mixed (meaning the middle portions of the tongue), tense, unrounded.

l. 8. [strɛɪndʒ]. In American pronunciation the vowel would be [eɪ] or [eː].

l. 9. [ʌtmoʊst]. The first element of the diphthong is described by Mr. Jones as half-close (i.e., half-high), back, slack, rounded, and it therefore corresponds pretty exactly to [ɔ] as this symbol is used in the present book. But it did not seem advisable to change it to [ɔ], for Mr. Jones uses this symbol also, for a sound which he describes as open (i.e., low), back, slack, with slight lip rounding. The difference between his [o] and his [ɔ] cannot be great, but in any case the first element of his [oʊ] must not be taken as meaning the sound represented in our alphabet by [o], but a sound nearer to [ɔ].

## XVIII

### 'sɑnɪt

(*a*)

mʌtʃ hæv ɑɪ trævəld ɪn ðə rɛlmz əv goʊld,
   ənd mɛnɪ gʊdlɪ steɪts ənd kɪŋdəmz siːn;
   rɑʊnd mɛnɪ wɛstən ɑɪləndz hæv ɑɪ biːn,
ʍɪtʃ bɑːdz ɪn fiːəltɪ tu əpɔlo hoʊld.
5 ɔːft əv wʌn wɑɪd ɛkspæns hæd ɑɪ biːn toʊld
   ðət diːp-brɑʊd hoʌmə ruːld əz hɪz dɪmiːn;
   jɛt dɪd ɑɪ nɛvə briːð ɪts pjuə sɪriːn
tɪl ɑɪ hʌːd tʃæpmən spiːk ɑʊt lɑʊd ənd boʊld:
ðən fɛlt ɑɪ lɑɪk sʌm wɔtʃər əv ðə skɑɪz
10    ʍɛn ə njuː plænɪt swɪmz ɪntu hɪz kɛn;
ɔ lɑɪk stɑʊt kɔːtɛz ʍɛn wɪð iːgəl ɑɪz
   hiː stæːd ət ðə pəsɪfɪk — ənd ɔːl hɪz mɛn
lukt ət iːtʃ ʌðə wɪð ə wɑɪld səmɑɪz,
   sɑɪlənt əpən ə piːk ɪn dɑːrɪɛn.

(*b*)

| | |
|---|---|
| l. 1. goːld. | l. 4. hoːld. |
| l. 2. steːts. | l. 5. ɪkspæns, bɪn, toːld. |

l. 6. hoːmə.
l. 7. pjuːə.
l. 8. boːld.
l. 14. deːrɪɛn.

(*c*)

l. 3. wɛstəɹn.
l. 4. bɑːɹdz.
l. 6. hoːməɹ.
l. 7. pjuːɹ.
l. 8. həɹd.
l. 11. ɔɹ, kɔːɹtɛz.
l. 12. stæːɹd.
l. 13. ʌðəɹ, səɹmɑɪz.

## Sonnet

Much have I traveled in the realms of gold,
And many goodly states and kingdoms seen;
Round many western islands have I been,
Which bards in fealty to Apollo hold.
Oft of one wide expanse had I been told
That deep-browed Homer ruled as his demesne;
Yet did I never breathe its pure serene
Till I heard Chapman speak out loud and bold:
Then felt I like some watcher of the skies
When a new planet swims into his ken;
Or like stout Cortez when with eagle eyes
He stared at the Pacific — and all his men
Looked at each other in a wild surmise,
Silent upon a peak in Darien.

### REMARKS

This sonnet, by Keats, is transcribed here as given in a *Report of a Joint Committee representing the National Educational Association, the American Philological Association,* and *the Modern Language Association of America, on the Subject of a Phonetic English Alphabet,* New York, 1904. The first version gives the sonnet "as read by an Englishman — a graduate of Oxford — whose utterance may be taken as fairly representing that of educated Londoners"

(p. 38). The set of variant readings under (*b*) are those differences from the pronunciations of (*a*) which occurred in the reading of the same sonnet by "a New Englander — a member of the Harvard faculty." The readings under (*c*) are those differences from (*b*) which occurred in the reading of the sonnet by "a Michigan man some time resident in New York."

l. 1 [ɑɪ]. In the phonetic alphabet used in the above report, the diphthong known as 'long i,' is regularly transcribed with [ɑ] as its first element. This transcription is retained in the present passage, though the author's observation is that the vowel is ordinarily [a].

[goʊld]. Note the diphthongal character of long vowels in the Englishman's pronunciation as compared with that of (*b*) and (*c*).

l. 6. [hoʌmə]. The second element of the diphthong as recorded here is the vowel of **much**, **one**, etc.

l. 12. [stæːd]. The *Report*, p. 21, recognizes the similarity of the vowel in this word to [ɛː]. Might not this word have been transcribed ['stɛːəd]?

l. 14. [əpən]. So recorded in all three pronunciations, which means that it was pronounced by all three readers without stress. But it might be pronounced [ə'pɔn].

## XIX

### wɪnd ænd sʌn

(*a*)

**Southern British**

ðə nɔːθ wɪnd ənd ðə sʌn wʌː dɪs'pjuːtɪŋ wɪtʃ wəz ðə 'strɔŋgə, wɛn ə 'trævlə keɪm ə'lɔŋ ræpt ɪn ə wɔːm kloʊk. ðeɪ ə'griːd ðət ðə wʌn huː fʌːst meɪd ðə 'trævlə teɪk ɔːf (h)ɪz kloʊk ʃʊd bɪ kən'sɪdəd 'strɔŋgə ðən ðɪ
5 'ʌðə. ðɛn ðə nɔːθ wɪnd bluː wɪð ɔːl hɪz maɪt, bət ðə mɔː hiː bluː, ðə mɔː 'kloʊslɪ dɪd ðə 'trævlə foʊld (h)ɪz kloʊk ə'raʊnd hɪm; ənd ət lɑːst ðə nɔːθ wɪnd geɪv ʌp ðɪ ə'tɛm(p)t. ðɛn ðə sʌn ʃɔn aʊt 'wɔːmlɪ, ənd ɪ'miː-

djətlɪ ðə ˈtrævlə tʊk ɔːf (h)ɪz kloʊk; ənd soʊ ðə nɔːθ
10 wɪnd wəz əˈblaɪdʒd tə kənˈfɛs ðət ðə sʌn wəz ðə
ˈstrɔŋgər əv ðə tuː.

(*b*)

**Northern British**

ðə nɔɹθ wɪnd ənd ðə sʌn wɛɹ dɪsˈpjuːtɪŋ ʍɪtʃ wəz ðə
strɔŋgəɹ, ʍɛn ə ˈtravləɹ keːm əˈlɔŋ rapt ɪn ə wɔɹm
kloːk. ðeː əˈgriːd ðət ðə wʌn huː fəɹst meːd ðə ˈtravləɹ teːk ɔf hɪz kloːk ʃʊd bɪ konˈsɪdəɹd ˈstrɔŋgəɹ ðən
5 ðɪ ˈʌðəɹ. ðɛn ðə nɔɹθ wɪnd bluː wɪθ ɔːl hɪz maɪt, bʌt
ðə mɔːɹ hiː bluː, ðə mɔːɹ ˈkloːslɪ dɪd ðə ˈtravləɹ foːld
hɪz kloːk əˈraʊnd hɪm; ənd ət last ðə nɔɹθ wɪnd geːv
ʌp ðɪ ətɛm(p)t. ðɛn ðə sʌn ʃɔn aʊt ˈwɔːrmlɪ, ənd
ɪˈmiːdjətlɪ ðə ˈtravləɹ tʊk ɔf hɪz kloːk; ənd soː ðə nɔɹθ
10 wɪnd wəz ɔˈblaɪdʒd tʊ konˈfɛs ðət ðə sʌn wəz ðə
ˈstrɔŋgəɹ əv ðə tuː.

(*c*)

**American English**

ðə nɔɹθ wɪnd ən ðə sʌn wəɹ dɪsˈpjutɪŋ əz tə ʍɪtʃ
wəz ðə ˈstɹɔːɪŋgɪst, ʍɛn ə ˈtɹævələɹ keːm əˈlɔːŋ, ɹæpt
ɪn ə wɔɹm kloʊk. ðe əˈgɹiːd ðət ðə wʌn hu meːd ðə
ˈtɹævləɹ teɪk ɔf ɪz koʊt fəɹst ʃəd bɪ kənˈsɪdəɹd ˈstrɔːɪŋgəɹ
5 ðən ðə ˈʌðəɹ. ðɛn ðə nɔɹθ wɪnd bljuː wɪð ɔl ɪz mɑɪt;
bət ðə mɔːɹ ɪ bljuː, ðə mɔːɹ ˈkloʊslɪ ðə ˈtɹævləɹ ˈfoʊldɪd
ɪz kloʊk əˈɹɑʊnd ɪm; ənd ət læst ðə nɔɹθ wɪnd geɪv ʌp
ðɪ əˈtɛmpt. ðɛn ðə sʌn ʃoːn ɑʊt ˈwɔɹmlɪ (or bəˈgæn
tə ʃɑɪn ɑʊt hɑt), ənd ɪn ə fju ˈmoːmənts ðə ˈtɹævləɹ
10 tʊ̈k ɔf ɪz kloʊk. so ðə nɔɹθ wɪnd wəz əˈblɑɪdʒd tə
kənˈfɛs ðət ðə sʌn wəz ðə ˈstrɔːɪŋgəɹ əv ðə tuː.

## Wind and Sun

The North Wind and the Sun were disputing which was the stronger, when a traveller came along wrapped in a warm cloak. They agreed that the one who first made the traveller take off his cloak should be considered stronger than the other. Then the North Wind blew with all his might, but the more he blew, the more closely did the traveller fold his cloak around him; and at last the North Wind gave up the attempt. Then the Sun shone out warmly, and immediately the traveller took off his cloak; and so the North Wind was obliged to confess that the Sun was the stronger of the two.

### REMARKS

These three versions of the fable of the Sun and Wind are taken from a pamphlet, *The Principles of the International Phonetic Association*, pp. 20–22, published as a supplement to the *Maître Phonétique*, Sept.–Oct., 1912. They are supposed to represent "the average pronunciation of educated persons in each case," the first Southern English in England, the second Northern English in England, the third American English "for New York State and the central portion of the United States." They are presented here for comparative study, the most interesting conclusion from such study probably being the close similarity to be observed between American English and British Northern English. The version in American English is in some respects a travesty. It is throughout on a more colloquial level than the other two versions, but besides is needlessly changed in other details. In the first sentence, "as to which was the strongest" is dialectal American usage, not that of "educated persons." Similar uncalled-for changes are "began to shine out hot" for "shone out warmly," and "in a few moments" for "immediately." The phonetic details of the version of American English are also open to criticism in some respects. The sound of **r** is not the same in all positions; the vowel of **the** before **other** would not be [ə]; **blew** would be [bluː], not [bljuː]; the diphthong in **might** is [maɪt], not [mɑɪt]; the vowel of **strongest, stronger** is short, not long; and the diphthongal character of [eː] and [oː] is less marked and general than the transcription would lead one to suppose. The transcriptions also make a distinction between British and American use in the vowel of **wind, which,** etc., which is supposed to be slightly lower in American than in British use, being high slack in British pronunciation and between high slack and high-mid slack in American usage. The reality of this distinction seems very doubtful, and the author has disregarded it in his versions of the transcriptions. For the vowel of words like **bird, hurt,** when the **r** is not pronounced, the symbol [ʌː] has been substituted for [əː]. Note the Northern British use of [a] where Southern British and American have [æ].

# INDEX OF WORDS

The numbers refer to sections

a 146
abject 89
about 20, 66, 109, 146
abrasion 333
absent 87
absolutely 85, 192
abstract 87
abuse 312
abusive 321
accept 308
access 87
acclimate 91
account 263
accurate 234
accuse 263, 318
acknowledge 264
acorn 90
acoustic 194
across 343
action 338
actual 327, 338
acute 232
adamantine 166
add 83
added 52, 173
address 87
admirable 93
adobe 174
adult 89
adverse 89
advertisement 96
advice 312
advise 312
aeroplane 144
aerostat 144
Æschylus 163
Æsculapius 163
Æsop 163
æsthetic 163
again 134, 135
against 134, 135 ]
agile 212
ague 234
Alabama 121
Albany 174
albumen 92
all 45, 185
allege 329
allies 87
alloy 87
ally 87
almond 115, 274
alms 115, 274
aloof 193
Altamaha 188
altruistic 192
always 134, 146
amateur 327
ambergris 315
amenable 162
amend 109
amenity 162
America 148
American 201
anapæst 163
ancient 327
angel 246
anger 249
angina 166
angle 249
angry 249
annex 87
annoy 75
answer 369
ant 126, 284
Anthony 348
anxiety 267
anxious 267, 327
anything 297
aplomb 235

appendicitis 166
applicable 93
appreciate 327
appreciation 327
approbation 176
apricot 130
apron 304
aqueduct 344
archaic 131
arctic 265
aren't 112
Argentine 166
argot 337
argue 234
aristocrat 95
Arkansas 325
armistice 92
ashen 327
Asia 327
asked 109, 346
asphalt 130
aspirant 92
associate 327
association 327
assume 327
assumption 300
asthma 354
astute 327
ate 137
athlete 151
athletic 151
attack 99, 343
attention 327
audacious 181
audit 185
auditory 181
Audubon 181
Augean 222
augur 185
aunt 124, 126
aural 185, 190
aurochs 222
authentic 181
author 185
authority 62
automatic 181
autumn 288
autumnal 288
auxiliary 269
avoirdupois 315, 326
awe 63, 80
awful 80
ax-handle 86
axiom 270, 327
axiomatic 270
ay 134
aye 134
azure 333

baby 21
backed 239
Baconian 131
bad 128
bade 130
baize 318
baked 239
bakery 131
balk 273
Balkan 273
balky 273
ballet 337
balm 115, 274
banal 130
band-box 243
bank 289
banquet 293
Banquo 293
barge 246
basket 52
bas-relief 120
bath 128, 352
bathe 351
baths 31, 124, 352
battle 47
bawl 371
bay-berry 131
be 5
bead 80
bean 161
bear 69
beat 80
beatific 51
Beaulieu 107
beauteous 327
beauty 229
beds 35
beef-steak 86
been 171

beet 21, 80
befogged 15
beg 139
begin 52, 172, **173**
belated 240
belch 341
Belvoir 107
bench 341
bend 135
Bennett 108
best 308
better 14, 206
between 365
bib 12, 21
bilge 246
bird 154, 155
Birmingham 97, **257**
Birrell 108
bison 210
Bithell 108
bitter 240
black 263
blackguard 268
blather– 114
blouse 226
blue 20
boat 74
boil 70, 75, 211, 228
Bologna 285
bomb 111, 235
bombard 204
bombast 204
book 60, 193
booklet 66
book-shelf 86
boor 196, 197
boot 192, 193
borough 199, 220
Boswell 111
both 180, 349
bother 111, 114
bough 222
bought 122, 187
Boulogne 285
bounteous 327
bouquet 194
Bourchier 107
bourgeois 315
Bourgogne 285
bowie-knife 179
bowl 74, 224, 371
boy 75
Bradbury 97
branch 124, 127, 128
brand-new 243
bran-new 243
breath 30, 135, 352
breathe 351
breaths 352
breeches 171
breeching 171
bridge 329
bringer 249
Broadway 86
Bronx 289
brooch 194
broom 193
broth 111
Brough 357
brown 371
bruit 192
brusque 195
Buckingham 257
buffet 337
bulge 246
bull 195
buoy 228
buoyant 228
Burgoyne 285
Burgundy 285
burned 241
Burnett 108
burnt 241
burr 154
burrow 199, 220
burst 303
Bury 136
bury 136, 200, 201
bush 37, 60, 195
business 171
busy 171, 174
but 198
butcher 193
butte 229
butter 64, 206
butter-knife 86
buxom 308
buy 72

buzz 198
by 72
Byron 153

cab 128
cacao 149
Cædman 309
calculate 273
calf 57, 58, 124, 276
Calhoun 105
call 9, 22, 263, 309
calm 115, 274
calmative 274
calves 124
camouflage 334
Campagna 285
camphor 299
can 309
cañon 285
cant 126
can't 124, 128
capillary 96
car 42, 119
caret 129
carriage 129
carrier 259
carry 129, 306
cart 302
carter 123
cartridge 307
case 318
cases 318
casual 333
cats 319
caught 63, 122, 187, 302
caulk 273
ceiling 308
celibacy 96
cell 33, 309
Celt 309
Celtic 309
cement 88
cemetery 98
cereal 136, 167
Ceres 136
certain 206
chagrin 327
chaise 327
chalet 327, 337
chalk 273, 305
chalk-line 185
cham 263
chamois 327
champagne 285, 327
Champlain 327
chandelier 327
chaotic 131
charade 327
Charlevoix 327
Charlotte 327
chary 55, 133, 141
chassis 327
chasten 340
Chatauqua 327
château 177
Chatham 257
Chattanooga 327
chauffeur 327
chauvinism 327
Cheboygan 327
chef 327
chemise 327
chemist 137, 263
Chenango 327
chequer 369
Cherokee 327
cheroot 327
chest 139
chestnut 340
cheval 327
chevalier 327
Cheyenne 327
chic 327
Chicago 327
chicanery 327
chicken 295
Chicopee 327
chiffon 327
chiffonier 327
Chillicothe 327
chimney 287
chin 8
Chinese 324
chip 37
Chippewa 327
chivalry 327
chocolate 110
Choctaw 188

choir 27, 367
Christian 327
church 49, 65
cinch 308, 309
Cincinnati 174
cincture 308
circle 308
cite 72
citron 309
city 52, 175
clapboard 298
Clara 129
claret 129
Clark(e) 116, 117
Claverhouse 105
cleanly 138
clerk 67, 117
climb 235, 236
climber 236
climbing 236
clique 162
close 312, 343
closure 333
clothe 351
clothes 355
Coburn 105
Cockburn 105
cocoa 13, 149
coco-nut 149
coffee 111
cognac 285
coign 75
coin 75
coincidence 75
coke 309
college 173
collier 259
colonel 278
color 42
Colorado 121
Colquhoun 105
column 261
comb 235
combat 203
combatant 92
combative 92
combine 87
come 198
comfortable 307
commissure 327
companion 259
company 203
comparison 322
compass 203
compensate 91
complacent 53
completely 51
compliable 93
comptroller 281
concave 292
conceit 309
concentrate 91
conch 289
conclave 292
conclusive 321
concord 292
concourse 292
concrete 292
concubine 292
condemn 288
condemning 288
condign 248, 284
confession 327
confiscate 91
Conger 291
Congo 291
congregate 291
congregational 291
congress 291
congressional 291
Congreve 291
congruous 291
congruity 291
conjure 202
Connecticut 265
connotative 176
conquer 293, 369
conqueror 293
conquest 293, 365
conscience 327
conscious 327
constable 202
consular 327
consummate 91
contact 344
contemplate 91
contemplative 95
convene 161

convention 327
convict 265
cook 309
cool 192
coop 193
Cooper 193
cord 42
cordial 333
corn 44, 189
Cornell 108
coroner 111
corp 298
corps 298
corpse 298
corpuscle 266
corpuscule 266
corpuscular 266
corrosive 321
cortege 334
cost 111
cot 302
cotillion 262
cotillon 262
cough 111, 357
coughed 336
could 279
count 223
couple 198
coupon 232
courage 173, 199
court 302
courteous 157, 327
courtezan 157
courtier 157
cousin 198
cow 73, 222, 223
Cowan 371
cowardice 214
cows 319
creature 327
creek 162
crept 342
cruel 147
crumb 235
crumble 237
crustaceous 327
Cuba 146
cube 232
cucumber 232
culinary 232
culm 274
cuneiform 232
cunning 198
cup 198, 309
cupboard 86, 238, 298
cupola 149
cur 206, 301
curaçao 149
cure 196, 230
curse 65, 303
cushion 195
cut 64
cycle 309
cylinder 52
Cymric 309
Cynewulf 309
czar 326

damage 173
damn 288
damning 288
dance 56, 57, 58, 124, 127, 128
Dane 134
danger 246
Danish 134
dare 140
dart 152
dash 126
data 120
daub 111
daughter 187
daunt 186
day 132
dead 80
deaf 138
deal 147
death 352
deaths 352
debate 173
debt 54, 80, 235
debtor 22
deceive 51
decide 52, 173, 309
decision 38
declamatory 97
deduct 265
deed 161
defensive 321

deficit 92
deify 51
delighted 85
demonstrate 91
demur 42
deniable 93
dense 54, 312, 341
deny 209
depict 265
depot 337
Derby 117
derision 333
derogatory 97
description 109
desist 172
Des Moines 314
despicable 93
despise 318
device 312
devotional 61
diamond 147
diary 147
diction 338
did 12, 21
differentiation 327
difficulty 95
diffusive 321
dig 13
dignitary 97
dimension 327
dinner 42
diocesan 95
diphtheria 359
diphthong 359
dirigible 170
dirt 65, 67, 69, 206
discursive 321
discussion 327
disgusted 173
disreputable 93
dissoluble 93
dissuade 27
distinct 289
distressed 316
dived 360
dizzy 35, 318
do 5, 20, 21, 192
docile 111
doe 177
dog 62, 63, 111, 182, 305
doing 296
doll 111
done 198
door 191, 197
double 198
doubt 235
dough 13, 177
dough-nut 176
drachm 263
drama 120
draw 185, 370
dreamt 299
dreary 167
dress 40
dressy 83
drown 245
drowse 371
Du Bois 107
dumb 235
dune 192
duteous 327
duty 231
dynasty 210
dysentery 97

eagle 161
economy 161
ecstatic 271
eczema 92
educate 135
e'er 362
eery 167
egg 83, 139
egg-glass 83
eggs 6
Egypt 161
eighth 346
either 164
elect 173
Elizabethan 164
elk 273
elm 151, 282
emaciated 327
emend 109
endure 196
engage 173
engine 332
England 138, 249

English 138, 249
enough 198, 225
enow 225
enthusiasm 231
enunciate 327
enunciation 327
envelope 92
epistle 340
epoch 138
equation 333
era 148, 167
erasure 333
ere 69
erosion 333
err 69
errata 120
essential 327
Esther 348
eternal 161
evasive 321
exact 269
exactly 85
excellent 271
except 173, 308
excess 87, 89
exchequer 263
exhale 258
exhaust 258
exhaustion 339
exhibit 7, 258, 269
exhibition 7, 258, 271
exhort 258
exhume 258
exigency 271
exile 269, 270
exit 271
expansive 321
expediency 161
expedient 333
expire 271
exquisite 85
extra 148
extraordinary 97
extreme 271

face 132
fade 53, 71, 132
fair 55, 140, 143
fairy 55, 141
faith 347
falcon 273
falconry 273
Falkland 273
famish 28
fancy 33, 124
far 301
fare 55
farina 210
farm 44
Farrar 108
farther 302
fashion 56, 99, 126, 128, 327
fast 50, 56, 57, 58
fasten 340
fatally 53, 131
fate 71
father 5, 20, 31, 57, 114, 302
fatigue 21, 162
fault 185
Faust 222
favorite 98, 214
fear 301
feat 80
feather 31, 155
feature 259, 327
febrile 212
February 306
feeble 45
feed 80
feet 80
feign 284
fellow 66, 146, 220
fern 206
ferry 54, 135
fetid 164
fetish 164
fetter 10
few 229, 370
fiery 153
fifth 349
figure 234
filch 341
film 151, 274, 282
finally 146
find 357
fine 216
finger 249
finish 52

fir 42, 65, 67, 69, 154, 155, 206
fire 153, 160, 301
fired 304
first 303
fish 327
fissure 327
fit 28
fitted 240
fixture 339
flaccid 263
flange 125
flapped 239
flaunt 186
fleece 208
floe 177
floor 191, 197
flour 160
flourish 199
flow 177
flower 160
fog 15
folk 273
folks 180
follow 111
food 193
foot 193
fop 110
for 191, 301
force 189
Fordham 257
fore 191
forehead 111, 253
foreign 111, 200, 248, 284
forest 111
forge 246
formidable 93
fort 302
fortune 327
fought 302
foully 280
four 152, 191, 301
fowl 280
fragile 212
fragmentary 95
France 124
Frasier 333
Frazier 333
freak 208
freeze 208
freight 253
frontier 90
frost 63
froth 347
frothed 239
Frothingham 257
frothy 347
frown 73
fruit 192
fuchsia 327
full 60, 195
fully 280
fulsome 195
function 289, 338
fur 42, 65, 67, 69, 154, 155, 206, 301
furl 206
Furness 108
furniture 327
furry 306
fury 196
fusion 229, 333

gage 329
garage 120
garden 123, 295
gas 126, 318
gases 318
gather 114
gaunt 186
gauntlet 186
geese 21
gem 8, 329
Geneva 332
gentile 212
gentle 212
genuine 98, 214
get 135, 139
ghetto 253
ghost 253
ghostly 253
gibber 332
gibbering 332
gibberish 332
gibbet 332
gibe 332
giblets 332
gig 247
gill 332

Gillett 108
gin 332
ginseng 332
girl 156
gist 332
give 364
glacier 134
glass 128
glazier 333
glimpse 300
glory 190
Gloucester 106
gnarled 248
gnash 248
gnat 248
gnaw 248, 284
gnome 248
gnostic 248
gun 248, 370
go 5, 218
go-cart 176
God 63, 111
goes 319
golf 276
gondola 92
gone 247
gong 21
good 60, 193
Goodenough 225
Goodenow 225
goodness 173
Goodnow 225
goose 193
gooseberry 6
got 110
Goth 352
Gothic 111
Goths 352
gout 223
government 288
gown 227, 245
gracious 327
Graham 257
grand 125, 128
grandeur 333
grandmother 243
grass 124
grave 132
gray 207
grease 312
greasy 311
Greenwich 369
grew 370
grey 207
griefs 361
grisly 310
gristle 310
groom 193
group 192
grovel 111
guano 366
guard 233, 366
guava 366
gubernatorial 233
Guelph 366
guess 54, 233, 366
guest 366
guide 366
guile 366
gulch 341
gun 233
gush 233
guy 209
gymnasium 333
gyrate 170

ha 24
hair 140, 142, 143
hairy 141
half 80, 124, 276
halibut 130
halve 80
halves 124
Hampden 300
Hampshire 300
handkerchief 243
handsome 243
hanger 249
Hannah 305
harangue 250
hard 42, 119, 302
hare 140
harp 119
Harry 141
hart 116
Harvard 119
has 56, 125, 126

hat 24, 50, 56, 82, 128
hath 30, 126
haughty 122
haul 10
haunt 186
have 125, 126
hawk 371
hay 207
hazard 318
haze 132
he 10, 11, 20, 161
hear 167
heard 42, 69, 154, 155
hearing 167
heart 116
hearth 116, 117, 119
heaven 12
heavens 295
heavy 29, 174
heed 24
height 350
heir 254
heiress 254
helm 274, 282
her 67
herald 256
heraldic 256
herb 254
herbaceous 327
herbage 254
herbalist 254
herbarium 254
hero 168
Hertford 117
hew 24
hiccough 357
hid 80
higher 160
hilly 45
him 16
hinge 246
hire 160
hired 304
his 35, 318
hissed 239
history 159, 256
hit 22, 80
hod 302
hog 111
hollow 111
holly 280
holm 274
Holmes 180, 274
holy 280
honest 173, 254
honor 254
hood 80
hoof 193, 361
hoofs 361
hook 80
hoop 193, 373
Hooper 193
hooping-cough 373
hooves 361
horrid 111
horse 189
hosier 333
hospitable 93
hospital 46, 111
host 343
hostile 212
hot 50, 57, 110, 182
hound 227
hour 254
house 70, 73, 222, 318
houses 318
hovel 111
hover 111
howl 224, 371
hue 24
huge 24
Hugh 24
hulk 273
Hulme 274
human 254
humble 237, 254
humor 24, 254
Humphrey 254, 299
Humphries 254, 299
hundred 306
hurry 41, 64, 199
hurt 50, 65, 67
husband 86, 198
hustle 340
hut 50
hymn 288
hymnal 288
hymning 288

iamb 238
Iceland 146
idea 92, 305
ill 46
Illinois 314
illustrate 91
impinge 246
impugn 248
impulsive 321
incisive 321
income 290
incubate 290
incubus 290
indict 265
individual 333
indulge 246
infer 67, 206
Ingalls 249
Inglis 249
initial 172
injunction 267
ink 169
inkwell 84
inquest 290
inquiry 92, 290
insect 344
instead 139
institute 327
institution 327
insular 327
interest 98
interesting 98
invasion 333
inveigle 164
Iowa 148
iron 304
irony 304
Isaiah 134
issue 327
isthmus 348
Italian 175

Jacob 238
Jacobs 238
Jacobson 238
jamb 235
January 306
Japanese 324
jaundice 175
Jenny 137
jenny 137
Jesuit 333
jettison 322
John 111
join 211, 228, 329
jostle 340
jowl 224
judge 38, 49, 329
jug 8
juice 59
juncture 338
jury 196
just 205, 343

Kansas 325
keel 22
keg 139
Kenesaw 188
kept 342
key 5, 161
khan 263
kill 9
killed 241
kiln 286
kind 215, 217
king 263
kitchen 295
knee 264, 284
knell 284
Knickerbocker 107
knight 264
knock 284
knoll 284
know 74, 218, 219, 284, 370
knowledge 261
Koch 107

laggard 56
lair 55, 140
lamb 235
lambkin 235
lamentable 93
lamps 300
land 45
landlady 243
landlord 243
language 27, 250, 365
languid 250, 365

languish 250
languor 250
large 116, 246, 301
latent 134
lathe 351
lather 114, 125
laud 302
laugh 124, 127, 357
laughs 361
launch 186, 341
laundry 186
Laura 186
lava 120
law 46, 63, 185
lazy 318
lead 54
league 80, 208
leak 80
learned 241
learnt 241
lease 318
leases 318
lecture 338
led 54, 80
ledge 329
leek 80
leg 139
legume 233
leguminous 233
leisure 164, 333
length 272, 294
lengthen 294
lense 135
Leominster 106
lessee 83
let 80
letter 14, 240
lettuce 173, 336
library 306
lichen 210
lie 209
lieutenant 357
life 80
limber 236
limped 300
Lincoln 277
linger 249, 330
lingo 250
lingual 250, 293
linguist 250
linguistic 293
linked 267
liquor 369
listen 340
lit 46
literature 327
live 29, 360
lives 80
lizard 318
load 302
loaf 80, 361
loam 179
loaves 361
locomotive 176
locust 343
log 111, 182
long 62, 63, 183, 289
longer 249
longest 249
longevity 332
longitude 332
looked 15
loose 318
looses 318
lord 302
Louisville 314
Lucy 231
ludicrous 59
lugubrious 233
Luke 231
lumber 236
lunar 192
lung 289
lure 60, 196
luscious 327
Lusitania 192
lute 231
luxury 270, 327
luxurious 269, 270, 333
lye 209
lymph 299
lyric 169

mad dog 83
magic 329
Maher 105
malinger 330
Maltese 324

manage 173
mansion 327
manufactory 327
manufacture 327, 338
margarine 331
Marjoribanks 105
marred 116, 119
marry 129
Martha 148
Mary 55, 133, 141
Mather 114
mattock 83
mature 327
may 48
meadow 135
Meagher 105
medial 333
medicine 54
medium 333
Meeker 105
memoir 368
menage 334
meningitis 166
mention 327
mercy 67
merit 135
merry 129, 201
mewl 371
Michigan 327
middle 47
mignonette 285
Millard 108
million 45
milk 152, 273
mince 341
mine 215
minute 173
minx 289
miracle 170, 201
mirage 120, 334
mirror 170
miry 153
misery 318
miss 308
missed 336
misses 320
mission 37, 169, 327
Missouri 174, 313, 318
mistletoe 310
mistress 308
mixture 339
mnemonic 281
modulate 333
moisten 340
moisture 327
money 198
monger 202
mongrel 202
monk 289
monkey 289
Montana 121, 174
month 347
months 349
mood 59, 193
moon 193
moor 60, 196, 197
Moore 197
moose 318
moose's 318
moral 45, 147, 190
more 191
More 197
Mosher 335
Mosier 335
moss 182
most 180
moth 111, 352
moths 352
Mozier 335
Mrs. 320
mule 229
municipal 96
murmur 67
muscle 266
music 25, 35, 229
musician 59, 229, 327
mustache 327
mute 78
myrrh 154, 206
myrtle 154
myth 30, 347
mythology 347
myths 319

naked 173
naphtha 359
nation 66, 327
national 66, 109

nature 259, 327
naught 185
naughty 122
nausea 327
Nebraska 121, 174
negotiation 327
neither 164
nephew 357, 360
Nero 168
nestle 340
neuritis 166
Nevada 121, 174
never 42, 155, 206
new 229, 231
New Orleans 314
news 323
newspaper 323
newt 371
next 343
nimble 237
no 48, 74, 284
Noah 148, 305
nobby 111
nod 182
nodule 333
nook 193
Norwich 369
not 57, 110, 182
notable 61
notation 61
note 61, 74
nothing 297
nourish 199
novel 111
now 370
noxious 327
nude 231
nurse 303
nutmeg 139

oath 219
oaths 355
obedient 176, 333
obligatory 96
oblige 99
oblique 166
occasion 333
occult 89
occur 83
ocean 327
oceanic 327
œcumenical 163
Œdipus 163
Œnone 163
o'er 362
œsophagus 161, 163
of 7, 363
off 7, 111
officiate 327
often 111, 340
Omaha 188
omniscient 327
on 111, 182
once 343, 367
one 27, 367
onion 259
only 180
opera 148
opponent 92
oral 190, 306
orange 111, 173
Ossian 327
ostrich 111
otiose 327
otium 327
Ottawa 188
our 160
Owen 371

pacient 327
pair 55, 69, 140
palace 173
palfrey 276
palm 57, 115, 274
Palmyra 274
pansy 125
pant 126
pantry 126
paper 13
paradigm 248
pare 55, 140
parent 129, 133, 153
Paris 129
parish 129
parochial 327
parquet 337
part 42, 119, 302
particular 307

partner 345
partridge 307
party 301
passion 327
patent 134
path 56, 124, 347, 352
paths 6, 124, 319, 352
patriot 53, 134
patriotic 134
patriotism 134
patter 128
Paul 185
pay 5, 22, 71
pay-roll 131
peace 80
peach 13
peal 147
pear 55, 140
peas 80
peer 167
peeress 153
Pelham 257
penal 164
penalize 164
penalty 164
pendulum 333
peninsula 327
pen-knife 83
penny 83, 284
pensive 321
people 45
peremptory 96
perfect 344
perfection 338
perfume 87
period 136, 153
perish 54, 129, 135
Persia 327
persiflage 334
person 65, 69, 154, 155
persuade 27, 365
persuasive 321
pert 67
phase 132, 318
philosophy 28, 357
phlebitis 166
phlegm 248
phlegmatic 248
phthisic 359
phthisis 359
physiognomy 248
piano 66, 120, 146, 176, 220
picked 265
pier 167
pile 215
pincers 317
pinch 317, 341
piñon 285
pip 12
pirate 170
pitch 82
piteous 327
pity 172
place 53
plait 130
pleasure 5, 38, 333
pleat 130
plebiscite 92
plenteous 327
plumb 235, 236
plumber 235, 236
plumbing 236
pneumatic 298
pod 57
poem 147, 173
poignancy 248
poignant 248, 284
Polish 134, 179
polish 179
Polk 180
polka 180
pollen 111
pomp 111
pool 13
poor 60, 196, 197
pop 13
pope 22
pore 191
port 189
position 327
positive 62
pot 42, 302
potato 13, 146
pour 191
power 371
prairie 174
precinct 165
preciosity 327

precious 327
predecessor 165
predicate 165
predigested 165
predilection 165
pre-eminent 70
prefect 165
preferable 93
preference 165
prefix 165
prehistoric 165
prejudice 165
prelate 173
prelude 165
premature 165
premise 87
premiss 87
preparation 165
prepay 165
preposition 165
prescience 327
presentation 165
pressure 327
preterite 165
pretty 138
priest 161
prize 5
probate 178
problem 178
proceed 87
proceeds 178
process 178
produce 178
product 178
profile 178
program 90, 178
programme 90, 178
progress 178
project 178
prolix 178
prologue 178
pronoun 178
pronunciation 327
proof 193
prophet 178
prospect 178
protest 87, 178
proverb 178
provost 178
Prussia 327
psalm 33, 115, 274, 275, 298
psalmist 275
psalmody 275
psalter 275
psaltery 275
pseudo– 298
psychology 298
ptarmigan 298
pterodactyl 298
ptomaine 298
pumpkin 283
punctilious 267
punctual 267
puncture 338
Purcell 108
pure 25, 196, 230
Purnell 108
purr 67, 206
purslane 303
pursy 303
put 195
putty 14, 240

quack 365
qualm 274
quarrel 111, 147
quay 161
query 167
question 327, 339, 365
quick 8
quinine 90, 213
quire 365
quit 27
quoit 134

rabbit 173
racial 327
radish 130
radium 333
raid 53, 132
raided 240
raillery 130
Ralph 276
rang 289
raspberry 298
rate 132
rated 240
rather 114, 125

ratio 327
ratiocination 327
rational 126, 327
rations 130
read 40
real 147
really 147
realm 151
rebuke 229
receive 33
recess 87
recluse 312
recognition 251
recognizance 251
recognize 251
reconnaissance 251
recrudescence 192
red 40
referable 93
refuse 87
refutable 93
reign 248
reliable 93
remonstrate 91
renown 227
Rensselaer 317
reptile 212
reservoir 368
reveille 262
revocable 93
rhomb 238
rhythm 353
rhythmic 353
rhythmical 353
rice 5, 308
rich 169
riches 173
ride 70, 72
rides 319
right 209, 253
righteous 327
rile 211, 228
ringer 249
rinse 317
rise 5, 312
rite 209
Rivaulx 105
road 61, 74
roar 191
rob 111
rod 80
rode 61, 74, 177
roil 211, 228
Rolfe 276
roll 177, 219
romp 111
rood 193
roof 193
rook 193
room 193
rooster 193
root 193
rose 74, 219
rosin 111
rot 80
rote 177
rouge 334
rough 28, 357
round 227
route 194
rude 231
rule 192, 231
rune 192, 231
rural 196
ruse 231
Russia 327

sacerdotal 309
sacrifice 210, 312
said 54
salmon 115, 274
salt 185
salvage 276
salvation 276
salve 276
samphire 299
sanctify 267
sanctimonious 267
Sargent 117
Saturday 307
sauce 185
saucy 185
saw 50
saying 296
scarf 361
scarfs 361
scarves 361
scene 308

scenic 164
schedule 263, 333
Schenectady 174
schism 263, 308
schist 327
schnapps 327
schottische 327
Schurman 107
Schuyler 107
Schuylkill 107
scissors 308, 318
scurry 199
scythe 308
sea 51, 76, 208
seal 147
seasonable 51
seat 9, 208
sedentery 97
see 20, 50, 51, 76, 208
seed 51, 208
seethe 51
sell 45
señor 285
sensual 327
sentient 327
sergeant 117
serial 136, 167
series 136, 167
serious 136
serpent 154
serum 136
service 308
servile 212
set 50, 54
sew 219
sexual 327
shackle 327
shady 21
shan't 124
shawl 37
sheathe 351
shepherd 255
shew 179
shew-bread 179
ship 37, 327
shirt 67, 206
shone 179
shook 193
should 279
shoved 360
shovel 111
Siamese 324
sieve 33
sigh 72
sight 72
sin 16, 33
sinew 234
sing 5, 16, 48, 249, 289
singer 249
singing 249, 289, 297
single 249
sir 67, 154
siren 170
sirup 170
sit 11, 52, 169
site 72
sixth 349
skiffs 319
sky 209, 217
slather 114
slaughter 187
sleek 162
slept 342
slew 222
slipped 336
sloo 222
sloth 179
slothful 179
slough 198, 222
slue 222
slur 67
sniffed 239, 357
so 219
soar 191
sob 111
social 327
sod 111
sofa 146
soft 111, 182, 305
soften 340
solder 279
soldier 333
solely 280
solemn 288
solemnize 288
some 64, 198
son 64
song 16, 48, 62, 183

sonnet 173
soon 192, 193
soot 193
sore 191
sorrow 220
sort 302
Soudanese 324
sought 253, 302
soul 280
soup 192
sovereign 248
sow 219, 370
spa 120
Spain 134
Spanish 134
special 47
speech 13
spelled 241
spelt 241
spilled 241
spilt 241
spoil 211
spoiled 241
spoilt 241
Spokane 130
spoke 61
spook 193
spool 13, 192
spoon 193
spume 229
spur 206
spurious 229
spurt 67
squab 111
squalor 184
squirrel 201
staff 361
staffs 361
stair 142
stamp 111
stamped 300
star 116
staves 361
Stephen 360
steps 319
stiff 28, 357
sting 13
stir 67
stirrup 201
St. Louis 314
stock 110
stole 152
stood 193
stop 57
store 191
story 190
straight 71
strange 246
strawberry 185
strayed 71
strength 272, 294
strengthen 294
stringer 249
stripped 6
strong 111
stronger 68, 249
strongest 249
suave 120
substantiation 327
subtle 235
subtly 235
success 87
such 205
suction 338
sufficient 327
suffragan 252
suffrage 252
sugar 327
suggest 109, 316, 329
suggestion 327
suit 192, 231
sumach 327
sun 64
sunk 289
supper 68
supple 195
sure 196, 327
surprised 307
surveillance 262
swallow 111
swamp 111
swan 111
swing 365
swollen 184
sword 367
syllable 169
sylph 357
symphony 299

symposium 333
synagogue 169
Syracuse 201
syringe 170
syrup 170, 201

table 12, 45, 47
tacks 6
tactile 212
tags 6
talk 185, 187, 273, 336
tar 119
tare 55
tarry 129
taught 185, 187
taunt 186
taut 185
taw 42, 302
tax 8, 263, 308
tea 5, 20, 161
tear 55, 167
tea-table 161
tedious 333
tedium 333
temporary 97
ten 135
tenable 138
tenet 138
terrible 135, 142, 201
Texas 325
Thames 348
than 351
that 31, 351, 356
their 55
then 5, 8, 351
there 50, 55, 69, 140, 142, 143, 301
they 132, 351
thimble 237
thin 5, 8, 347
thing 30
think 289, 356
this 351
thistle 310, 340
Thomas 348
Thompson 348
thorough 146, 199, 220
thou 351, 370
though 74, 219, 351
thought 63, 185
three 41
throng 183
thus 31
thyme 348
tie 72
tier 167
timber 236
time 216
timid 169
tin 13
tincture 289
tirade 170
tired 304
tissue 327
Titian 327
to 192
toe 13, 74, 177, 302
tomato 146
tomb 235
ton 284
tongue 249, 250
too 20, 76
tooth 76
toothsomeness 76
tore 42, 302
torrid 111
tory 190
tough 198
tour 194
tow 74, 177
tow-path 176
towel 147, 371
Townsend 318
toy 13
trait 337
tramp 111
transfer 87
transient 327
tread 40, 135
treasure 333
tremble 237
trench 54
trouble 198
troupe 192
trow 225
trowel 73
tube 59, 231
tuber 327

tubs 319
Tudor 327
tulle 195
tunic 327
turn 206
turret 199
tutor 327
twice 343
twig 365
two 76, 367
tyranny 170
tyrant 170

union 259
unison 322
unkempt 300
up 64
upon 109
urge 246
usage 173, 322
use 229, 259, 312
used 242
usual 333
Utah 188

vacation 53, 131
vagary 92, 133
valet 337
value 234
vary 133, 141
vat 29
vehement 92, 255
venison 322
verdigris 315
very 40, 41, 135, 142, 201, 306
vest 343
vex 270
vexation 270
vicious 327
victuals 265
view 229
vignette 285
violet 147
virile 170
virtuous 327
virus 170
vision 29, 333
visor 318
visual 333
vitiate 327
vivid 360
void 75
vowel 173

wabble 111
waif 132
waistcoat 343
waive 132
walk 273
walked 6
walks 319
Waltham 257
want 111
war 301
warmth 299
wary 55, 133, 141
was 113
wash 111, 305
Washington 111, 305
wasp 111, 308
watch 111, 182
water 14, 111, 182, 240
wave 132
weary 167
Wednesday 244
weigh 207
welch 341
well 82
Welsh 341
wen 27
were 145
Westcott 343
wet 27
what 372
wheat 372
when 27
where 140, 142
wherry 141
whet 27
whey 132
which 26, 27, 255, 372
while 26
whirl 206
whisper 372
whistle 310
whit 26, 27, 372
white 372
who 373

whole 179, 180, 373
wholly 280
whoop 373
whooping-cough 373
wife 361
wife's 361
Wilbraham 257
Willamette 94
win 365
window 146, 176, 220, 305
Windsor 243
winter 12, 14, 68
wire 153
wired 304
wiry 153
wish 5, 37, 343
wished 239, 336
wit 27
witch 27
with 31, 351, 356
wives 319, 361
Woodward 369
woof 193
Woolwich 369
Woolworth 369
Wooster 106
Worcester 106
worst 316
worth 67, 206
worthy 154
would 279
wound 194
wrap 367
wrath 30
wreathe 351
wrench 317
Wrentham 257
wring 367
wrist 343, 367
write 209, 367
wrong 183, 249
Wyndham 257

Xanthippe 326
Xavier 326
Xebec 326
Xenophon 326
Xerxes 326

yacht 263
yawl 25, 259, 371
yearn 259
yeast 260
yelk 136
yellow 66, 146, 176
yes 139, 259, 308
yet 139
yield 25
yolk 136, 273
young 249
younger 249
youngest 249
your 196, 197
youth 259
Ypsilanti 174

zealous 35
zebra 146
zebu 370
zero 168
zinc 35
zone 318
zoology 194